PROPORTIONALITY A.
IN INVESTOR-STATE ARBITRATION

In this study, Caroline Henckels examines how investment tribunals have balanced the competing interests of host states and foreign investors in determining state liability in disputes concerning the exercise of public power. Analyzing the concepts of proportionality and deference in investment tribunals' decision-making in comparative perspective, the book proposes a new methodology for investment tribunals to adopt in regulatory disputes, which combines proportionality analysis with an institutionally sensitive approach to the standard of review. The author argues that adopting a modified form of proportionality analysis would provide a means for tribunals to decide cases in a more consistent and coherent manner, leading to greater certainty for both states and investors. Affording due deference to host states in the determination of liability would address the concern that the decisions of investment tribunals unjustifiably impact on the regulatory autonomy of states.

CAROLINE HENCKELS is a Vice-Chancellor's Postdoctoral Research Fellow in Law at the University of New South Wales, and in 2016 will commence as a Senior Lecturer in Law at Monash University.

CAMBRIDGE STUDIES IN INTERNATIONAL AND COMPARATIVE LAW

Established in 1946, this series produces high-quality scholarship in the fields of public and private international law and comparative law. Although these are distinct legal sub-disciplines, developments since 1946 confirm their interrelations.

Comparative law is increasingly being used as a tool in the making of law at national, regional and international levels. Private international law is now often affected by international conventions, and the issues faced by classical conflicts rules are frequently dealt with by the substantive harmonization of law under international auspices. Mixed international arbitrations, especially those involving state economic activity, raise complex questions of public and private international law, while in many fields (such as the protection of human rights and democratic standards, investment guarantees and international criminal law), international and national systems interact. National constitutional arrangements relating to 'foreign affairs', and to the implementation of international norms, are the focus of attention.

The series welcomes works of a theoretical or interdisciplinary character, and those focusing on the new approaches to international or comparative law or conflicts of law. Studies of particular institutions or problems are equally welcome, as are translations of the best work published in other languages.

General Editors James Crawford SC FBA
Whewell Professor of International Law, Faculty of Law, University of Cambridge

John S. Bell FBA
Professor of Law, Faculty of Law, University of Cambridge

A list of books in the series can be found at the end of this volume.

PROPORTIONALITY AND DEFERENCE IN INVESTOR-STATE ARBITRATION

Balancing Investment Protection and Regulatory Autonomy

CAROLINE HENCKELS

CAMBRIDGE
UNIVERSITY PRESS

CAMBRIDGE
UNIVERSITY PRESS

University Printing House, Cambridge CB2 8BS, United Kingdom

One Liberty Plaza, 20th Floor, New York, NY 10006, USA

477 Williamstown Road, Port Melbourne, VIC 3207, Australia

314-321, 3rd Floor, Plot 3, Splendor Forum, Jasola District Centre, New Delhi - 110025, India

79 Anson Road, #06-04/06, Singapore 079906

Cambridge University Press is part of the University of Cambridge.

It furthers the University's mission by disseminating knowledge in the pursuit of education, learning and research at the highest international levels of excellence.

www.cambridge.org
Information on this title: www.cambridge.org/9781107458178

First published 2015
First paperback edition 2018

A catalogue record for this publication is available from the British Library

Library of Congress Cataloging in Publication data
Henckels, Caroline, 1982– author.
Proportionality and deference in investor-state arbitration : balancing investment protection and regulatory autonomy / Caroline Henckels.
pages   cm. – (Cambridge studies in international and comparative law)
Includes bibliographical references and index.
ISBN 978-1-107-08790-3 (hardback)
1. Investments, Foreign (International law)   2. International commercial arbitration.
3. Proportionality in law.   4. Respect.   I. Title.
K3830.H45   2015
346´.092 – dc23   2015014536

ISBN 978-1-107-08790-3 Hardback
ISBN 978-1-107-45817-8 Paperback

For Casper and Silas

CONTENTS

ACKNOWLEDGEMENTS

I would like to thank many people and institutions for their support and assistance with this project, which began as a PhD thesis at the University of Cambridge and concluded during my postdoctoral fellowship at the University of New South Wales. First and foremost, I would like to thank my supervisor, Lorand Bartels, for his thoughtful and comprehensive criticism of the work (and for his inimitable sense of humour). Federico Ortino and Michael Waibel, my thesis examiners, provided invaluable advice on revising the thesis for publication. My first-year examiners, John Bell and Zachary Douglas, gave useful feedback that assisted me in sharpening the focus of this work.

Many thanks are due to Andrew Mitchell of Melbourne Law School, who was a great source of advice throughout the process. I would also like to thank Carolyn Evans and Tania Voon of Melbourne Law School for their assistance and advice, and Jürgen Kurtz, whose excellent teaching during my LLM inspired my interest in international investment law.

I am very appreciative of the assistance provided by Shawn Rajanayagam and Natalie Hodgson in the final stages of preparing the book manuscript. Thank you also to the team at Cambridge University Press and to the anonymous reviewers, who provided useful suggestions on the book proposal.

This research would not have been possible without the generous financial support I received from the Cambridge Commonwealth Trust Scholarship, the New Zealand Federation of Graduate Women Fellowship Award, the Stephen Körner Scholarship, the Murray Edwards College Research Fund and the Faculty of Law's Yorke Fund. I am also very grateful to Melbourne Law School for supporting my research in 2012 by way of a Visiting Scholarship, for conference funding from the Centre for International Law at the National University of Singapore, and for research funding from the University of New South Wales.

During the course of the research, I benefitted greatly from discussions with many people, particularly José Manuel Álvarez Zárate,

Jonathan Bonnitcha, Caroline Foster, Susan Franck, Lukas Gruszczynski, Jonathan Ketcheson, Jonathan Liberman, Andrew Mitchell, Federica Paddeu, Joshua Paine, Cecily Rose, Stephan Schill, Elizabeth Sheargold, Bart Smit Duijzentkunst, Muthucumaraswamy Sornarajah, Valentina Vadi, Geraldo Vidigal, Tania Voon and Markus Wagner.

I am also greatly indebted to Jonathan Bonnitcha, Cecily Rose, Joshua Paine and Markus Wagner for reading and commenting on chapters of the manuscript. Any errors or omissions are, of course, my sole responsibility.

In developing my thinking on these issues, earlier versions of parts of this book were published as 'Indirect Expropriation and the Right to Regulate: Revisiting Proportionality Analysis and the Standard of Review in Investor-State Arbitration' in (2012) 15 *Journal of Economic Law* 223, as 'Balancing Investment Protection and the Public Interest: The Role of the Standard of Review and the Importance of Deference in Investor-State Arbitration' in (2013) 4 *Journal of International Dispute Settlement* 197, with a revised version published in Wouter Werner and Lukasz Gruszczynski (eds.), *Deference in International Courts and Tribunals: Standard of Review and Margin of Appreciation* (Oxford University Press, 2014) 113; and as 'Balancing Investment Protection and Sustainable Development in Investor-State Arbitration: The Role of Deference', in Andrea K. Bjorklund (ed.), *Yearbook of International Investment Law and Policy 2012–2013* (Oxford University Press, 2014) 305. Research undertaken for this book was also published in an article co-authored with Andrew Mitchell entitled 'Variations on a Theme: Comparing the Concept of "Necessity" in International Investment Law and WTO Law' (2013) 14 *Chicago Journal of International Law* 287.

I am thankful to friends in Cambridge, London, Melbourne and Sydney who kept me relatively sane throughout the process of researching and writing. Finally, I would like to thank my family (especially Sonja and Greg) for their unfailing support.

TABLE OF ARBITRAL AWARDS AND CASES

Investor-state arbitrations

xiii

Other investor-state dispute documents

Other international arbitrations

International Court of Justice and Permanent Court of International Justice

Court of Justice of the European Union

European Court of Human Rights

World Trade Organization and General Agreement on Tariffs and Trade

GATT Panel Reports

WTO Panel Reports

Appellate Body Reports

Domestic cases

Canada

United Kingdom

United States

TABLE OF TREATIES, LEGISLATION, AND UN DOCUMENTS

Treaties

United Nations documents

Arbitration rules

Domestic laws

Ecuador

United Kingdom

United States

ABBREVIATIONS

ASEAN	Association of South East Asian Nations
BIT	Bilateral Investment Treaty
CEPA	Closer Economic Partnership Agreement
CJEU	Court of Justice of the European Union
COMESA	Common Market for Eastern and Southern Africa
EC	European Communities
ECHR	European Convention on Human Rights
ECtHR	European Court of Human Rights
EU	European Union
FCN	Treaty of Friendship, Commerce and Navigation
FIPA	Foreign Investment Protection Agreement
FTA	Free Trade Agreement
GATS	General Agreement on Trade in Services
GATT	General Agreement on Tariffs and Trade
IACtHR	Inter-American Court of Human Rights
ICJ	International Court of Justice
ICSID	International Centre for the Settlement of Investment Disputes
NAFTA	North American Free Trade Agreement
OECD	Organization for Economic Cooperation and Development
PCIJ	Permanent Court of International Justice
SPS Agreement	Agreement on Sanitary and Phytosanitary Measures
TBT Agreement	Agreement on Technical Barriers to Trade
TFEU	Treaty on the Functioning of European Union
UK	United Kingdom
UN	United Nations
UNCITRAL	United Nations Commission on International Trade Law
UNCTAD	United Nations Commission on Trade and Development
UNHRC	United Nations Human Rights Committee
USA	United States of America
VCLT	Vienna Convention on the Law of Treaties
WTO	World Trade Organization

1

Introduction

1.1 Investor-state arbitration in context

Investment treaties aim to promote foreign investment by providing legal protection to foreign investors from the abuse of public power by host states. They also empower arbitral tribunals to review and rule upon the legality of government conduct affecting foreign investors and investments. Foreign investors have brought claims against states in relation to a wide variety of areas of government policy, including the devaluation of currency in a financial crisis, the protection of cultural heritage, regulatory controls on drinking water and sewerage services, bans on the marketing of harmful substances, and decisions taken in relation to hazardous waste. High profile pending cases include challenges to tobacco control laws enacted by Australia and Uruguay and to Germany's decision to phase out the use of nuclear power. These cases, among others, illustrate the broad reach of international investment law into all aspects of legislation, government policy and service delivery. They also illustrate that foreign investors have, in recent years, begun to challenge not only individual treatment by host state authorities, but also generally applicable laws and regulations – in many cases, in circumstances where domestic investors do not enjoy the same substantive and procedural rights.

The decisions of investment tribunals can significantly affect the regulatory autonomy of states for several reasons. Investment treaty provisions that set out states' obligations toward foreign investors are typically framed in broad and open-textured language that does not address the relationship between investment protection and the continuing powers of host states to regulate and take other actions to promote public welfare. These vaguely worded provisions give investment tribunals a high degree of discretion in interpreting the obligations of states and, therefore, significant authority to control the exercise of regulatory and administrative power by states.[1] Investment tribunals have, in a number of cases, found states liable to pay compensation to foreign investors in respect of non-discriminatory measures directed at public welfare objectives.

Successful claims by foreign investors may also affect the willingness of governments to enact or maintain public welfare measures. A finding against a state may incentivize the state to repeal the measure so as not to attract further claims, and the prospect of investor-state arbitration may – although this is difficult to measure – have a chilling effect on the resolve of other states to implement measures incidentally affecting foreign investors or to maintain them in the face of challenges to similar measures adopted by other states.[2] A damages award may divert the state's budget from its own policy priorities and may give rise to new situations of sovereign indebtedness.[3]

Moreover, the current institutional structure of investor-state arbitration does not permit investment tribunal decisions to be appealed against; decisions may be annulled or set aside only on very limited grounds.[4] The effect of this structure, combined with the vaguely worded standards of investment protection, is that tribunals enjoy broad interpretive discretion that is practically immune from review.

At the same time, investment tribunals have been criticized for significant inconsistencies in the way in which they have decided cases, in terms

---

[1] For example, Montt, *State Liability in Investment Treaty Arbitration: Global Constitutional and Administrative Law and the BIT Generation* (2009) 165; Roberts, 'Power and Persuasion in Investment Treaty Arbitration: The Dual Role of States' (2010) 104 *American Journal of International Law* 179.

[2] See e.g. Van Harten, 'Investment Treaty Arbitration, Procedural Fairness and the Rule of Law' in Schill (ed.), *International Investment Law and Comparative Public Law* (2010) 627; Tienhaara, 'Regulatory Chill and the Threat of Arbitration: A View from Political Science' in Brown and Miles (eds.), *Evolution in Investment Treaty Law and Arbitration* (2011) 607; Bonnitcha, *Substantive Protection under Investment Treaties* (2014) 113–33. For example, New Zealand has delayed the passage of its proposed plain tobacco packaging legislation pending the outcome of the *Philip Morris* v. *Australia* dispute. New Zealand Government, 'Government Moves Forward with Plain Packaging of Tobacco Products' (2013).

[3] See e.g. Van Harten, *Investment Treaty Arbitration and Public Law* (2007) 7; Van Harten, *Sovereign Choices and Sovereign Constraints: Judicial Restraint in Investment Treaty Arbitration* (2013) 114.

[4] Awards for claims brought under the auspices of the Convention on the Settlement of Investment Disputes between States and Nationals of other States (ICSID Convention) are binding and final and are amenable to annulment on very limited grounds (Articles 49–53). Non-ICSID arbitrations (such as those taking place under UNCITRAL rules) are normally challengeable in domestic courts, but again on limited grounds.

of both the content that they have ascribed to standards of investment protection and the methodologies they have adopted in determining state liability. Although tribunals increasingly rely on previous cases in their decision-making,[5] they continue to generate inconsistent interpretations of the same standards of investment protection[6] and differing conclusions as to state liability in relation to cases with identical or similar fact situations.[7] The decided cases evidence low coherence and, often, little consideration of the systemic implications of decision-making, other relevant areas of international law or the intentions of the treaty parties.[8] This incoherence has resulted in uncertainty both for states, who find it difficult to know whether their conduct will be adjudged lawful, and for investors, who cannot have confidence that recourse to arbitration will be fruitful. These uncertainties also appear to contribute to the law's chilling effect on public welfare regulation.[9]

A prominent example of these concerns is the series of claims against Argentina arising from its 2001–2002 economic crisis, in which foreign investors successfully challenged emergency laws enacted to restore domestic order and economic stability. Tribunals adopted a strict approach to whether Argentina should be liable for financial losses sustained by foreign investors as a result of the crisis and the emergency laws enacted to avert it. Several tribunals found Argentina liable to compensate foreign investors in the electricity and gas sectors for failing to maintain a stable regulatory environment or failing to comply with the

---

[5] For example, Cheng, 'Precedent and Control in Investment Treaty Arbitration' (2006) 30 *Fordham International Law Journal* 1014, 1030–47; Kaufmann-Kohler, 'Arbitral Precedent: Dream, Necessity or Excuse?' (2007) 23 *Arbitration International* 357, 368, 372–3; Bjork-lund, 'Investment Treaty Arbitral Decisions as Jurisprudence Constante' in Picker, Bunn and Arner (eds.), *International Economic Law: the State and Future of the Discipline* (2008) 265.

[6] See e.g., in relation to inconsistent approaches taken by tribunals to the concept of fair and equitable treatment, Kläger, *Fair and Equitable Treatment in International Investment Law* (2011) 86–7; Paparinskis, *The International Minimum Standard and Fair and Equitable Treatment* (2013) 116.

[7] See Van Harten, *Investment Treaty Arbitration and Public Law*, pp. 122–3; Kurtz, 'The Use and Abuse of WTO Law in Investor-State Arbitration: Competition and its Discontents' (2009) 20 *European Journal of International Law* 749, 771; van Aaken, 'International Investment Law Between Commitment and Flexibility: A Contract Theory Analysis' (2009) 12 *Journal of International Economic Law* 507, 514. While these inconsistencies might be attributed in part to textual differences across the body of investment treaties, there is substantial commonality in the obligations and wording of relevant treaty provisions: see e.g. Schill, *Multilateralization of International Investment Law* (2009) 70–1.

[8] Roberts, 'Power and Persuasion', pp. 179, 190–1.

[9] Bonnitcha, *Substantive Protection under Investment Treaties*, pp. 122–7.

claimants' legitimate expectations that the existing regulatory framework would remain in place. Some of these tribunals appeared to take the view that the state's reasons for its actions were irrelevant to the question of liability for breach; others held that the state should have maintained the regulatory regime and adhered to the terms of concession agreements and licences held by these investors in spite of the crisis. These tribunals also took divergent approaches to whether Argentina could escape liability by relying on an exception clause in the Argentina-US Bilateral Investment Treaty (BIT). Argentina is liable for millions of dollars in damages arising from these and other cases, despite strong evidence that several tribunals made serious legal errors in determining liability[10] and despite the widespread criticism that these tribunals adopted an unduly broad interpretation of the state's treaty obligations that did not take Argentina's interests into account, and employed an excessively strict approach to the standard of review.

Recent tribunals have generally taken a more moderate approach to these issues, for example, by holding that an investor can establish a legitimate expectations claim only in more limited circumstances, or that the state has the right to make reasonable changes to the regulatory environment affecting investors. Yet these cases, among others, raise some of the sharpest questions about the relationship between international investment law and the right of host states to regulate and take other action to promote public welfare. These cases also highlight the significant inconsistencies in the way in which tribunals approach the determination of liability under the various standards of investment protection.

As disenchantment with international investment law and investor-state arbitration continues, finding a way to deal with these problems is a crucial issue confronting the discipline. States have adopted various strategies in response to these concerns, ranging from radical to reformist. Argentina has failed to comply with most of the awards rendered against it in relation to the emergency measures it adopted in response to its economic crisis of 2001–2002, only recently settling five of the numerous awards.[11] Some states have terminated bilateral investment treaties[12] or

---

[10] See e.g. Kurtz, 'Adjudging the Exceptional at International Investment Law: Security, Public Order and Financial Crisis' (2010) 59 *International and Comparative Law Quarterly* 325, 371. These issues are discussed further in Chapter 4.

[11] Peterson, 'After Settling Some Awards, Argentina Takes More Fractious Path in Bond-Holders Case, with New Bid to Disqualify Arbitrators', *Investment Arbitration Reporter*, 30 December 2013.

[12] See e.g. UNCTAD, *Recent Developments in Investor-State Dispute Settlement (ISDS)* (2014) 114.

have denounced the ICSID Convention.[13] Increasing numbers of African, Asian and Latin American states are disengaging from negotiations for new investment treaties.[14] As the numbers of claims filed against them have increased, states that were historically net exporters of capital have changed their approaches to treaty negotiations, seeking to clarify the substantive standards of investment protection and related procedural matters so as to reduce the interpretive discretion enjoyed by tribunals.[15] Commentators have also proposed changes to the institutional archi-tecture of international investment law, such as the establishment of an international investment court[16] or a body that would hear appeals from tribunal decisions.[17] These proposals aim to promote greater con-sistency in decision-making and to discipline adventurous interpretations of investment treaties in the first instance.

Yet, these recent developments and proposals do nothing to affect the 3200-plus other investment treaties currently in existence for those states who choose to remain part of the system.[18] Amending those treaties would require the consent of those treaty parties and would, naturally, take place on a treaty-by-treaty basis.[19] And although the language of

---

[13] See UNCTAD, *World Investment Report 2012: Towards a New Generation of Investment Policies* (2012) 87; UNCTAD, *World Investment Report 2014: Investing in the SDGs: An Action Plan* (2014) 114.

[14] UNCTAD, *World Investment Report 2014*, p. xxiii.

[15] See, e.g. in relation to the evolution in states' approach to negotiating investment treaties, UNCTAD, *World Investment Report 2014*, p. 116; Alvarez, 'The Return of the State' (2011) 20 *Minnesota Journal of International Law* 223, 234–8.

[16] For example, Franck, 'The Legitimacy Crisis in Investment Treaty Arbitration: Privatizing Public International Law Through Inconsistent Decisions' (2005) 73 *Fordham Law Review* 1521, 1617–25; Van Harten, *Investment Treaty Arbitration and Public Law*, pp. 180–4.

[17] Brower, 'Structure, Legitimacy, and NAFTA's Investment Chapter' (2003) 36 *Vanderbilt Journal of Transnational Law* 37, 91–3; International Centre for Settlement of Investment Disputes Secretariat, *Possible Improvements of the Framework for ICSID Arbitration* (2004) 14–16; Gantz, 'An Appellate Mechanism for Review of Arbitral Decisions in Investor-State Disputes: Prospects and Challenges' (2006) 39 *Vanderbilt Journal of Transnational Law* 39; Tams, 'An Appealing Option? The Debate about an ICSID Appellate Mechanism' (2006) 57 *Martin-Luther-Universität Halle-Wittenburg Beiträge zum Transnationalen Wirtschaft-srecht*; Miles, *The Origins of International Investment Law: Empire, Environment and the Safeguarding of Capital* (2013), pp. 349–50, 381–2. See also McRae, 'The WTO Appellate Body: A Model for an ICSID Appeals Facility?' (2010) 1 *Journal of International Dispute Settlement* 371 (noting the limitations of an ICSID appeal facility).

[18] At the end of 2014, there were approximately 3268 known BITs and other investment treaties (principally preferential trade agreements with investment chapters) in force: UNCTAD, *Recent Trends in IIAs and ISDS*, p. 2.

[19] See Kingsbury and Schill, 'Investor-State Arbitration as Governance: Fair and Equitable Treatment, Proportionality, and the Emerging Global Administrative Law' in Van Den Berg (ed.), *50 Years of the New York Convention* (2009) 5, 9–10.

many newer treaties indicates that tribunals should be loath to interfere with *bona fide* measures adopted to promote public welfare, these provisions generally indicate neither how tribunals should balance public and private interests in their decision-making in disputes concerning regulatory or administrative measures (hereinafter 'regulatory disputes'),[20] nor how intensively they should scrutinize a government's justification for its actions in such cases. This suggests that pending any future reform of investment treaties – either on an *ad hoc* basis or through multilateral efforts[21] – consideration needs to be given to how these concerns may be addressed within the current system of investor-state arbitration itself, without amending treaties or changing institutional structures.[22]

Two issues that have received increasing attention in recent years are the related questions of the appropriate *method of review* (i.e. the technique used by adjudicators to balance competing public and private interests) and the *standard of review* (i.e. the intensity with which the method of review is applied in terms of the scrutiny applied to the justification for the measure advanced by the responding government). Investment tribunals are in need of a workable methodology with which to deal with competing public and private interests in regulatory disputes, and the decided cases demonstrate that tribunals have been grappling with this question. Tribunals have increasingly referred to concepts such as necessity, reasonableness, balancing and proportionality in determining state liability, but they have not generally elaborated upon the methodologies they have adopted or attempted doctrinal justification for their choice of technique, and their approaches have frequently been incoherent.[23] Although a

---

[20] Van Harten, *Investment Treaty Arbitration and Public Law*, p. 4 (referring to regulatory disputes as those engaging public law considerations); Roberts, 'Clash of Paradigms: Actors and Analogies Shaping the Investment Treaty System' (2013) 107 *American Journal of International Law* 45, 65 (describing 'public arbitrations' in international investment law as those that 'involve significant matters of public concern that transcend the private rights and obligations of the disputing parties'); Maupin, 'Differentiating Among International Investment Disputes' in Douglas, Pauwelyn, and Viñuales (eds.), *The Foundations of International Investment Law: Bringing Theory into Practice* (2014) 468, 490 (describing regulatory disputes as those involving 'ordinary governmental regulatory activities').

[21] UNCTAD has called for a multilateral approach to building consensus on appropriate reforms to investment treaties (though not the negotiation of a multilateral investment agreement): UNCTAD, *World Investment Report 2014*, pp. 130–2.

[22] In this respect, see Schill, 'The Sixth Path: Reforming Investment Law from Within' in Kalicki and Joubin-Bret (eds), *Reshaping the Investor-State Dispute Settlement System: Journeys for the 21st Century* (2015) 621, 624–5.

[23] See Stone Sweet, 'Investor-State Arbitration: Proportionality's New Frontier' (2010) 4 *Law and Ethics of Human Rights* 47, 68. See also Bomhoff, *Balancing Constitutional Rights: The Origins and Meanings of Postwar Legal Discourse* (2013) 16–21, distinguishing between

number of tribunals have referred to concepts such as the standard of review, the margin of appreciation and deference to host states, they have only infrequently articulated the rationale for their approaches or the reasons why it might be appropriate for a tribunal to afford a measure of deference in the determination of liability.[24]

Without a coherent, consistent approach to the method and standard of review, states find it difficult to predict the consequences of their actions, foreign investors have little certainty as to the likely prospects of a successful claim, and other interested parties will find it difficult to determine the likely impact of international investment law on public welfare regulation. The question arises, therefore, as to how investment tribunals should approach the method and standard of review. The first port of call must be rules of treaty interpretation, given that the basis for investment tribunals' jurisdiction is the relevant investment treaty.

1.2   Treaty interpretation and the role of comparative law

1.2.1   *The relevance of the rules of treaty interpretation to the question of the method and standard of review*

Like all treaties, provisions of investment treaties must be interpreted in accordance with the ordinary meaning in their context and in light of the treaty's object and purpose, as required by Article 31(1) of the Vienna Convention on the Law of Treaties (VCLT).[25] Article 31(1) is regarded as a single rule comprising various techniques that should all be considered rather than prescribing any particular methodology or the weight to be attributed to the various factors,[26] although the ordinary meaning of the text is the starting point.[27]

---

the discourse of balancing and the application of proportionality analysis as a method of review.

[24] See Schill, 'Deference in Investment Treaty Arbitration: Re-Conceptualizing the Standard of Review' (2012) 3 *Journal of International Dispute Settlement* 577, 579–80: investment tribunals invoke the concept of deference 'as a mantra rather than . . . as part of a theoretical framework structuring the power relations between states and tribunals'.

[25] The VCLT rules of treaty interpretation are regarded as reflecting customary international law on the interpretation of treaties, see e.g. *Avena and Other Mexican Nationals (Mexico v. US)*, para. 83; *Sovereignty over Pulau Ligitan and Pulau Sipadan (Indonesia v. Malaysia)*, para. 37. The VCLT provisions are not exhaustive of treaty interpretation principles, see e.g. Sinclair, *The Vienna Convention on the Law of Treaties* (1984) 153.

[26] For example, Aust, *Modern Treaty Law and Practice* (2007) 234; Gardiner, *Treaty Interpretation* (2010) 9, 141.

[27] See Territorial Dispute (*Libyan Arab Jamahiriya v. Chad*), para. 41; Weeramantry, *Treaty Interpretation in Investment Arbitration* (2012) p. 42.

However, this approach may pose difficulties in relation to many of the substantive provisions of investment treaties which, as noted above, are drafted in vague and non-specific terms.[28] The ordinary meaning of typical investment treaty protections such as fair and equitable treatment, indirect expropriation and discrimination do little to clarify the substance of these obligations.[29] Even where the text does provide some guidance, such as exception clauses that permit a state to adopt an otherwise non-conforming measure where 'necessary' to promote a particular policy objective, the decided cases demonstrate that there may be a range of possible meanings attributable to the treaty terms and a range of possible approaches that a tribunal could take to the applicable standard of review.[30]

But a treaty interpreter cannot determine the ordinary meaning of a treaty provision in the abstract and must pay attention to the object and purpose of the treaty as a whole.[31] Many investment treaty preambles (a contextual source of interpretation)[32] refer to aims and objectives such as the protection and promotion of investment or the deepening of economic relations between the signatory states. Such references are frequently made in instrumental terms, referring to investment protection and promotion as a means to welfare, development or prosperity of state parties.[33] Even where the object and purpose of an investment treaty are less than clear or the treaty does not refer to non-investment objectives, an argument can be made that the purpose of the regime of

---

[28] Schill, *Multilateralization of International Investment Law*, pp. 264–5; Roberts, 'Clash of Paradigms', pp. 50–2.

[29] Schill, *Multilateralization of International Investment Law*, pp. 264–5; Kläger, *Fair and Equitable Treatment*, pp. 44–5.

[30] See Burke-White and von Staden, 'Investment Protection in Extraordinary Times: The Interpretation and Application of Non-Precluded Measures Provisions in Bilateral Investment Treaties' (2008) 48 *Virginia Journal of International Law* 307, 337–49 (noting the different meanings attributable to the concept of 'necessary').

[31] Gardiner, *Treaty Interpretation*, p. 190. See e.g., on the dominant hermeneutics that animate the process of treaty interpretation (the objective approach, the subjective approach and the teleological approach), Fitzmaurice, 'The Law and Procedure of the International Court of Justice: Treaty Interpretation and Certain Other Treaty Points' (1951) 28 *British Yearbook of International Law* 1, 1–2; Sinclair, *The Vienna Convention on the Law of Treaties*, pp. 114–15; Shaw, *International Law* (2008), 932–33 (with further references).

[32] The context of the treaty includes its preamble and 'any agreement relating to the treaty which was made between all the parties in connection with the conclusion of the treaty' (Article 31(2) VCLT).

[33] See e.g. the preambles to the US-Argentina BIT and UK-Jamaica BIT. More recent treaties also refer to other objectives such as protecting the environment, see e.g. the preambles to the Australia-Chile FTA and Energy Charter Treaty.

international investment law is to promote the economic development and prosperity of states, and that the promotion and protection of foreign investments are specific manifestations of this broader purpose.[34] The International Centre for the Settlement of Investment Disputes (ICSID) (the body under whose auspices the majority of investor-state arbitrations are conducted) was established by the World Bank with the aim of fostering economic development, and the ICSID Convention preamble refers to 'the need for international cooperation for economic development, and the role of private international investment therein'.[35] At the very least, this broader context indicates that the obligations of host states toward foreign investors should not be viewed solely through the lens of investment protection at the expense of other legitimate objectives.

Investment tribunals have frequently looked at a treaty's preamble in order to determine its object and purpose. Earlier tribunals often took the view that the sole or dominant purpose of the treaty in question was to maximize the protection afforded to foreign investors and investments, a perspective that strongly influenced their interpretations of states' obligations and one which has been subject to criticism.[36] More recently, however, tribunals have demonstrated a willingness to take into account the object and purpose of the relevant treaty in interpreting its operative provisions in a manner that is more supportive of regulatory autonomy.[37] However, tribunals' approaches have been less than methodologically clear in terms how the rules of treaty interpretation have informed their

---

[34] Brower, 'Obstacles and Pathways to Consideration of the Public Interest in Investment Treaty Disputes' in Sauvant (ed.), *Yearbook on International Investment Law & Policy 2008–2009* (2009) 274, 373–6; Salacuse, *The Law of Investment Treaties* (2010), pp. 112–15; Radi, 'Realizing Human Rights in Investment Treaty Arbitration: A Perspective from within the International Investment Law Toolbox' (2012) 37 *North Carolina Journal of International Law and Commercial Regulation* 1107, 1138–9; Ortino, 'The Investment Treaty System as Judicial Review' (2013) 24 *American Review of International Arbitration* 437, 440–5.

[35] Lowenfeld, 'The ICSID Convention: Origins and Transformation' (2010) 38 *Georgia Journal of International and Comparative Law* 47, 49–50, 53; Radi, 'Human Rights in Investment Treaty Arbitration', pp. 1138–9.

[36] For example, *SGS Société Générale de Surveillance S.A.* v. *Philippines*, Jurisdiction, para. 116; *MTD Equity Sdn. Bhd. & MTD Chile S.A.* v. *Chile*, Award, para. 104; *Siemens A.G.* v. *Argentina*, Award, para. 81; *CMS Gas Transmission Company* v. *Argentina*, Award, para. 274; *Sempra* v. *Argentina*, Award, para. 300; *LG&E* v. *Argentina*, Liability, para. 124; *Azurix Corporation* v. *Argentina*, Award, para. 372. See e.g. Kurtz, 'On the Evolution and Slow Convergence of International Trade and Investment Law' in Sacerdoti (ed.), *General Interests of Host States in International Investment Law* (2014) 104, 109–10.

[37] See e.g. *Saluka Investments BV (The Netherlands)* v. *Czech Republic*, Partial Award, para. 300; *Joseph Charles Lemire* v. *Ukraine*, Jurisdiction and Liability, paras. 272–3; *Continental Casualty* v. *Argentina*, Award, para. 258.

decision-making.[38] And, in any event, reference to the object and purpose of an investment treaty – beyond suggesting the need for a balanced approach that takes into account the rights of both states and investors – does little to actually concretize states' obligations and is unlikely to provide much assistance to the question of how to balance state and investor interests in the determination of liability.[39] Nor do supplementary means of interpretation, such as the *travaux préparatoires* to the treaty usually assist in this regard,[40] either because they are not available[41] or due to a reluctance on the part of states to produce them in litigation.[42]

1.2.2   The role that comparative law can play

1.2.2.1   The comparative method

Given that the principles of treaty interpretation do not provide much assistance in clarifying how state and investor interests should be taken into account in the determination of state liability, a comparative inquiry into the way in which other legal systems performing functionally similar tasks deal with the question of the method and standard of review may be useful.[43] In recent years, commentators have used a comparative methodology to elaborate on various substantive and procedural issues arising in investor-state arbitration,[44] and several tribunals have employed

---

[38]   See Fauchald, 'The Legal Reasoning of ICSID Tribunal: An Empirical Analysis' (2008) 19 *European Journal of International Law* 301, 322–4.

[39]   See Schill, *Multilateralization of International Investment Law*, p. 265.

[40]   In terms of Article 32 VCLT (either to confirm the meaning of a provision or to determine its meaning in cases of ambiguity or obscurity of meaning or manifest absurdity or unreasonableness of result).

[41]   Kläger, *Fair and Equitable Treatment*, p. 46; Roberts, 'Clash of Paradigms', p. 51, but see Burke-White and von Staden, 'Private Litigation in a Public Law Sphere: The Standard of Review in Investor-State Arbitrations' (2010) 35 *Yale Journal of International Law* 283, 296 (noting that the *travaux* to the 1998 US Model BIT suggest that the parties intended that a flexible necessity test be applied in the context of treaty exceptions).

[42]   Weeramantry, *Treaty Interpretation in Investment Arbitration*, pp. 183–4 (noting inequality of access to the *travaux* and the likely reluctance of an investor's home state to provide them).

[43]   To the extent that the provisions of the investment treaty so permit. Where a relevant treaty provision is clear-cut, comparative law can, however, only assist in terms of providing a normative perspective on what the law should be, rather than as an aid to the interpretation of existing law: see e.g. Schill, 'Enhancing International Investment Law's Legitimacy: Conceptual and Methodological Foundations of a New Public Law Approach' (2011) 52 *Virginia Journal of International Law* 57, 89–90.

[44]   See e.g. the contributions in Schill (ed.), *International Investment Law and Comparative Public Law* (2010).

a comparative approach as a means of fleshing out the normative content of certain substantive obligations in investment treaties, such as fair and equitable treatment.[45] There is also a burgeoning body of literature that employs comparative approaches to the question of the method and standard of review in international investment law.[46]

How, then, should one selected the legal systems from which to draw inspiration in relation to these matters? Those who take a functionalist approach to comparative law argue that every legal system faces similar problems and that it is legitimate to consider how other legal systems have dealt with functionally similar issues.[47] However, the functionalist approach has been criticized for exaggerating the extent to which different legal systems face similar problems or the ways in which they have dealt with these problems.[48] Critics of the functionalist approach also emphasize the need to bear in mind the unique cultural, economic, political and social context of each legal system because without consideration of

---

[45] *SD Myers* v. *Canada*, Partial Award; *International Thunderbird Gaming Corporation* v. *Mexico*, Award and Separate Opinion of Arbitrator Wälde; *Pope & Talbot, Inc* v. *Canada*, Merits; *Methanex* v. *US*, Final Award; *Continental* v. *Argentina*, Award; *Total* v. *Argentina*, Liability; *Toto Costruzioni Generali S.p.A.* v. *Lebanon*, Award.

[46] See Kingsbury and Schill, 'Investor-State Arbitration as Governance'; Stone Sweet, 'Investor-State Arbitration'; Kingsbury and Schill, 'Public Law Concepts to Balance Investors' Rights with State Regulatory Actions in the Public Interest–The Concept of Proportionality' in Schill (ed.), *International Investment Law and Comparative Public Law* (2010) 75; Schill, 'International Investment Law and Comparative Public Law: An Introduction' in Schill (ed.), *International Investment Law and Comparative Public Law* (2010) 3; Schill, 'Cross-Regime Harmonization through Proportionality Analysis: The Case of International Investment Law, the Law of State Immunity and Human Rights' (2014) 27 *ICSID Review* 87; Pirker, *Proportionality Analysis and Judicial Review: A Comparative Study in Domestic Constitutional, European and International Economic Law* (2013) (method of review); Burke-White and von Staden, 'Private Litigation'; Burke White and von Staden, 'The Need for Public Law Standards of Review in Investor-State Arbitrations' in Schill (ed.), *International Investment Law and Comparative Public Law* (2010) 689; Schill, 'Deference in Investment Treaty Arbitration'; Vadi and Gruszczynski, 'Standards of Review in International Investment Law and Arbitration: Multilevel Governance and the Commonweal' (2013) 16 *Journal of International Economic Law* 613; Gruszczynski and Vadi, 'Standard of Review and Scientific Evidence in WTO Law and International Investment Arbitration: Converging Parallels?' in Gruszczynski and Werner (eds.), *Deference in International Courts and Tribunals: Standard of Review and Margin of Appreciation* (2014) 152 (standard of review).

[47] See Zweigert and Kötz, *Introduction to Comparative Law* (1998) 34.

[48] Frankenburg, 'Critical Comparisons: Re-thinking Comparative Law' (1985) 26 *Harvard International Law Journal* 411, 436; Michaels, 'The Functionalist Method of Comparative Law' in Reimann and Zimmermann (eds.), *The Oxford Handbook of Comparative Law* (2006) 339, 369–71; Whytock, 'Legal Origins, Functionalism, and the Future of Comparative Law' (2009) 34 *Brigham Young University Law Review* 1879, 1886 (with further references).

these factors, any solutions that are proposed may lead to unintended consequences.[49] They also caution that when seeking to apply solutions from one or more legal systems to another legal system, there is a need to determine whether those solutions worked well in the original legal system in terms of solving the relevant problem.[50] These limitations must be kept in mind both in relation to the selection of comparators and to the evaluation of the methods and standards of review that the comparators have adopted.

1.2.2.2   Selecting the comparators

As adjudicators performing first-instance review of government action, investment tribunals function (*de facto*) as part of the system of governance of domestic public law in host states. To a certain extent, their role in adjudicating regulatory disputes may be analogized to domestic courts hearing constitutional and administrative law disputes, given that tribunals adjudicate challenges brought by individuals to legislation, regulations, policies, procedures and administrative decisions.[51] However, investment tribunals adjudicate treaty-based disputes and determine state liability at international law, meaning that they are not bound by and are arguably less likely to take into account public law principles developed in domestic legal systems, such as the separation of powers.[52] Moreover, the international dimension adds increased sensitivity to the adjudication of regulatory disputes due to investment arbitrators' lack of embeddedness in the host state polity.[53]

---

[49] Michaels, 'The Functionalist Method', 365–6. This is, however, acknowledged by functionalists, see e.g. Zweigert, 'Des solutions idéntiques par des voies différentes (Quelques observations en matière de droit comparé)' (1966) 18 *Revue internationale de droit comparé* 5, 13–14.

[50] Michaels, 'The Functionalist Method', pp. 373–6; Whytock, 'Legal Origins, Functionalism', pp. 1886–90.

[51] For example, Van Harten, *Investment Treaty Arbitration and Public Law*, p. 5; Montt, *State Liability in Investment Treaty Arbitration*, pp. 21–2; Schill, 'International Investment Law and Comparative Public Law – An Introduction', p. 24.

[52] Roberts, 'Clash of Paradigms', p. 68; Roberts, 'The Next Battleground: Standards of Review in Investment Treaty Arbitration' in Van Den Berg (ed.), *Arbitration: The Next Fifty Years*, p. 178.

[53] Burke-White and von Staden, 'Public Law Standards', pp. 714–15. See also (in relation to this issue in WTO adjudication) Bohanes and Lockhart, 'Standard of Review in WTO Law' in Bethlehem, McRae, Neufeld and Van Damme (eds.), *The Oxford Handbook of International Trade Law* (2009) 378, 381; Lovric, *Deference to the Legislature in WTO Challenges to Legislation* (2010) 60.

This book takes the perspective that the comparable legal systems to the regime of international investment law are those that require the adjudication of domestic regulatory and administrative measures for compliance with a government's treaty obligations, whether in terms of individually held rights and interests or more diffuse rights such as foreign market access. Where the challenged measure concerns the exercise of public power by a host state, investor-state arbitration functions as a form of international public law adjudication.[54] Accordingly, the book examines the adjudication of national measures derogating from freedom of movement by the Court of Justice of the European Union (CJEU),[55] the approach of the European Court of Human Rights (ECtHR) to measures interfering with the right to property, and the approaches of World Trade Organization panels and the Appellate Body (WTO tribunals) to certain measures interfering with liberalized trade. Like investment tribunals, these bodies must all deal with institutional limitations including their lack of embeddedness in the relevant polity, their weak democratic legitimacy and their comparatively weak evidence-gathering capacities.

These legal systems also have various other parallels. European Union (EU), European Convention on Human Rights (ECHR) and international investment law all trump domestic law in the case of conflict and permit individuals to bring proceedings directly against states.[56] ECHR law and international investment law both establish a minimum level of treatment that governments must afford to individuals, although the interests protected by each regime have a different normative quality.[57]

---

[54] Various scholars have referred to this perspective as one of international judicial review or international public law adjudication: see *Thunderbird* v. *Mexico*, Separate Opinion of Arbitrator Wälde, para. 13; Wälde, 'Investment Arbitration under the Energy Charter Treaty: An Overview of Selected Key Issues Based on Recent Litigation Experience' in Horn and Kröll (eds.), *Arbitrating Foreign Investment Disputes* (2004) 193, 211; Schill, 'Enhancing International Investment Law's Legitimacy', p. 78. See also Van Harten and Loughlin, 'Investment Treaty Arbitration as a Species of Global Administrative Law' (2006) 17 *European Journal of International Law* 121 and Montt, *State Liability in Investment Treaty Arbitration* (adopting an approach based on global administrative law); Roberts, 'Clash of Paradigms', pp. 69–74 (describing 'the emergence of the international public law paradigm').

[55] The Treaty establishing the European Economic Community (Treaty of Rome) provides that goods, services, capital and people should be able to move freely across the internal borders of the EU. By 'CJEU', this book also refers to cases decided when the Court was known as the European Court of Justice.

[56] Kulick, *Global Public Interest in International Investment Law* (2012) 110–12, 122–3.

[57] Van Harten, *Investment Treaty Arbitration and Public Law*, pp. 136–43; Roberts, 'Clash of Paradigms', p. 71.

WTO tribunals and investment tribunals both rule on the lawfulness of government action impacting on foreign businesses, both WTO law and international investment law oblige states to afford national treatment and most-favoured nation treatment, and proceedings may be brought in both arenas in relation to the same matter.[58] The ECtHR and investment tribunals, too, can hear cases arising from the same dispute.[59]

However, differences between these three regimes and international investment law must be taken into account, particularly as they relate to the applicable method and standard of review. The EU is unique both as an institution and in relation to its substantive legal order in that it has a regional basis that builds on a comparatively strong consensus concerning economic and political integration.[60] These institutional goals are imperatives that have provided the basis for EU judicial activism in relation to national measures restricting free movement.[61] Such an activist approach is, arguably, inappropriate in the context of international investment law – which neither possesses such an overarching purpose nor a relationship to a central legislature.[62] Like the CJEU, the ECtHR can draw on a relatively closer degree of consensus among treaty parties that might make it more legitimate to engage in activist decision-making compared

---

[58] See *Philip Morris Asia Limited* v. *Australia*, pending and *Australia-Certain Measures Concerning Trademarks and Other Plain Packaging Requirements Applicable to Tobacco Products and Packaging*, pending; *Australia-Certain Measures Concerning Trademarks, Geographical Indications and Other Plain Packaging Requirements Applicable to Tobacco Products and Packaging*, pending. See also *GAMI Investments, Inc.* v. *Mexico*, Final Award; *Archer Daniels Midland Company and Tate & Lyle Ingredients Americas, Inc.* v. *Mexico*, Award; *Corn Products International, Inc.* v. *Mexico States*, Decision on Responsibility and Panel Report, *Mexico-Anti-Dumping Investigation of High-Fructose Corn Syrup (HFCS) from the United States*; Appellate Body Report, *Mexico-Tax Measures on Soft Drinks and Other Beverages*.

[59] For example, *Yukos Universal Limited (Isle of Man)* v. *Russia*, Final Award and *OAO Neftanaya Kompaniya Yukos* v. *Russia*; Kriebaum, 'Is the European Court of Human Rights an Alternative to Investor-State Arbitration?' in Dupuy, Petersmann and Francioni (eds.), *Human Rights in International Investment Law and Arbitration* (2009) 219; Tomuschat, 'The European Court of Human Rights and Investment Protection' in Binder, Kriebaum, Reinisch and Wittich (eds.), *International Investment Law for the 21st Century: Essays in Honour of Christoph Schreuer* (2009) 636.

[60] For example, Button, *The Power to Protect: Trade, Health and Uncertainty in the WTO* (2004) 211–12; Kurtz, 'Adjudging the Exceptional', pp. 367–8. Moreover, the EU has its own legal order including doctrines such as direct effect and supremacy of EU law.

[61] Kurtz, 'Adjudging the Exceptional', pp. 367–8.

[62] Kurtz, 'Adjudging the Exceptional', pp. 367–8. See also Button, *The Power to Protect*, pp. 211–12 (comparing the WTO and EU); Kapterian, 'A Critique of the WTO Jurisprudence on "Necessity"' (2010) 59 *International and Comparative Law Quarterly* 89, 97–8.

to investment tribunals. The normative value ascribed to the protection of certain human rights may also indicate a stricter standard of review than may be appropriate for investor-state arbitration. However, the ECHR requires applicants for review to have exhausted local remedies, which may indicate that the ECtHR affords a deferential standard of review in part because the challenged measure has already been reviewed by another independent body.[63] As WTO law provides a system of inter-state dispute settlement, WTO tribunals determine whether measures hamper international trade at a general level rather than determining whether an individual has been harmed through the actions of the state, which suggests that the approach of WTO tribunals to the standard of review might be moderated to a greater extent by sovereignty considerations.

However, a notable similarity is that each of these bodies – like a variety of other international, supranational and domestic courts and tribunals[64] – employs proportionality analysis as a method of review to decide disputes, either in the context of the contours of the norm itself or in the determination of the lawfulness of limitations upon the norm. The CJEU, ECtHR and WTO tribunals all employ proportionality analysis in the absence of specific treaty language directing such an approach. The CJEU uses proportionality analysis to determine whether measures derogating from freedom of movement are 'justified', and has created the mandatory requirements doctrine without reference to specific treaty language.[65] The ECtHR employs proportionality analysis in its review of almost all alleged interferences with ECHR rights.[66] Although WTO tribunals have not (outside of the context of anti-dumping and countervailing duties and suspension of concessions) explicitly embraced the principle of proportionality,[67] they have used proportionality analysis to determine cases under the general exceptions provisions of the General

---

[63] Schill, 'Deference in Investment Treaty Arbitration', p. 597.

[64] See e.g. Stone Sweet and Matthews, 'Proportionality Balancing and Global Constitutionalism', pp. 72–5, 87–8, 160–1.

[65] Articles 36, 45(3), 52, 62, and 65 TFEU. The CJEU also uses proportionality analysis as a method of review when reviewing EU measures (and national measures implementing EU instruments) affecting individuals, in the determination of discrimination and rights claims and in cases involving charges and penalties. The principle of proportionality is now enshrined in Article 5 TFEU in relation to acts of EU institutions.

[66] Most significantly under Articles 8–11, Article 1, 1st Protocol and Articles 2(3) and 2(4), 4th Protocol ECHR. See e.g. Rivers, 'Proportionality and Variable Intensity of Review' (2006) 65 *Cambridge Law Journal* 174, 179–82.

[67] See, generally, Mitchell, 'Proportionality and Remedies in WTO Disputes' (2007) 17 *European Journal of International Law* 985.

Agreement on Tariffs and Trade (GATT) and the General Agreement on Trade in Services (GATS) and in relation to provisions of the Sanitary and Phytosanitary (SPS) and Technical Barriers to Trade (TBT) agreements that require measures to be 'necessary' to achieve their objectives.[68] Moreover, these bodies all approach the appropriate standard of review in a manner that respects both the need for scrutiny of the state's compliance with its treaty-based obligations and the desirability of national regulatory autonomy.

The approaches adopted by the courts and tribunals studied in this book are not always as coherent and consistent as they could be. Nevertheless, many aspects of the ways in which these bodies approach proportionality and deference in regulatory disputes have a lot to offer to investment tribunals in terms of the development of a certain, coherent and institutionally sensitive approach to determining state liability. The approaches of these bodies demonstrate that, provided that a proportionality-based approach is not otherwise precluded,[69] there should be no impediment to investment tribunals using this methodology in situations where they take state and investor interests into account in determining liability in regulatory disputes. A review of the jurisprudence of these courts and tribunals demonstrates that they can provide useful guidance to investment tribunals in their development of an approach to balancing public and private interests that provides greater coherence and certainty and reflects a fair balance between the interests of states and investors.

1.2.2.3 The relevance of domestic legal systems

Commentators have also argued that domestic legal systems are relevant comparators to international investment law in relation to the method and standard of review, given the functional similarities between these regimes in terms of their role in controlling government action by adjudicating regulatory disputes.[70] This approach might also point to the relevance of proportionality analysis, which is said to be evolving as the dominant method of review in public law adjudication in domestic legal

---

[68] Article XX GATT; Article XIV GATS; Articles 2.2 and 5.6 SPS Agreement; Articles 2.2 and 2.3 Agreement TBT Agreement.

[69] These circumstances are discussed further in Chapter 6.

[70] For example, Montt, *State Liability in Investment Treaty Arbitration*, pp. 371–2; Kingsbury and Schill, 'Investor-State Arbitration as Governance', p. 28; Burke-White and von Staden, 'Private Litigation', pp. 314–22; Schill, 'Enhancing International Investment Law's Legitimacy', pp. 78, 85–8; Schill, 'Deference in Investment Treaty Arbitration', pp. 589–91, 596–7.

systems in cases where competing public and private rights or interests are at issue.[71] Although courts in the United States (US) have resisted using the language of proportionality and balancing, their scrutiny of measures interfering with certain constitutionally protected rights and measures interfering with interstate commerce bears substantial similarities with proportionality analysis.[72] Moreover, the concept of the standard of review – in terms of the allocation of authority between governments and adjudicators in regulatory disputes – is relevant to both domestic and international adjudication. Much of the theory underpinning the concept of deference discussed in this book comes from domestic public law scholarship. This theory is relevant to the context of international adjudication, with modification to the extent that international and domestic adjudication relevantly differ.[73]

However, this book does not adopt domestic legal systems as comparators for three reasons. First, the international dimension is crucial, particularly with respect to the question of the appropriate standard of review. Second, the approach taken by a domestic court to the method and standard of review will be innately tied to the role of that court in the constitutional context, meaning that domestic approaches may not be very helpful: in the US, for example, legislation may be struck down as unconstitutional, whereas in the UK, courts respect the constitutional principle of parliamentary sovereignty. Third, there is a risk that reliance on domestic legal systems will be especially selective, entailing comparisons with legal systems with which the writer is most familiar or can

---

[71] Stone Sweet and Matthews, 'Global Constitutionalism', pp. 73–5; Cohen-Eliya and Porat, *Proportionality and Constitutional Culture* (2013) 10–13 (documenting the adoption of proportionality analysis by many domestic legal systems).

[72] Sullivan and Frase, *Proportionality Principles in American Law: Controlling Excessive Government Actions* (2009) 53–66; Cohen-Eliya and Porat, 'American Balancing and German Proportionality: The Historical Origins' (2010) 8 *International Journal of Constitutional Law* 263, 265, 267–70; Matthews and Stone Sweet, 'All Things in Proportion? American Rights Review and the Problem of Balancing' (2011) 60 *Emory Law Journal* 101–102; Cohen-Eliya and Porat, *Proportionality and Constitutional Culture*, p. 19 (constitutional rights); Trachtman, 'Trade and . . . Problems, Cost-Benefit Analysis and Subsidiarity' (1998) 9 *European Journal of International Law* 69, 63–4; Fallon, 'Strict Judicial Scrutiny' (2006) 54 *UCLA Law Review* 1267, 1330–2; Mathis, 'Balancing and Proportionality in US Commerce Clause Cases' (2009) 35 *Legal Issues of Economic Integration* 273, 277–8; Matthews and Stone Sweet, 'All Things in Proportion?', pp. 127, 137 (interstate commerce).

[73] See Legg, *The Margin of Appreciation in International Human Rights Law: Deference and Proportionality* (2012) 70–1 (discussing rationales for deference in domestic constitutional law and their relationship to rationales for the margin of appreciation in international human rights law). These differences are discussed further in Chapter 2.

access materials in her or his own language.[74] Indeed, comparative public law research in the context of international investment law has already attracted the criticism that it has been too narrowly focused on European systems of law to the exclusion of legal systems in the developing world.[75] This approach also risks collapsing into an approach based on general principles of law which, as discussed below, encounters both normative and methodological criticisms.

To be sure, the criticism of selectivity might also be levelled at the international and supranational legal systems selected as comparators for this study, two of which are European legal systems. However, other international legal regimes that hear claims between individuals and states or that concern economic interests have produced limited case law at this time. In any event, there are indications that these courts and tribunals and other bodies hearing individual claims against states are increasingly employing proportionality analysis as a method of review, and that these fora give consideration to the appropriate standard of review in their determination of state liability. For example, the Inter-American Court of Human Rights (IACtHR) and the United Nations Human Rights Committee (UNHRC)[76] have increasingly used proportionality analysis to determine the permissibility of interferences with rights, and have afforded deference to states in certain circumstances.[77] Decisions from other courts and tribunals of regional economic and political integration will also be relevant to the comparative exercise, although to date these bodies have produced only a very small number of cases.[78] Future research into the jurisprudence of these bodies would, undoubtedly, add to and refine the approach that this book develops.

---

[74] See e.g. Vadi, 'Critical Comparisons: The Role of Comparative Law in Investment Treaty Arbitration' (2010) 39 *Denver Journal of International Law and Policy* 67, 77–8.

[75] See Alvarez, 'Beware: Boundary Crossings' (2013) in Kahana and Schnicov (eds.), *Boundaries of Rights, Boundaries of State* (forthcoming), pp. 56–7. See also Kurtz, 'The Shifting Landscape of International Investment Law and Its Commentary' (2012) 106 *American Journal of International Law* 686, 693.

[76] The UNHRC hears individual communications against states under the International Covenant on Civil and Political Rights.

[77] See Legg, *Margin of Appreciation*, pp. 4–6, 31–6, 80–1, 122, 125–6, 150–67, 178–9, 197–8. Duhaime notes that the IACtHR has applied a doctrine of deference 'using a great variety of names and designations, making such references sometimes difficult to recognize': Duhaime, 'Subsidiarity in the Americas: What Room is There for Deference in the Inter-American System?' in Gruszczynski and Werner (eds.), *Deference in International Courts and Tribunals: Standard of Review and Margin of Appreciation* (2014) 289, 301.

[78] See Baudenbacher and Clifton, 'Courts of Regional Economic and Political Integration Agreements' in Romano, Alter and Shany (eds.), *The Oxford Handbook of International Adjudication* (2014) 250.

1.2.2.4   The relevance of general principles of law

It has also been argued that comparative law can be used to elucidate general principles of law that will, as a source of international law,[79] assist in fleshing out the substantive obligations of states under international investment law and related issues such as the appropriate method and standard of review.[80] In this respect, some commentators have argued that proportionality is itself a general principle of law,[81] but this view is not uniformly held and no in-depth study of this issue has been conducted.[82] However, reliance on general principles is controversial in terms of both the problem of subjectivity in selecting the relevant legal systems from which to distil general principles[83] and the appropriate methodology by which to identify and apply them.[84] In any event, it is not necessary for the purpose of the arguments made in this book to form a conclusion on whether proportionality has crystallized as a general principle of law or whether the appropriate standard of review can be distilled and applied from general principles. The key point is that, in the absence of

---

[79] In terms of Article 38(1)(c) of the Statute of the International Court of Justice, which provides that the Court shall apply, *inter alia*, 'the general principles of law recognized by civilized nations'.

[80] Schill, 'General Principles of Law and International Investment Law', in Gazzini and De Brabandere (eds.), *International Investment Law: The Sources of Rights and Obligations* (2012) 133, 137–8.

[81] Gazzini, 'General Principles of Law in the Field of Foreign Investment' (2007) 10 *Journal of World Investment and Trade* 103 118; Franck, 'On Proportionality of Countermeasures in International Law' (2008) 102 *American Journal of International Law* 715, 718, 731, 736; Stone Sweet and Mathews, 'Global Constitutionalism', pp. 74, 109; Kingsbury and Schill, 'Investor-State Arbitration as Governance', p. 32; Kulick, *Global Public Interest*, p. 171; Schill, 'General Principles of Law', p. 178; Cohen-Eliya and Porat, *Proportionality and Constitutional Culture*, p. 12; de Nanteuil, *L'expropriation indirecte en droit international de l'investissement* (2014) 395; Stone Sweet and della Cananea, 'Proportionality, General Principles of Law, and Investor-State Arbitration: A Response to José Alvarez' (2014) 46 *New York University Journal of International Law and Politics* 911, 914, 918, 938. It is beyond doubt that proportionality is a general principle of EU law: see (among many others) Cases C-96/03 & C-97/03, *Tempelman and van Schaijk v. Directeur van de Rijksdienst voor de keuring van Vee en Vlees*, para. 47. Others have argued that proportionality is a general principle of *international* law: Engle, 'History of the General Principle of Proportionality: An Overview' (2012) 10 *Dartmouth Law Journal* 1, 3; Meron, *Human Rights and Humanitarian Norms as Customary Law* (1989) p. 65.

[82] See Higgins, *Problems and Process: International Law and How We Use It* (1994) p. 236.

[83] Sornarajah, *The International Law on Foreign Investment* (2010) 85–7, 418; Schneiderman, 'The Global Regime of Investor Rights: Return to the Standards of Civilised Justice?' (2014) 5 *Transnational Legal Theory* 60, 64, 74–7; See Paine, 'The Project of System-Internal Reform in International Investment Law: An Appraisal' (2015) 6 *Journal of International Dispute Settlement* 332, 339–40.

[84] Stone Sweet and della Cananea, 'General Principles of Law', p. 912; Paine, 'The Project of System-Internal Reform, pp. 340–2.

assistance from the rules of treaty interpretation, it is legitimate to examine how other legal regimes that deal with functionally similar issues approach these questions.

1.3   Book methodology and structure

The book examines tribunals' approaches to the method and standard of review in the determination of liability in regulatory disputes in relation to a subset of investment treaty provisions: fair and equitable treatment and arbitrary measures clauses, indirect expropriation, non-discrimination and treaty exceptions. These are the key areas of tension between regulatory autonomy and the protection of foreign investment in international investment law, and are frequently the basis of claims in regulatory disputes – or, in the case of treaty exceptions, have been relied upon by the state in a number of high-profile cases that have attracted criticism in terms of the approaches taken by tribunals to the method and standard of review.

This book does not undertake any in-depth analysis of the normative question of the ideal level of protection of investors' interests under the various standards of investment protection, instead examining how the method of review and standard of review can inform adjudication in relation to currently predominant understandings of states' substantive obligations under investment treaties. In focusing on regulatory disputes, the book does not examine claims based solely on interferences with contracts or other acts of the state in a private law capacity, although it does analyze cases involving regulatory or administrative measures affecting contractual relationships between investors and states. Nor does the book focus on challenges to decisions of domestic courts or explore how tribunals have balanced state and investor interests in determining the appropriate quantum of compensation payable in the event of a breach.[85]

The study undertaken for the present book primarily has a doctrinal and comparative methodology. The research involved qualitative analysis of cases and review of the secondary literature on investor-state arbitration. Cases were identified for analysis initially through a review of the secondary literature, followed by monitoring cases decided after the

---

[85] In relation to the latter issue, see Kriebaum, 'Regulatory Takings: Balancing the Interests of the Investor and the State' (2007) 8 *Journal of World Investment and Trade* 717, 732; Kulick, *Global Public Interest*, pp. 199, 201–2, 208–9; UNCTAD, *Fair and Equitable Treatment: A Sequel* (2012) xvi (suggesting that investment tribunals should rely on proportionality considerations in this determination).

initial literature review was conducted in 2011. The secondary literature and decided cases were monitored until December 2014. Searches of the Investor-State Law Guide database were periodically performed for terms and phrases including balancing, proportionality, deference, standard of review and margin of appreciation, but the results of these searches were not the only way in which relevant cases were identified. Approximately 180 investment tribunal decisions were identified and analyzed further; 97 are discussed in this book in relation to various issues.

The rest of this book is structured as follows. Chapter 2 investigates how courts and tribunals use proportionality analysis as a method of review to determine the legality of limiting a right or interest protected by a given legal regime or the permissibility of a derogation from it. This chapter discusses how the stages of proportionality analysis are applied and evaluates some of the critical literature concerning this method of review. This chapter also introduces the concept of the standard of review and explores rationales for deference in international and supranational adjudication. Chapter 3 then examines how the CJEU, the ECtHR and WTO tribunals employ proportionality analysis and approach the standard of review, analyzing how different rationales for deference are applied to the various stages of proportionality analysis. These chapters provide a doctrinal and theoretical underpinning for the subsequent analysis of the decision-making of investment tribunals in Chapters 4 and 5.

Chapter 4 assesses the present state of the decided investment cases in terms of the methods of review that investment tribunals have employed, noting the gradual (yet inconsistent and somewhat incoherent) moves towards a proportionality-based methodology. Chapter 5 then disaggregates tribunals' approaches to the various stages of proportionality analysis in terms of the degree of deference afforded to states and other relevant factors influencing the determination of liability in order to construct an institutionally sensitive approach to proportionality analysis that investment tribunals could adopt. Chapter 6 reflects on the emergence of proportionality analysis as a method of review in international investment law and discusses the circumstances in which proportionality analysis will (and will not) be an appropriate method of review in regulatory disputes. This chapter also discusses other factors influencing the standard of review in investment cases, and addresses criticisms of proportionality analysis and deference as they relate to investor-state arbitration.

The main argument made in this book is that investment tribunals should adopt proportionality analysis as the applicable method of review and take an appropriately deferential approach to the standard of review in the determination of regulatory disputes, provided that this is not precluded by the treaty text, customary international law or the terms of an applicable contract.

According to this approach, investment tribunals would assess the legitimacy of the host state's regulatory objective, the suitability of the measure to achieve that objective, and whether there were less restrictive measures reasonably available that would achieve the objective. They would not, however, undertake the proportionality *stricto sensu* stage that is employed in some other jurisdictions.[86] Arbitrators would also afford a measure of deference to host states in situations of normative or empirical uncertainty. They would do so on the basis of the desirability of regulatory autonomy and of embedded decision-makers having primary decision-making responsibility, and on the basis of the practical advantages that flow from reliance upon primary decision-makers with greater institutional competence and/or expertise in relation to the issues to be determined. Although the decided cases hint at elements of this approach, such an approach does not by any means predominate at this time and, as such, it would represent a significant change in the manner in which investment tribunals approach the determination of state liability in regulatory disputes.

Combining the method of proportionality analysis with an institutionally sensitive approach to the standard of review could respond to both of the concerns about investment tribunals' decision-making identified above. Proportionality analysis provides a more coherent, consistent method of review in regulatory disputes than its alternatives, providing greater certainty to states and investors. The adoption of an appropriately deferential approach to the standard of review could address concerns about the incursion of investment tribunal decisions into the regulatory autonomy of host states. It would permit governments greater discretion in selecting regulatory objectives and designing measures to achieve them, while at the same time providing for adequate scrutiny of their conduct for compliance with international law, so as to control misuse of public power.

---

[86] This approach is elaborated on further in Chapters 2, 3 and 5.

2

Proportionality and deference in theoretical perspective

2.1 Introduction

Every legal system requires adjudicators to second-guess governmental decision-making when determining the permissibility of interferences with legally protected rights or interests. In regulatory disputes, courts and tribunals use methods of review such as proportionality analysis to determine whether an interference with a right or interest is justifiable, or whether the government has overstepped the bounds of its discretion. At the same time, adjudicators in all legal systems are frequently confronted with the question of how strictly they should scrutinize legislation and other government conduct, and thus the appropriate standard of review.[1] This chapter discusses the use of proportionality analysis as a means of deciding cases involving competing public and private interests, including its advantages and disadvantages as a method of review. The chapter then addresses the question of the standard of review; in particular, the circumstances in which an international court or tribunal might afford a measure of deference to a state in the determination of liability.

2.2 The structure of proportionality analysis

Originating in German administrative law, proportionality analysis is now employed as a method of review by international, supranational and domestic courts and tribunals in a variety of contexts, including disputes between individuals and governments and disputes between states.[2] As well as the areas of law discussed in this book, the concept of proportionality is used in international law to determine the legality of self-defence,[3]

---

[1] King, 'Institutional Approaches to Judicial Restraint' (2008) 28 *Oxford Journal of Legal Studies* 409.
[2] See e.g. Stone Sweet and Matthews, 'Global Constitutionalism', pp. 72–5, 87–8, 160–1.
[3] *Military and Paramilitary Activities in and against Nicaragua (Nicaragua v. US)*, Merits, paras. 176, 194. See Crawford, *The International Law Commission's Articles on State*

armed conflict,[4] countermeasures[5] and in maritime delimitation proceedings.[6] Proportionality analysis is generally understood to comprise a three- or four-fold test or set of questions that a court or tribunal applies in reviewing a measure: an assessment of the legitimacy of the objective of the measure, an analysis of the suitability of the measure to achieve this objective, a determination of the necessity of the measure in light of available alternatives, and a balancing test that evaluates the importance of achieving the objective vis-à-vis the importance of avoiding the harm to the protected right or interest caused by the measure (proportionality *stricto sensu*).[7] Each stage is assessed cumulatively, and failure of a measure to comply with that stage will render the measure unlawful.

The preliminary stage of the evaluation of the *legitimacy of the regulatory objective* – in terms of whether the objective serves the public interest – aims at filtering out illegitimate or impermissible purposes. An illegitimate regulatory objective will lack proportionality if it infringes upon a protected right or interest. Where the relevant treaty or statutory provision sets out a list of permissible regulatory objectives, an adjudicator's role is limited to assessing whether the stated objective falls within the relevant category, because the stipulated objectives are, at a general level, already determined to be legitimate by virtue of their inclusion in the provision.[8] In circumstances where the provision does not stipulate permissible objectives, an adjudicator will determine whether the objective

---

Responsibility: Introduction, Text and Commentaries (2002) 296; Kretzmer, 'The Inherent Right to Self Defence and Proportionality in *Jus Ad Bellum*' (2013) 24 *European Journal of International Law* 235; Newton and May, *Proportionality in International Law* (2013) 7–8, 82–3, 291–2.

[4] *Legality of the Threat or Use of Nuclear Weapons*, Advisory Opinion, para. 78. See Franck, 'Rights, Balancing and Proportionality' (2010) 4 *Law and Ethics of Human Rights* 230, 232–4; Newton and May, *Proportionality in International Law*, pp. 172–3.

[5] *Gabčíkovo-Nagymaros Project (Hungary v. Slovakia)*, para. 85; *Armed Activities on the Territory of the Congo (Democratic Republic of the Congo v. Uganda)*, para. 147; Crawford, *Articles on State Responsibility*, pp. 294–6; Franck, 'Rights, Balancing and Proportionality', p. 232; Newton and May, *Proportionality in International Law*, pp. 182–9.

[6] *Maritime Delimitation in the Black Sea (Romania v. Ukraine)*, para. 122; *Territorial and Maritime Dispute (Nicaragua v. Colombia)*, paras. 191–93; *Continental Shelf (Libyan Arab Jamahiriya v. Malta)*, paras. 55–66, 74–5; *North Sea Continental Shelf (Germany v. Denmark, Germany v. Netherlands)*, paras. 98, 101. The International Court of Justice (ICJ) also employed this method of review in *Navigational and Related Rights (Costa Rica v. Nicaragua)*, para. 87.

[7] On the stages of proportionality analysis, see e.g. Stone Sweet and Matthews, 'Global Constitutionalism', p. 75; Barak, *Proportionality: Constitutional Rights and Their Limitations* (2012) 132–3.

[8] Kumm, 'Political Liberalism', p. 138.

of the measure is legitimate by reference to prevailing societal standards. This is a normative question, reflecting the view that not every regulatory objective can justify limiting a protected right or interest.[9]

The stage of *suitability* requires an adjudicator to determine whether the challenged measure is rationally connected to its objective. This involves the determination of whether the measure has the capacity to achieve its objective or whether there is a causal relationship between the measure and the objective.[10] A measure will be unlawful if it cannot advance its stated objective.[11] The suitability stage can also be used to identify whether the measure's stated objective is a pretext for another (impermissible) objective, by examining the measure as designed and applied in light of its pleaded objective.[12]

The *necessity* stage of review, also known as least-restrictive means analysis, requires that in circumstances where there is another measure or measures available that would achieve the objective, the government must select the option that intrudes the least upon the right or interest. The measure will be unlawful if an alternative measure is available that has a less restrictive effect on the right or interest. Least-restrictive means analysis is the heart (and in some circumstances, the limit) of the approaches of the CJEU, the ECtHR and WTO to proportionality analysis.[13]

The *proportionality stricto sensu* stage requires an adjudicator to ascribe value to the competing interests, weigh them and decide whether the measure's impact is proportionate to or too severe relative to the gain that the measure seeks to achieve. This is done by assessing the social importance of achieving the measure's objective against the social importance of avoiding harm to the right or interest.[14] While the necessity stage limits

---

[9] Barak, *Proportionality*, pp. 245–6.

[10] See e.g. Jans, 'Proportionality Revisited' (2000) 27 *Legal Issues of Economic Integration* 239, 240, 244; Andenas and Zleptnig, 'Proportionality: WTO Law in Comparative Perspective' (2007) 42 *Texas International Law Journal* 371, 388–9; Rivers, 'Variable Intensity of Review', p. 198; Kumm, 'Political Liberalism', p. 138; Barak, *Proportionality*, p. 303.

[11] Rivers, 'Variable Intensity of Review', p. 198; Barak, *Proportionality*, pp. 303, 316.

[12] See e.g. Jans, 'Proportionality Revisited', pp. 244, 249; Mountfield, 'Regulatory Expropriations in Europe: The Approach of the European Court of Human Rights' (2002) 11 *New York University Environmental Law Journal* 136, 140–1; Ortino, *Basic Legal Instruments for the Liberalisation of Trade: A Comparative Analysis of EC and WTO Law* (2004) 445–66.

[13] For example, Lovric, *Deference to the Legislature*, p. 140; Matthews and Stone Sweet, 'All Things in Proportion?', p. 107.

[14] Barak, *Proportionality*, pp. 8, 357, 484. See also Sunstein, *After the Rights Revolution: Reconceiving the Regulatory State* (1990) 181, defining proportionality as requiring that aggregate social benefits be proportionate to aggregate social costs; Trachtman, 'Trade and . . . Problems', p. 74; Alexy, *A Theory of Constitutional Rights* (2002) 100, 401.

the relevant inquiry to *how* the objective may be achieved (the relationship of means to ends), the proportionality *stricto sensu* stage is concerned with whether the objective itself may lawfully be achieved, given its impact on the relevant right or interest.[15] Although the challenged measure may be the least-restrictive means available to achieve the objective, its impact on the protected right or interest may nevertheless be too high a price to pay.[16] This stage of analysis can, therefore, render unlawful the only possible way of achieving what has already been judged to be a legitimate objective.[17]

2.3   The desirability of proportionality analysis as a method of review

Methods of review such as proportionality analysis are trade-off devices that operate as aids to problem solving and to express the reasoning processes of adjudicators.[18] One of the main arguments made in support of proportionality analysis is that this method of review can rationalize decision-making by restricting reasoning and argumentation to a pre-determined analytical structure.[19] Proportionality analysis can also make value judgements more explicit by formalizing the decision-making

---

[15] Elliott, 'Proportionality and Deference: The Importance of a Structured Approach' in Forsyth, Elliott, Jhaveri, Ramsden and Scully Hill (eds.), *Effective Judicial Review: A Cornerstone of Good Governance* (2010) 264, 267; Barak, *Proportionality*, p. 343.

[16] Rivers, 'A Theory of Constitutional Rights and the British Constitution' in Alexy, *A Theory of Constitutional Rights* (2002) xvii, xxxiii. See also Cohen-Eliya and Porat, *Proportionality and Constitutional Culture*, pp. 68–70, describing the proportionality *stricto sensu* stage as one that can identify pretextual objectives: 'Because a rational actor would not ordinarily make an extremely poor tradeoff, it can be assumed that the government actor in such circumstances was motivated by goals other than what was alleged'; Brems and Lavrysen, '"Don't Use a Sledgehammer to Crack a Nut": Less Restrictive Means in the Case Law of the European Court of Human Rights' (2015) 15 *Human Rights Law Review* 139, 147, arguing that the necessity test can similarly be deployed because 'if the hidden objective is to strike at the individuals concerned, the measure will often go further than strictly required to advance the stated objective'.

[17] See Elliott, 'The HRA 1998 and the Standard of Substantive Review' (2002) 7 *Judicial Review* 97, 107; Rivers, 'Variable Intensity of Review', p. 200; Elliott, 'The Importance of a Structured Approach', p. 267.

[18] See Trachtman, 'Trade and . . . Problems', pp. 39, 82; Trachtman, 'Regulatory Jurisdiction and the WTO' (2007) 10 *Journal of International Economic Law* 631, 646–8; Legg, *Margin of Appreciation*, pp. 312–14; Panaccio, 'In Defence of Two-Step Balancing and Proportionality in Rights Adjudication' (2011) 24 *Canadian Journal of Law and Jurisprudence* 109, 119.

[19] Harbo, 'The Function of the Proportionality Principle in EU Law' (2010) 16 *European Law Journal* 158, 160–1; Matthews and Stone Sweet, 'All Things in Proportion?', p. 111.

process, which may reduce the perception of a predisposition in favour of certain ideologies or at least facilitate public debate about the values underpinning a particular decision.[20] Greater transparency in decision-making through applying the analytical structure of proportionality analysis may assist litigants and broader communities affected by a court or tribunal's decision to understand how adjudicators have reached a conclusion about the legality of a measure.[21] The constraints imposed by the structure of proportionality analysis can also legitimize adjudicatory authority by promoting greater certainty and coherence in the application of norms.[22]

Yet despite these apparent benefits, proportionality analysis has attracted a number of criticisms, particularly in the context of human rights law.[23] One criticism that has particular resonance beyond the human rights context is that proportionality analysis involves balancing incommensurable values – values that do not share a common measure and therefore cannot be ranked in terms of importance.[24] This concern relates to the proportionality *stricto sensu* stage of proportionality analysis, which, as noted above, has not been wholly embraced in the international and supranational legal contexts. In undertaking the

---

[20] See e.g. Stone Sweet and Matthews, 'Global Constitutionalism', pp. 80, 84, 95; Bomhoff, 'Balancing the Global and Local: Judicial Balancing as a Problematic Topic in Comparative (Constitutional) Law' (2008) 31 *Hastings International and Comparative Law Review* 555, 559; Kavanagh, *Constitutional Review under the UK Human Rights Act* (2009) 257; Harbo, 'Proportionality Principle in EU Law', pp. 162–4; Bomhoff, 'Genealogies of Balancing as Discourse' (2010) 4 *Law and Ethics of Human Rights* 108, 117–18; Matthews and Stone Sweet, 'All Things in Proportion?', p. 108.

[21] Jackson, 'Being Proportional About Proportionality: Review of Beatty, The Ultimate Rule of Law' (2004) 21 *Constitutional Commentary* 803, 831; Barak, 'Proportionality (2)' in Rosenfeld and Sajo (eds.), *The Oxford Handbook of Comparative Constitutional Law* (2012) 739, 749.

[22] For example, Harbo, 'Proportionality Principle in EU Law', p. 162. See, in relation to the importance of coherence and clarity for legal legitimacy, Franck, *The Power of Legitimacy Among Nations* (1990) 30–5, 49, 147–8, 152–3; Franck, 'Legitimacy in the International System' (1988) 82 *American Journal of International Law* 705, 706; Franck, *Fairness in International Law and Institutions* (1998) 38.

[23] See Habermas, *Between Facts and Norms: Contributions to a Discourse Theory of Law and Democracy* (1996) 259–61; Dworkin, *Taking Rights Seriously* (1977) 197–200; Dworkin, 'Rights as Trumps' in Waldron (ed.), *Theories of Rights* (1984); Tsakyrakis, 'Proportionality: An Assault on Human Rights?' (2009) 7 *International Journal of Constitutional Law* 468, 474, 476, 493; Panaccio, 'In Defence of Two-Step Balancing', pp. 114–15.

[24] On incommensurability, see e.g. Raz, *The Morality of Freedom* (1986) 321–69; Finnis, 'Natural Law and Legal Reasoning' (1990) 38 *Cleveland State Law Review* 1, 9–13; Luban, 'Incommensurable Values, Rational Choice, and Moral Absolutes' (1990) 38 *Cleveland State Law Review* 65, 67–8; Raz, *Engaging Reason* (2001) 46.

proportionality *stricto sensu* stage, an adjudicator must attempt to ascribe values on the same scale to both interests and then judge their relative importance, which may give rise to legitimacy concerns. The concern is that to directly balance competing interests in this way assumes either that these interests will be commensurable, or that it will always be possible to make rational judgements about incommensurable interests.[25] But it may be conceptually difficult and risk arbitrariness to directly balance competing interests in this way, which may undermine the argument that proportionality analysis provides an objective and coherent structure to guide adjudicators.[26] It might be argued that adjudicators can deal with the problem of incommensurability by attempting to assess the costs and benefits of the competing interests on their own terms, then producing an abstract scale against which to weigh their relative social importance.[27] Arguably, however, determining whether the importance of avoiding harm to the claimant's interests outweighs the importance of achieving the objective in the circumstances is a highly subjective matter that is open to different interpretations; to perform it legitimately suggests that adjudicators need to have a high degree of familiarity with the values held dear by local communities and the circumstances that preceded the introduction of the measure. This issue leads to another criticism: that employing proportionality analysis places too much discretion in adjudicators to engage in value judgements when deciding cases. Proportionality analysis can be a very far-reaching method of review in terms of its intrusiveness into governmental policy-making because the method permits adjudicators to substitute their judgment with respect to each stage of review.[28]

The stages of suitability and necessity are factual questions, in the sense that it can be objectively ascertained whether the measure is rationally

---

[25] See e.g. Rivers, 'Proportionality, Discretion and the Second Law of Balancing' in Pavlakos (ed.), *Law, Rights and Discourse: The Legal Philosophy of Robert Alexy* (2007) 167, 185; Panaccio, 'In Defence of Two-Step Balancing', pp. 114–15.

[26] For example, Habermas, *Between Facts and Norms*, p. 259; Çali, 'Balancing Human Rights? Methodological Problems with Weights, Scales and Proportions' (2007) 29 *Human Rights Quarterly* 251, 253, 256–7, 264–5; Tsakyrakis, 'An Assault on Human Rights?', pp. 482–4; Webber, 'Proportionality, Balancing and the Cult of Constitutional Rights Scholarship' (2010) 23 *Canadian Journal of Law and Jurisprudence* 179, 183, 194; Harbo, 'Proportionality Principle in EU Law', p. 165.

[27] For example, Alexy, 'On Balancing and Subsumption: A Structural Comparison' (2003) 16 *Ratio Juris* 433, 442; Barak, *Proportionality*, pp. 357, 483–4.

[28] For example, Regan, 'The Meaning of "Necessary" in GATT Article XX and GATS Article XIV: The Myth of Cost–benefit Balancing' (2007) 6 *World Trade Review* 347, 349; Elliott, 'Proportionality and Deference', p. 264; Stone Sweet and Matthews, 'Global Constitutionalism', p. 100; Matthews and Stone Sweet, 'All Things in Proportion?', p. 110.

connected to its objective or whether there are other measures available that would achieve the objective. These issues are not always clear-cut, however, as there may be uncertainty or disagreement as to the effectiveness of the challenged measure or the availability of alternative measures. The government may have more resources at its disposal that make it better placed to answer these questions.

The more value-oriented stages of proportionality analysis (legitimate objective and proportionality *stricto sensu*) are even more problematic in this respect. These stages of proportionality analysis involve asking normative questions to which the answer will depend on a number of implicit political, moral, ideological and economic beliefs and assumptions held by adjudicators.[29] This scope for subjectivity and reliance on judicial intuition may lead to decisions being rendered that are at odds with the expectations not only of litigants, but also of society more broadly. In international and supranational legal settings, adjudicators cannot rely on the fact that they are embedded within the local community as a means to bolster their adjudicative legitimacy in making value judgements.[30] In this respect, consideration of the appropriate standard of review – including the relevance of deference – is necessary in order to deal with situations where there is uncertainty as to whether a particular stage or stages of the proportionality test are satisfied. Arguably, adopting an appropriately deferential approach to proportionality analysis can resolve – or at least attenuate – these concerns.

2.4 The relevance of the standard of review to adjudicating regulatory disputes

2.4.1 *Method of review, standard of review and grounds of review*

In this book, 'standard of review' refers to the degree of scrutiny of the decision of a primary decision-maker by an adjudicator in relation to the evaluation of factual and legal issues, which will fall on a continuum

---

[29] For example, de Búrca, 'The Principle of Proportionality and its Application in EC Law' (1993) 13 *Yearbook of European Law* 105, 108–9; Elliott, 'Proportionality and Deference', p. 281; Webber, 'The Cult of Constitutional Rights Scholarship', p. 185.

[30] See e.g. Greer, *The Margin of Appreciation: Interpretation and Discretion under the European Convention on Human Rights* (2000) 414; Neumann and Türk, 'Necessity Revisited: Proportionality in World Trade Organization Law after *Korea-Beef, EC-Asbestos* and *EC-Sardines*' (2003) 37 *Journal of World Trade* 199, 231–3; Marceau and Trachtman, 'A Map of the World Trade Organization Law of Domestic Regulation of Goods' in Bermann and Mavroidis (eds.), *Trade and Human Health and Safety* (2006) 9, 49; Regan, 'The Meaning of "Necessary"', p. 349; Harbo, 'Proportionality Principle in EU Law', p. 165.

bounded by total reliance on the decision the primary decision-maker at one end, and substitutionary (*de novo*) review at the other.[31] The standard of review employed by a court or tribunal reflects the horizontal allocation of authority between the court or tribunal and the legal system's primary decision-makers.[32] In international and supranational legal systems, the standard of review also influences the vertical relationship between adjudicators and states, and, ultimately, the relationship between state responsibility and state sovereignty.[33]

In the context of international adjudication, the standard of review must strike an appropriate balance between oversight of compliance with a state's international obligations and respect for national autonomy in terms of the right to regulate at international law.[34] An overly lenient approach to the standard of review may undermine the negotiated balance of the rights and obligations set out in the relevant treaty.[35] However, international regimes also depend on a degree of deference to national governments by adjudicators in structuring relationships between states and international courts and tribunals.[36] Intrusive approaches to the standard of review adopted by international adjudicators not only give adjudicators more power, but also give greater authority to international over domestic governance.[37] The repeated application of a strict standard of review may give rise to compliance issues, reform of legal instruments to curtail adjudicative discretion, or withdrawal of states from the court or tribunal's jurisdiction – all situations that have arisen in international

---

[31] See e.g. Oesch, *Standards of Review in WTO Dispute Resolution* (2003) 14–15; Kavanagh, 'Deference or Defiance? The Limits of the Judicial Role in Constitutional Adjudication' in Huscroft (ed.), *Expounding the Constitution: Essays in Constitutional Theory* (2008) 184, 184–6, 190; Taggart, 'Proportionality, Deference, *Wednesbury*' (2008) 1 *New Zealand Law Review* 423, 451; Bohanes and Lockhart, 'Standard of Review in WTO Law', p. 379.

[32] For example, Oesch, *Standards of Review in WTO Dispute Resolution*, p. 23; Bohanes and Lockhart, 'Standard of Review in WTO Law', p. 379.

[33] For example, Croley and Jackson, 'WTO Dispute Procedures, Standard of Review, and Deference to National Governments' (1996) 90 *American Journal of International Law* 193–7; Oesch, *Standards of Review in WTO Dispute Resolution*, p. 28; Bohanes and Lockhart, 'Standard of Review in WTO Law', p. 381; Lovric, *Deference to the Legislature*, p. 60; Roberts, 'The Next Battleground', pp. 175–8.

[34] For example, Bohanes and Lockhart, 'Standard of Review in WTO Law', p. 381.

[35] Chen, 'The Standard of Review and the Roles of ICSID Arbitral Tribunals in Investor-State Dispute Settlement' (2012) 5 *Contemporary Asia Arbitration Journal* 23, 30; Roberts, 'The Next Battleground', p. 180.

[36] Schill, 'Deference in Investment Treaty Arbitration', pp. 589–60.

[37] See Roberts, 'The Next Battleground', p. 173.

investment law.[38] The standard of review is, therefore, a critical factor in an investment tribunal's determination of whether a government may permissibly regulate or take other actions in the public interest without being liable to compensate a foreign investor. Employing a standard of review that reflects an appropriate allocation of authority between tribunals and states may be one way for the regime of international investment law to deal with concerns that the law has an unjustifiably intrusive effect on regulatory autonomy.

Conceptually, the *standard of review* differs from the applicable *method of review*. Each serves a distinct purpose.[39] Commentators and adjudicators have, however, used a variety of terms to describe these concepts and frequently conflate them.[40] As noted in Chapter 1, a method of review is a technique used by adjudicators (such as proportionality analysis) to determine the permissibility of interference with a right or interest, whereas the standard of review refers to the intensity with which the method of review is applied – whether taking a strict or more deferential approach.[41] However, the method of review and the standard of review are closely intertwined, because when courts and tribunals employ a method of review in assessing the legality of an impugned measure, they must also determine the relevant standard of review.[42] The standard of review cannot be seen in isolation and must be addressed alongside the method of review used by a court or tribunal to decide cases. The standard of review also

---

[38] See Burke-White and von Staden, 'The Need for Public Law Standards of Review in Investor-State Arbitrations' in Schill (ed.), *International Investment Law and Comparative Public Law* (2010) 689, 711.

[39] See e.g. (noting the difference between the concepts) Kavanagh, *Constitutional Review*, p. 237.

[40] See (describing proportionality analysis and other methods of review as standards of review) Van Harten, *Investment Treaty Arbitration and Public Law*, pp. 81–2; Burke-White and von Staden, 'Private Litigation', pp. 334–7; Moloo and Jacinto, 'Standards of Review', p. 552; Arato, 'The Margin of Appreciation in International Investment Law', p. 549; Shirlow, 'Deference and Indirect Expropriation Analysis in International Investment Law: Observations on Current Approaches and Frameworks for Future Analysis' (2014) 29 *ICSID Review* 595, 601. See also e.g. *Whaling in the Antarctic (Australia v. Japan)*, Separate Opinion of Judge Yusuf, para. 3.

[41] For example, in the investment award *Tecmed v. Mexico*, the tribunal took a non-deferential approach to proportionality analysis involving intensive scrutiny of the legitimacy of the state's objective and the balance of interests, whereas in the ECtHR decision *James v. UK*, the ECtHR adopted a deferential approach to these questions.

[42] See e.g. de Búrca, 'The Principle of Proportionality in EC Law', p. 110; Gunn, 'Deconstructing Proportionality in Limitations Analysis' (2005) 19 *Emory International Law Review* 465, 477–8; Andenas and Zleptnig, 'Proportionality: WTO Law in Comparative Perspective', pp. 392–8; Pirker, *Proportionality Analysis and Judicial Review*, p. 43.

differs from the *grounds of review* – the basis for review set out in the treaty, such as fair and equitable treatment or indirect expropriation, any further articulation of its normative content (whether in the treaty itself, by the tribunal, or by a formal interpretation of the treaty parties).[43] Like the method of review and standard of review, these two concepts can also be closely connected,[44] and have in several cases been conflated by investment tribunals.[45]

2.4.2   Determining the appropriate standard of review

A treaty may stipulate or provide guidance as to the applicable standard of review.[46] For example, Article 144(1) of the TFEU permits EU member states to take protective measures to address a sudden crisis in the balance of payments, as long as those measures 'cause the least possible disturbance in the functioning of the internal market' and are not 'wider in scope than is strictly necessary to remedy the sudden difficulties which have arisen'. The references to the 'least possible disturbance' and 'strictly necessary' indicate that a strict approach to the standard of review is envisaged in terms of determining the necessity of measures. The reference to the concept of necessity also provides guidance as to the method of review. Article 1 of the 1st Protocol to the ECHR refers in part to a state's right 'to enforce such laws as it deems necessary to control the use of property in accordance with the general interest', indicating that a deferential approach to review is envisaged. Article 17(6)(i) of the WTO Anti-Dumping Agreement is especially clear with respect to the applicable standard of review with respect to fact-finding, providing that 'the panel shall determine whether the authorities' establishment of the facts was proper and whether their evaluation of those facts was unbiased and objective. If this is the case, the panel must not overturn the authorities'

---

[43] Such as the NAFTA parties' *Note of Interpretation* concerning Article 1105 of the NAFTA (2001) (discussed further in Chapter 6).

[44] See Ortino, 'The Investment Treaty System as Judicial Review', pp. 458–61, 467 (discussing the interrelated nature of the grounds of review and standard of review); Schill, 'Deference in Investment Treaty Arbitration', p. 582 (arguing that an investment tribunal's approach to the scope of fair and equitable treatment in terms of what this book terms the grounds of review will be influential or even determinative of the standard of review). See also Shirlow, 'Deference and Indirect Expropriation', p. 614 (appearing to view the grounds of review and standard of review as one broader concept); Cheyne, 'Deference and the Use of the Public Policy Exception in International Courts and Tribunals' in Gruszczynski and Werner (eds.), *Deference in International Courts and Tribunals* (2014) 38, 53–4 (describing the grounds of review as the standard of review).

[45] This issue is discussed further in Chapter 6.

[46] The treaty may additionally or alternatively stipulate the applicable method of review.

conclusions as to these matters 'even though the panel might have reached a different conclusion'. Article 22(2)(b) of the Australia–United States Free Trade Agreement provides a very relaxed standard of review, stating that a party may adopt 'measures that it considers necessary for . . . the protection of its own essential security interests'. The use of the language 'that it considers necessary' indicates that the adjudicator's role is confined to determining whether the party invoking the provision has done so in good faith.[47]

However, these examples are relatively isolated. Treaties rarely specifically stipulate or provide explicit guidance as to the standard of review. Rather, the authority of international courts and tribunals to determine the applicable standard of review derives from their inherent powers. International courts and tribunals enjoy inherent powers to make and exercise rules that are necessary for the administration of justice, to determine their own procedures and to effectively exercise jurisdiction.[48] These powers exist without reference to the text of the tribunal's constitutive document, or may be regarded as implicit within it.[49] The Appellate Body has taken the view that the determination of the applicable standard of review is an inherent power of WTO tribunals.[50] Investment tribunals have affirmed the existence of inherent powers, although not specifically in relation to the standard of review.[51] Procedurally, the standard of review could also, as it relates to the burden and standard of proof, be viewed in terms of the inherent judicial authority to settle the method of handling the evidence.[52]

---

[47] See *Mutual Assistance in Criminal Matters (Djibouti v. France)* Judgment of 4 June 2008, para. 145: 'while it is correct . . . that the terms of [the self-judging clause] provide a State to which a request for assistance has been made with a very considerable discretion, this exercise of discretion is still subject to the obligation of good faith'; Schill and Briese, '"If the State Considers": Self-Judging Clauses in International Dispute Settlement' (2009) 13 *Max Planck United Nations Yearbook* 61.

[48] Shany, 'Toward a General Margin of Appreciation Doctrine in International Law?' (2006) 16 *European Journal of International Law* 907, 911. It might also be argued that where the treaty text provides no guidance as to how to take competing interests into account in the determination of liability, a court or tribunal may rely on its inherent powers to determine the appropriate method of review.

[49] See Brown, 'The Inherent Powers of Courts and Tribunals' (2005) 76 *British Yearbook of International ad Comparative Law* 195, 225–7.

[50] Appellate Body Report, *EC-Measures Affecting Livestock and Meat (Hormones)*, paras. 114–17.

[51] See e.g. *Libananco Holdings Co. Limited v. Turkey*, Award, para. 78. See also Paparinskis, 'Inherent Powers of ICSID Tribunals: Broad and Rightly So' in Laird and Weiler (eds.), *Investment Treaty Arbitration and International Law* (2012) 11 (arguing for a broad understanding of the inherent powers of ICSID tribunals).

[52] Shany, 'Margin of Appreciation', p. 911 (with further references).

The approach that a court or tribunal takes to the standard of review in a given case will depend on one or more of a number of other factors. Most significantly, the characteristics of the primary decision-maker relative to the court or tribunal – in terms of relative suitability for deciding the relevant issues – will also influence the standard of review. This is the concept of deference, which is the focus of the inquiry undertaken in this book.[53] The extent of interference with the right or interest may also be a relevant consideration, with greater interferences being likely to attract more intensive scrutiny.[54] The level of dependence of the court or tribunal on other organs in the legal system may also affect the standard of review, in terms of whether adjudicators desire to manifest respect for the primary decision-maker for strategic reasons.[55]

2.5   Rationales for deference in international and supranational adjudication

Deference involves an adjudicator exercising restraint where the adjudicator's judgment is different from that of the primary decision-maker in circumstances where there is uncertainty as to what the right conclusion should be, or there is no objectively correct answer to an issue.[56] Deference may be justified where there are particular reasons why the view of the primary decision-maker should be preferred to the view of the adjudicator in relation to the reliability of assessments of factual and value-based matters.[57] However, deference is not a concept that is amenable to concretization in terms of a doctrine readily applicable to a

---

[53] It should be noted, however, that others define the concept differently, see e.g. Van Harten, *Sovereign Choices and Sovereign Constraints*, p. 20, equating the concept of the standard of review to what this book terms the concept of deference. This book takes the view that the standard of review is a broader concept than deference, as discussed in this section.

[54] Rivers, 'Variable Intensity of Review', pp. 205–6; Gerards, 'Pluralism, Deference and the Margin of Appreciation Doctrine' (2011) 17 *European Law Journal* 80, 112. This issue is discussed further in Chapter 5 in relation to proportionality analysis.

[55] This issue is discussed further in Chapter 6. Additionally, where a legal regime protects more than one type of right or interest, the nature of that right or interest compared to others protected by the regime may influence the standard of review, see e.g. Greer, *The European Convention on Human Rights: Achievements, Problems and Prospects* (2006) 210; Craig, *EU Administrative Law* (2012) 600–1, 629–31.

[56] See e.g. Rivers, 'Variable Intensity of Review', p. 199; Kavanagh, *Constitutional Review*, p. 170.

[57] Rivers, 'Variable Intensity of Review', p. 203; Kavanagh, 'Deference or Defiance?', pp. 185–6; Kavanagh, *Constitutional Review*, pp. 169, 171 (also arguing that deference is due (in the domestic constitutional context) on the basis of 'prudential reasons' or 'courtesy' in the absence of uncertainty, where the primary decision-maker's assessment of the issue differs from that of the adjudicator); Brady, *Proportionality and Deference under the UK Human*

given case.[58] Rather, adjudicators consider whether the qualities of and discretion enjoyed by the primary decision-maker make that decision-maker better qualified to have primary responsibility for deciding or determining a particular issue.[59]

If a court or tribunal determines that a measure of deference is appropriate, the degree of deference it will afford ranges from treating the views of the primary decision-maker in relation to an issue as persuasive (meaning that an adjudicator assesses the issue but takes due account of the primary decision-maker's views) to treating them as conclusive (where an adjudicator declines to assess the issue, relying solely on the assessment of the primary decision-maker).[60] For example, a court or tribunal might require only that certain procedures were followed, might place a low evidential burden on the government in relation to an issue for determination, might assess whether the primary decision-maker's conclusions were reasonable or might accord substantial weight to the views of the primary decision-maker.[61]

2.5.1 Epistemic deference: responding to normative and empirical uncertainty

This book adopts Alexy's approach to deference,[62] which divides the concept into structural deference and epistemic deference.[63] Epistemic

---

Rights Act: An Institutionally Sensitive Approach (2012) 68, 107; Van Harten, Sovereign Choices and Sovereign Constraints, p. 2.

[58] See Beloff, 'The Concept of Deference in Public Law' (2006) 11 Judicial Review 213, 223; Taggart, 'Proportionality, Deference, Wednesbury', p. 458.

[59] See Croley and Jackson, 'Deference to National Governments', pp. 194–5; Oesch, Standards of Review in WTO Dispute Resolution, p. 24; Shany, 'Margin of Appreciation', p. 913; Rivers, 'Variable Intensity of Review', p. 204; Kavanagh, 'Deference or Defiance?', p. 190; Burke-White and von Staden, 'Investment Protection in Extraordinary Times', pp. 370–1; Kavanagh, Constitutional Review, pp. 173, 240; Kavanagh, 'Defending Deference in Public Law and Constitutional Theory' (2010) 126 Law Quarterly Review 222, 241.

[60] Kavanagh, Constitutional Review, pp. 172–3; Bohanes and Lockhart, 'Standard of Review in WTO Law', p. 383.

[61] See Rivers, 'Variable Intensity of Review', pp. 177–82, 203; Andenas and Zleptnig, 'Proportionality: WTO Law in Comparative Perspective', pp. 392–3; Elliott, 'Proportionality and Deference', pp. 269, 282–4.

[62] Alexy describes deference as adjudicative 'discretion' in this context: Alexy, A Theory of Constitutional Rights, pp. 414–15). However, in the context of proportionality analysis, the terms 'discretion' and 'deference' are often used interchangeably: Rivers, 'Variable Intensity of Review', p. 191; Klatt and Meister, The Constitutional Structure of Proportionality (2012) 77.

[63] Structural deference applies only to certain situations that may arise in relation to proportionality analysis: where, in relation to the necessity and proportionality stricto sensu

deference comprises the two further sub-categories of *normative* deference and *empirical* deference.[64] Normative deference relates to the uncertainties that arise in relation to value judgements, whereas empirical deference relates to situations of uncertainty in relation to knowledge and factual findings.[65] The categories of normative and empirical deference are relevant to different issues that require determination by courts and tribunals, and to different stages of proportionality analysis.[66]

In the context of international adjudication, there are two key reasons why the views of national decision-makers may be more reliable than those of adjudicators in situations of normative or empirical uncertainty.[67] These are the desirability of regulatory autonomy and decision-making by actors that are proximate to or embedded in the national polity, and the practical advantages of relying on the decisions of actors with greater institutional competence or expertise.[68] These rationales for deference are relevant in situations of normative uncertainty and empirical uncertainty, respectively. Although these rationales for deference are not necessarily categorized and articulated as such, these themes frequently recur in the decisions of many international courts and tribunals, whether using the language of deference or the margin of appreciation, or more implicitly by recognizing the allocation of authority between primary

---

stages, there are two or more alternatives that comply with the relevant stage and uncertainty as to which alternative should be preferred. In such cases, an adjudicator affording deference will not interfere with the primary decision-maker's choice: Alexy, *A Theory of Constitutional Rights*, pp. 405–14. Structural deference will not be explored further in this book.

[64] Alexy, *A Theory of Constitutional Rights*, pp. 388–425.

[65] See Brady, *Proportionality and Deference*, p. 68.

[66] Although the concept of epistemic deference has broader application than proportionality analysis.

[67] Similar rationales for deference exist in domestic law, see e.g. Kavanagh, 'Deference or Defiance?'; Kavanagh, *Constitutional Review*.

[68] Cf. Van Harten, *Sovereign Choices and Sovereign Constraints* pp. 3–6. According to Van Harten, restraint (including deference) may be due on the basis of 'relative accountability', usually where the measure is a product of a legislature or is an act of the executive authorized by statute, and may be due on the basis of 'relative capacity', usually in the case of executive measures or actions. The categories of relative accountability and relative capacity loosely map onto the rationales for deference offered in this book, with the difference that this book does not tie the rationale for deference to the type of measure at issue and avoids relying on theories of democratic accountability, as discussed below. More importantly, however, Van Harten's work does not appear to distinguish between the appropriate basis for deference and the circumstances in which it is appropriate that a tribunal afford a measure of deference on that basis.

decision-makers and adjudicators.[69] Both bases for deference relate, at a broad level, to the legitimacy of an adjudicator having primary responsibility for deciding the issue at stake in light of the relative strengths of primary decision-makers. However, each rationale rests on a different theoretical basis and relates to different characteristics of primary decision-makers, different aspects of the decision-making processes of adjudicators and, in the context of proportionality analysis, different stages of review.[70]

2.5.2   Regulatory autonomy and proximity

Courts and tribunals exhibiting deference on the basis of regulatory autonomy do so with the view that national authorities should be the main determinant of the public interest in situations of normative uncertainty.[71] The concern is that the adversarial process may not be able to effectively substitute governmental decision-making where that decision-making entails a value judgement, such as whether the legislature should regulate in a particular area or the importance of a particular government policy as a reason for interfering with private interests.[72] A related issue is the proximity of the court or tribunal to the national polity or region. As discussed above, adjudicators who are not embedded within the state may not fully appreciate national debates or dialogues preceding the introduction of a particular measure, nor public sentiments or policy priorities.[73] In this respect, national governments may be more competent than adjudicators to discern and evaluate local conditions, as they are usually more closely acquainted with local issues, sensitivities and traditions.[74]

---

[69] For example, in *Navigational and Related Rights (Costa Rica v. Nicaragua)*, at para. 101, the ICJ observed that '[a] court examining the reasonableness of a regulation must recognize that the regulator . . . has the primary responsibility for assessing the need for regulation and for choosing, on the basis of its knowledge of the situation, the measure that it deems most appropriate to meet that need'.

[70] Elliott, 'Proportionality and Deference', pp. 268, 278.

[71] See e.g. Çoban, *Protection of Property Rights within the European Convention on Human Rights* (2004) 200.

[72] Gerards, 'Margin of Appreciation', p. 86.

[73] For example, Oesch, *Standards of Review in WTO Dispute Resolution*, p. 57; Gerards, 'Margin of Appreciation', p. 85.

[74] Shany, 'Margin of Appreciation', p. 919; Letsas, *A Theory of Interpretation of the European Convention on Human Rights* (2007) 80–4, 90–1; Burke-White and von Staden, 'Private Litigation', pp. 331–3; Gerards, 'Margin of Appreciation', pp. 85, 98, 110.

The claim for deference on the basis of regulatory autonomy and proximity is inherently weaker than the claim for deference on the basis of relative institutional competence and expertise, as it is not clear that primary decision-makers have any practical advantage over adjudicators on the basis of the former rationale for deference.[75] One criticism that might be made of this rationale for deference is that governments can always make a claim about the desirability of regulatory autonomy or that they enjoy greater proximity to communities affected by the decision at issue. Moreover, the non-embedded nature of adjudicators may also be important in assuring the neutrality of the court or tribunal. Indeed, this was the impetus for the establishment of investor-state arbitration rather than the use of domestic courts to resolve disputes between foreign investors and states.[76] In this respect, while it might be argued that governmental decisions are always worthy of a certain minimum level of deference on the basis of the desirability of regulatory autonomy and decision-making by embedded actors (a presumption in favour of a degree of deference for its own sake), only in situations where there is normative uncertainty should an adjudicator afford a greater degree of deference (where the issue entails a value judgement, such as where the matter is sensitive or controversial).[77] The appropriateness of deference in this area and the applicable degree of deference will depend on the nature of the particular issue before the court or tribunal, rather than applying as an overarching principle that mandates a universally deferential approach.

2.5.3   Relative institutional competence and expertise

The other key rationale for deference in international adjudication is the institutional competence and expertise of the primary decision-maker relative to the adjudicator, where this is relevant to the issue for determination.[78] Deference on the basis of relative institutional

---

[75] Daly, *A Theory of Deference in Administrative Law* (2012) 101.

[76] Roberts, 'The Next Battleground', p. 179. See also Burke-White and von Staden, 'Public Law Standards', pp. 713–14, noting that ICSID arbitrators cannot have the same nationality as a party to the dispute without the consent of the other party. Conversely, however, it is arguable that the institutional features of investor-state arbitration (such as lack of security of tenure and party appointment) call into question the independence of investment arbitrators: Van Harten, *Investment Treaty Arbitration and Public Law*, pp. 5–6, 167–75.

[77] Kavanagh, 'Deference or Defiance?', pp. 192–3; Kavanagh, *Constitutional Review*, pp. 190–6. See also Brady, *Proportionality and Deference*, pp. 25, 108.

[78] See e.g. Hunt, 'Sovereignty's Blight: Why Contemporary Public Law Needs the Concept of "Due Deference"' in Bamworth and Leyland (eds.), *Public Law in a Multi-Layered*

competence and expertise is a practical response to situations of empirical uncertainty.

Institutional features or greater expertise may mean that national authorities are better placed to have primary responsibility for making certain decisions or undertaking certain functions. These include gathering and evaluating complex information (including in relation to risk or harm), monitoring developing situations, engaging in consultation and investigating alternative courses of action.[79] Governments may have greater institutional capacity to apprehend the implications of policy-making where the interests of multiple stakeholders are engaged by the measure. Governments, or experts whom they rely on in decision-making, may also have greater expertise in relation to the subject matter of the measure, such as in relation to macroeconomic policy and science.[80]

By comparison, courts and tribunals are often constrained by time, resource, procedural and evidentiary limitations, which may inhibit a thorough examination of all relevant material.[81] Moreover, courts and

---

Constitution (2003) 337, 353–4; Kavanagh, *Constitutional Review*, pp. 182–90; Lovric, *Deference to the Legislature*, pp. 129–30.

[79] For example, Shany, 'Margin of Appreciation', pp. 918–19; Rivers, 'Variable Intensity of Review', p. 204; Guzman, 'Determining the Appropriate Standard of Review in WTO Disputes' (2009) 42 *Cornell International Law Journal* 45, 63–4; Lovric, *Deference to the Legislature*, p. 69; Gerards, 'Margin of Appreciation', p. 98; Shaffer and Trachtman, 'Interpretation and Institutional Choice at the WTO' (2011) 52 *Virginia Journal of International Law* 103, 148–9.

[80] See, in relation to international adjudication involving scientific questions, Viñuales, 'Foreign Investment and the Environment in International Law: An Ambiguous Relationship' (2010) 80 *British Yearbook of International Law* 244, 278–9 (international investment law); Wagner, 'Law Talk v. Science Talk: The Languages of Law and Science in WTO Proceedings' (2012) 35 *Fordham International Law Journal* 151, 160–3 (WTO law); Fukunaga, 'Standard of Review and "Scientific Truths" in the WTO Dispute Settlement System and Investment Arbitration' (2012) 3 *Journal of International Dispute Settlement* 559, 572–76 (international investment law and WTO law); Mbengue, 'Scientific Fact-finding by International Courts and Tribunals' (2012) 3 *Journal of International Dispute Settlement* 509 (international courts and tribunals generally). The issue of adjudicators' lack of expertise in relation to scientific questions was highlighted in two recent ICJ cases where dissenting judges questioned the Court's competence to decide matters involving the evaluation of competing scientific evidence: see *Pulp Mills on the River Uruguay (Argentina v. Uruguay)*, Joint Dissenting Opinion of Judges Al-Khasawneh and Simma, paras. 2–4, 7, 11–13 and Joint Dissenting Opinion of Judge *ad hoc* Vinuesa, paras. 67–95; *Whaling in the Antarctic (Australia v. Japan)*, Dissenting Opinion of Judge Owada, paras. 24–5, 37–8 and Dissenting Opinion of Judge Yusuf, para. 17.

[81] See, generally, Zleptnig, 'The Standard of Review in WTO Law: An Analysis of Law, Legitimacy and the Distribution of Legal and Political Authority' (2002) 6 *European Integration Online Papers*, p. 12; Shany, 'Margin of Appreciation', pp. 918–19; Gerards, 'Margin of Appreciation', pp. 90, 111.

tribunals take decisions only in relation to the narrow matter at issue, and through the lens of legal norms.[82] In particular, courts and tribunals may experience difficulties in fully apprehending the ramifications of a particular decision that has polycentric effects, due to the binary nature of adjudication.[83]

Where a court or tribunal affords deference to a primary decision-maker on the basis of expertise, it does so on the basis of the reliability of the assessment made by the primary decision-maker.[84] This suggests that an adjudicator should only be deferential in this respect where the authorities can demonstrate that they have the requisite expertise and that the primary decision-maker has relied on that expertise in making the decision, rather than simply because a particular government agency has responsibility for a particular area of government policy.[85] Conversely, deference will likely not be due where a government – although generally possessing superior competence or expertise – has not addressed the relevant issues, such as by not basing a measure on a risk assessment where risk is relevant to the decision.[86]

Nevertheless, where uncertainty remains after adjudicators have taken into account the evidence of the parties in relation to a particular matter, this rationale for deference suggests that a tribunal should afford a measure of deference to the state due to the state's greater expertise and institutional competence as a regulator.[87] Empirical deference may also be indicated where policy-makers have relied on their expertise to predict a likely outcome or have relied on their expertise and experience in pursuing novel or experimental initiatives. There may be no actual information or evidence of effectiveness available to policy-makers when promulgating a measure, and decisions may be based on predictions of how a measure might achieve its objective in future. If the primary decision-maker has greater expertise in relation to the type of issue or more resources at its disposal to decide the issue, the primary decision-maker's

---

[82] Shany, 'Margin of Appreciation', pp. 918–19.

[83] Polycentric decisions are those that have implications for a large network of relationships so that change to any one relationship causes changes to the others: see Fuller, 'The Forms and Limits of Adjudication' (1978) 92 *Harvard Law Review* 353, 395, 401; King, Judging *Social Rights* (2012) 189, 194.

[84] Brady, *Proportionality and Deference*, p. 114.   [85] See Daly, *Theory of Deference*, p. 87.

[86] See Hickman, 'The Substance and Structure of Proportionality' (2008) *Public Law* 694, 698.

[87] Cf. Chan, 'Deference, Expertise and Information-Gathering Powers' (2013) 33 *Legal Studies* 598, 603–4.

assessment of an uncertain matter will be more reliable than an adjudicator's assessment of it.[88] It is also arguable that the institutional competence of governments in performing certain functions can be presumed and need not be established before a court or tribunal, on the basis that in situations of uncertainty, one should afford a measure of deference if the institutional characteristics of the primary decision-maker suggest that it will be more likely to be correct in relation to the issue.[89] More generally, it is arguable that adjudicators should permit a margin for error, so that a good faith misjudgement by government would not result in liability.[90]

2.5.4   Privileging economically developed states?

The regulatory autonomy rationale for deference is frequently referred to as deference based on democratic legitimacy or democratic accountability, particularly in the domestic public law context but sometimes also in the context of international adjudication.[91] Although democracy is a core value of, for example, the EU and the ECHR,[92] other international legal systems such as the WTO and the UN human rights treaty bodies[93] have a membership comprising states with a broader range of systems of government. To be sure, the claim for deference may be stronger where the challenged measure is the product of a government elected through a

---

[88] Brady, *Proportionality and Deference*, p. 114. It should be noted that courts and tribunals may take steps to better equip or inform themselves in relation to relevant issues without relying on deference or the production of evidence by the parties, such as by appointing or consulting experts or through *amici curiae*, see e.g. Viñuales, 'Foreign Investment and the Environment in International Law', pp. 278–9.

[89] King, 'Institutional Approaches to Judicial Restraint', pp. 411–14, 425–6, cf. Brady, *Proportionality and Deference*, pp. 114–15.

[90] This issue is discussed further in Chapter 5.

[91] For example, Kavanagh, 'Deference or Defiance?', pp. 200–3. See, referring to the concept of deference on the basis of democratic legitimacy in the context of international adjudication, Neumann and Türk, 'Necessity Revisited', pp. 201, 232; von Staden, 'The Democratic Legitimacy of Judicial Review Beyond the State: Normative Subsidiarity and Judicial Standards of Review' (2012) 10 *International Journal of Constitutional Law* 1023, 1027, 1037; Van Harten, *Sovereign Choices and Sovereign Constraints*, pp. 49–79. Others refer to this rationale for deference as deference based on 'national sovereignty': von Staden, 'Democratic Legitimacy', p. 1046 or 'voice': Schill, 'Deference in Investment Treaty Arbitration', p. 600.

[92] See Preamble and Title I Article 2 TFEU; Preamble ECHR.

[93] The UNHRC nevertheless affords deference on the basis of democratic legitimacy in some cases, see Legg, *Margin of Appreciation*, pp. 80–1.

robust electoral process or where there had been public participation in the process of enacting the measure.[94]

But the concept of democratic legitimacy as a basis for deference by investment tribunals has attracted criticism on the basis that the appropriate degree of deference might depend on the democratic quality of the host state in question and that, consequently, the measures of some states might be subjected to more intense scrutiny than others, depending on the state's democratic credentials as adjudged by the tribunal.[95] Adopting a variegated approach to the standard of review in international investment law on this basis could result in arbitrators being more deferential to more economically developed states, fuelling claims that investor-state arbitration is structurally biased against the developing world.[96] Moreover, the internal political organization of states is a domestic matter at international law and it is questionable whether investment tribunals have the necessary competence to determine the democratic quality of states.[97] However, the normative desirability of regulatory autonomy and decision-making by embedded actors is a broader consideration relating to the right to regulate under international law, which is a basic attribute of state sovereignty.[98]

There are also some caveats to consider in relation to deference based on greater institutional competence or expertise in terms of the impact that this approach may have on certain states. Just as a theory of deference based on democratic accountability may have the effect of privileging certain systems of government over others, it might be argued that adjudicators will be less likely to exhibit deference on the basis of relative institutional competence and expertise in circumstances where the host state does not have the level of institutional apparatus and capacity comparable to that

---

[94] See e.g. Gerards, 'Margin of Appreciation', p. 86; Legg, *Margin of Appreciation*, p. 69; Kavanagh, 'Proportionality and Parliamentary Debates: Exploring Some Forbidden Territory' (2014) 34 *Oxford Journal of Legal Studies* 443, 470; Van Harten, *Sovereign Choices and Sovereign Constraints*, p. 56.

[95] Roberts, 'The Next Battleground', p. 178. See also Alvarez, 'Review: *Investment Treaty Arbitration and Public Law* by Gus Van Harten' (2008) 102 *American Journal of International Law* 909, 913.

[96] Roberts, 'The Next Battleground', p. 178.   [97] Roberts, 'The Next Battleground', p. 178.

[98] See *Military and Paramilitary Activities in and Against Nicaragua (Nicaragua v. US)*, Merits, paras. 258, 269: 'A State's domestic policy falls within its exclusive jurisdiction, provided of course that it does not violate any obligation of international law. Every State possesses a fundamental right to choose and implement its own political, economic and social systems . . . in international law there are no rules other than such rules as may be accepted by the State concerned, by treaty or otherwise.'

of the more economically powerful states.[99] These considerations will be essential for investment tribunals to bear in mind in developing an approach to deference, suggesting that tribunals should avoid privileging forms of bureaucratic decision-making and expertise with which they are most familiar.

2.6 Conclusion

Proportionality analysis provides a relatively transparent and coherent analytical structure for adjudicators to employ in regulatory disputes where the exercise of governmental power affects privately held rights or interests. By structuring the discretion of adjudicators, the adoption of proportionality analysis as a method of review could improve the quality of investment tribunals' legal reasoning and the coherence of their decisions, leading to greater certainty for host states, investors and civil society. However, proportionality analysis has attracted criticism, especially in relation to the more value-oriented stages that place a high degree of discretion in adjudicators.

By itself, proportionality analysis cannot address – and may even heighten – concerns about the impact of the decision-making of investment tribunals on the regulatory autonomy of host states. In international adjudication, an institutionally sensitive approach to proportionality analysis will be critical so as to avoid a court or tribunal overreaching its powers into the domain of domestic policy space. In the context of international investment law, the extremely limited opportunities for review or appeal of tribunal decisions mean that the manner in which arbitrators engage in proportionality analysis assumes even greater importance, and, in particular, how concerns about subjectivity and an overly strict approach to the standard of review may be assuaged.[100] This means that consideration of the appropriate standard of review is crucial in determining the manner in which proportionality analysis might be applied.

Deference, an aspect of the broader concept of the standard of review, is relevant where courts and tribunals make decisions in situations of normative or empirical uncertainty. This chapter has offered two reasons why international courts and tribunals might afford a measure of deference when reviewing government action in such circumstances: the

---

[99] I am grateful to José Manuel Álvarez Zárate for this point.

[100] See Montt, *State Liability in Investment Treaty Arbitration*, p. 286; Kurtz, 'Adjudging the Exceptional', p. 368; Kingsbury and Schill, 'Public Law Concepts', pp. 102–3.

normative desirability of regulatory autonomy and decision-making by embedded actors, and the practical benefits of relying on the views of decision-makers with greater institutional competence or expertise in relation to the issue to be determined. Chapter 3 analyzes the manner in which the CJEU, ECtHR and WTO tribunals approach proportionality analysis and deference, in order to demonstrate how this approach can operate in practice.

Operationalizing deference in the context of proportionality analysis

Comparative approaches

3.1 Introduction

Courts and tribunals have often attempted to soften the impact of their adjudicatory power by employing a deferential approach including specifically in relation to proportionality analysis.[1] For example, the ECtHR developed the margin of appreciation so as to permit national authorities to retain a degree of discretion with regard to their assessment of factual and normative issues as they relate to the different stages of proportionality analysis.[2] Other courts and tribunals have adopted similarly deferential approaches to proportionality analysis and related methods of review in the absence of the development of a more formalized doctrine.

Adjudicators can exercise deference when undertaking proportionality analysis in a number of ways: (1) by relying on or attaching weight to the decision of the primary decision-maker, such as by attaching weight to the government's conclusion that a measure was suitable or necessary to achieve its objective; (2) by undertaking proportionality analysis less stringently, such as by modifying the concept or one or more of its component stages so that a measure would be regarded as proportionate so long as it was not 'manifestly disproportionate'; or (3) by lowering the standard

---

[1] See Rivers, 'Proportionality and Discretion in International and European Law' in Tsagourias (ed.), *Transnational Constitutionalism: European and International Models* (2007) 107; Klatt and Meister, *The Constitutional Structure of Proportionality*, p. 84.

[2] See Yourow, 'The Margin of Appreciation Doctrine in the Dynamics of the European Human Rights Jurisprudence' (1988) 3 *Connecticut Journal of International Law*, 111, 118; Eissen, 'The Principle of Proportionality in the Case-Law of the European Court of Human Rights', in Macdonald, Matscher and Petzold (eds.), *The European System for the Protection of Human Rights* (1993) 125, 127–31, 145–6; Shany, 'Margin of Appreciation Doctrine', pp. 909–11; Letsas, *A Theory of Interpretation of the European Convention*, pp. 81, 90; Kavanagh, *Constitutional Review*, pp. 208–9.

of proof required to satisfy factual matters.[3] Proportionality analysis can also be used as a procedural framework within which a tribunal can seek justification from the authorities, such as by requiring a government to demonstrate that it had considered alternative measures or balanced the relevant interests in decision-making.[4]

This chapter reviews the approaches taken by the CJEU, the ECtHR and WTO tribunals to proportionality analysis and deference. It analyzes each stage of the proportionality test separately for heuristic purposes, although these courts and tribunals do not always analyze each stage in a discrete manner. In this respect, the comparative case law should not be regarded as embodying best practice in terms of a consistently applied and well-articulated approach to proportionality analysis, a point that should be kept in mind when evaluating their utility from a comparative perspective. The CJEU's approach is frequently terse, is at times imprecise and has been inconsistently applied. In some cases, the CJEU does not undertake the proportionality *stricto sensu* stage, bypasses least-restrictive means analysis, finds a measure to be 'necessary' where an alternative means is apparent or employs a different approach altogether.[5] The ECtHR's approach to proportionality analysis can also lack clarity: it does not always articulate all of the stages of the proportionality inquiry, and its decisions are sometimes stated summarily without further elaboration of the weight ascribed to the competing considerations.[6] In property cases, the ECtHR frequently folds the necessity and proportionality *stricto sensu* stages into one another, sometimes along with an assessment of the

---

[3] For example, Rivers, 'Variable Intensity of Review', pp. 203–4; Kavanagh, *Constitutional Review*, pp. 237–8; Young, 'Will You, Won't You, Will You Join the Deference Dance?' (2014) 34 *Oxford Journal of Legal Studies* 375, 389–90.

[4] Schueler, 'Methods of Application of the Proportionality Principle in Environmental Law' (2008) 35 *Legal Issues of Economic Integration* 231, 237; Gerards, 'How to Improve the Necessity Test of the European Court of Human Rights' (2013) 11 *International Journal of Constitutional Law* 466, 487–8.

[5] Maduro, *We the Court: The European Court of Justice and the European Economic Constitution* (1998) 103; van Gerven, 'The Effect of Proportionality on the Actions of Member States of the European Community: National Viewpoints from Continental Europe', in Ellis (ed.), *The Principle of Proportionality in the Laws of Europe* (1999) 37, 60; Ortino, *Basic Legal Instruments*, p. 433.

[6] McHarg, 'Reconciling Human Rights and the Public Interest: Conceptual Problems and Doctrinal Uncertainty in the Jurisprudence of the European Court of Human Rights' (1999) 62 *Modern Law Review* 671, 687; Arai-Takahashi, *The Margin of Appreciation Doctrine and the Principle of Proportionality in the Jurisprudence of the ECHR* (2002) 16, 193; Elliott, 'Proportionality and Deference', p. 266; Popelier and Van De Heyning, 'Procedural Rationality: Giving Teeth to the Proportionality Analysis' (2013) 9 *European Constitutional Law Review* 230, 234.

regulatory objective.[7] WTO case law is also less than clear on occasion. For example, although WTO tribunals have referred to weighing and balancing in a number of cases,[8] they have not engaged (with one possible exception) in the proportionality *stricto sensu* stage of review, instead adopting a relatively convoluted necessity test.

Further caveats apply in relation to the approaches of these bodies to the concept of deference. Both CJEU and the ECtHR case law lack a coherent framework establishing the factors that affect the standard of review, although these courts do frequently refer to factors influencing deference in their decision-making.[9] Under the SPS Agreement, where the Appellate Body has set out clear guidance as to the applicable standard of review to be used by panels in determining whether a measure is 'based on a risk assessment'[10] and in the context of trade remedies, it has allowed governments a degree of discretion in evaluating economic data.[11] Apart from these areas, however, WTO tribunals have not explicitly considered the circumstances in which reliance on the characteristics of primary decision-makers might affect the intensity of

---

[7] See Çoban, *Protection of Property Rights*, pp. 189–90; Ratner, 'Regulatory Takings in Institutional Context: Beyond the Fear of Fragmented International Law' (2008) 102 *American Journal of International Law* 475, 497; Elliott, 'Proportionality and Deference', p. 266. It should also be noted that in cases where there has been a 'deprivation' of property rather than a lesser interference, the ECtHR uses proportionality analysis to determine the quantum of compensation payable rather than in the determination of liability (though it is reluctant to find that a deprivation has taken place), see e.g. Mountfield, 'Regulatory Expropriations in Europe', p. 146; Freeman, 'Regulatory Expropriation Under NAFTA Chapter 11: Some Lessons from the European Court of Human Rights' (2003) 42 *Columbia Journal of Transnational Law* 177, 190–1, 193; Pita, 'Right to Property, Investments and Environmental Protection: The Perspectives of the European and Inter-American Courts of Human Rights', in Treves, Seatzu and Trevisanut (eds.), *International Investment Law and Common Concern* (2013) 553, 562–3.

[8] For example, Appellate Body Report, *Korea-Beef*, para. 164.

[9] See e.g. Greer, *The Margin of Appreciation*, pp. 5, 8, 32; Shany, 'Margin of Appreciation', p. 913; Rivers, 'Law of Balancing', p. 178; Letsas, *A Theory of Interpretation of the European Convention*, p. 3; Gerards, 'Margin of Appreciation', pp. 90–1.

[10] In relation to Article 5.1 SPS Agreement: Appellate Body Report, *US-Continued Suspension of Obligations in the EC-Hormones Dispute*, paras. 587–98. See Gruszczynski, *Regulating Health and Environmental Risks under WTO Law: A Critical Analysis of the SPS Agreement* (2010) 144, 146; Peel, 'Of Apples and Oranges (and Hormones in Beef): Science and the Standard of Review in WTO Disputes Under the SPS Agreement' (2012) 61 *International and Comparative Law Quarterly* 427, 446–8. See also Fukunaga, 'Scientific Truths', pp. 563–4, noting that earlier WTO panels determining SPS cases tended to take an approach close to *de novo* review.

[11] See Appellate Body Reports, *US-Measures Affecting Imports of Certain Passenger Vehicle and Light Truck Tyres from China*, paras. 123–5; *US-Safeguard Measure on Imports of Fresh, Chilled or Frozen Lamb from New Zealand*, para. 103 (safeguard measures); *US-Countervailing Duty Investigation on Dynamic Random Access Memory Semiconductors*

review – although the Appellate Body has, on several occasions, referred to the desirability of respecting the decisions of 'responsible and representative governments'.[12] Nor has the Appellate Body provided substantive guidance to panels with respect to the standard of review they should apply, apart from stating that the standard of review generally applicable in WTO disputes is neither *de novo* review nor 'total deference', because panels are poorly suited to engage in substitutionary review[13] and presumably because total deference would run counter to the expectations of WTO members.

3.2   Assessing the legitimacy of a regulatory objective: a residual role for adjudicators

Proportionality analysis is bifurcated in the sense that it requires both the making of value judgements (legitimate objective, proportionality *stricto sensu*) and the determination of factual questions (suitability, necessity).[14] These distinctions must be borne in mind in understanding how proportionality and deference might be combined and applied by investment tribunals.

Generally speaking, international and supranational courts and tribunals display a high degree of deference in relation to the assessment of the legitimacy of the objective of a challenged measure. There may be good reasons for a domestic court or tribunal to directly assess the value of a regulatory objective. However, in international and supranational contexts, this may be regarded as illegitimate on the basis that it transgresses the role of national authorities.[15] Even in the domestic sphere, given that legislatures enjoy a very wide discretion to act (as do administrative agencies within more limited powers authorized by statute), this stage

---

(*DRAMS*) *from Korea*, para. 186 (subsidies); Article 17.6 Anti-Dumping Agreement (stipulating the applicable standard of review for dumping investigations); Oesch, *Standards of Review in WTO Dispute Resolution*, pp. 137–9.

[12] Appellate Body Reports, *EC-Hormones*, paras. 124, 198; *US-Continued Suspension*, paras. 529, 680; *EC-Measures Affecting Asbestos and Asbestos-Containing Products*, para. 178.

[13] Appellate Body Report, *EC-Hormones*, para. 117. Article 11 Understanding on Rules and Procedures Governing the Settlement of Disputes provides that 'a panel should make an objective assessment of the matter before it, including an objective assessment of the facts of the case.' See Ehlermann and Lockhart, 'Standard of Review in WTO Law' (2004) 7 *Journal of International Economic Law* 491, 495; Zleptnig, 'Standard of Review in WTO Law', pp. 4, 7; Bohanes and Lockhart, 'Standard of Review in WTO Law', p. 383; Button, *The Power to Protect*, pp. 171–2.

[14] Elliott, 'Proportionality and Deference', p. 285.

[15] See e.g. Maduro, *We the Court*, p. 59; Çoban, *Protection of Property Rights*, p. 199.

of proportionality analysis is generally understood to function only to eliminate objectives that are inimical to the values of the legal regime, such as discrimination.[16]

Courts and tribunals usually afford deference in this area on the basis of the normative uncertainty inherent in determining the legitimacy of a particular regulatory objective.[17] This stage of review might, however, also attract empirical deference in circumstances where the treaty provision stipulates permissible objectives but there is uncertainty as to whether the pleaded objective comes within the relevant category, such as the question of the existence of a threat to national security.[18] The CJEU, the ECtHR (in relation to the right to property) and WTO tribunals exhibit deference in assessing the legitimacy of regulatory objectives on the basis of regulatory autonomy and proximity considerations, particularly in relation to polycentric issues and matters of sensitivity or controversy, such as social policy or the acceptable level of risk to health or the environment.

The TFEU provides that EU member states may derogate from freedom of movement where justified on grounds of, *inter alia*, public morality, public security and the protection of human health, provided that derogations do not constitute arbitrary discrimination or a disguised restriction on trade or otherwise violate EU law.[19] As well as the stipulated grounds of derogation, the judicially created mandatory requirements doctrine permits member states to adduce grounds of justification for non-discriminatory measures limiting free movement that do not have a basis in the treaty text.[20] What constitutes a mandatory requirement is theoretically open, but mandatory requirements must be of a non-economic nature.[21] The CJEU has repeatedly opined that, in the absence of European harmonization, it is up to member states to choose

---

[16] For example, Çoban, *Protection of Property Rights*, p. 98; Rivers, 'Variable Intensity of Review', p. 196; Montt, *State Liability in Investment Treaty Arbitration*, p. 352; Barak, *Proportionality*, p. 265.

[17] See Brady, *Proportionality and Deference*, pp. 71–2.

[18] Brady, *Proportionality and Deference*, pp. 70, 153–4.

[19] Articles 36, 45(3), 52, 62, and 65 TFEU. See Craig, *EU Administrative Law*, pp. 617–22. The CJEU may require evidence regarding the factual basis on which the derogation is claimed, see e.g. Case C-17/93, *Criminal Proceedings against JJJ Van der Veldt*, para. 17 (the government could not supply evidence to demonstrate the alleged risk to health). See also Case C-41/02, *Commission v. Netherlands (Vitamins)*, para. 49; Jans, 'Proportionality Revisited', p. 260.

[20] See Case 120/78, *Rewe-Zentrale AG v. Bundesmonopolverwaltung für Branntwein ('Cassis de Dijon')*, para. 8.

[21] See Tridimas, *The General Principles of EU Law* (2006) 207–8.

their own policy objectives and level of protection against various harms (environmental, health, and so on).[22] The CJEU will apply stricter scrutiny to the objective of the measure in policy areas where there are international standards and/or widespread consensus among member states, whereas it will take a more deferential approach in cases where there are no international standards or in situations of normative uncertainty.[23] Member states have been permitted to derogate from free movement on the basis of many policy areas that are familiar to the context of investor-state arbitration,[24] including addressing tax evasion,[25] the promotion of national and regional culture,[26] the protection of the environment[27] and on the basis of 'public security'.[28]

The ECHR permits states to limit the right to property in the 'public interest' or 'general interest', which does not predetermine the types of objectives that a rights-limiting measure must pursue.[29] The ECtHR has held that these concepts encompass a wide range of governmental activity and has repeatedly stated that it considers itself ill-equipped to second-guess the legitimacy of the objective of a measure interfering with property rights because national authorities are better placed to make this assessment 'due to their direct knowledge of their society and its needs'.[30] The lack of consensus among ECHR parties as to the matter

[22] For example, Cases C-491/06, *Danske Svineproducenter v. Justitsministeriet*, paras. 1, 31, 38, 40; C-275/92, *Her Majesty's Customs and Excise v. Gerhart Schindler and Jörg Schindler*, paras. 60–1; C-83/94, *Criminal proceedings against Peter Leifer, Reinhold Otto Krauskopf and Otto Holzer*, para. 35. See Jans, 'Proportionality Revisited', p. 249; Button, *The Power to Protect*, pp. 207–8; Tridimas, *The General Principles of EU Law*, p. 212.

[23] de Búrca, 'The Principle of Proportionality', p. 147; Jans, 'Proportionality Revisited', p. 253; Bermann, 'Proportionality and Subsidiarity', in Barnard and Scott (eds.), *The Law of the Single European Market: Unpacking the Premises* (2002) 75, 83.

[24] See e.g. *Feldman Karpa (Marvin Roy) v. Mexico*, (tax evasion); *Parkerings* v. *Lithuania* and *Glamis* v. *US* (national culture); *Metalclad* v. *Mexico* and *Tecmed* v. *Mexico* (environmental protection).

[25] For example, Case 120/78, *Cassis de Dijon*, para. 8.

[26] For example, Joined Cases C-60/84 and 61/84, *Cinéthèque SA and others* v. *Fédération nationale des cinémas français*, paras. 18, 23.

[27] Provided that such measures do not discriminate *de jure*, e.g. Case C-240/83, *Procureur de la République* v. *Association de défense des brûleurs d'huiles usagés (ADBHU)*, para. 13.

[28] Case 72/83, *Campus Oil Limited* v. *Minister for Industry and Energy*, paras. 34–5; Case C-503/99, *Commission* v. *Belgium (Golden Shares)*, paras. 46–7 and Case C-483/99, *Commission* v. *France (Golden Shares)*, paras. 47–8; Case C-394/97, *Criminal proceedings against Sami Heinonen*, para. 43.

[29] Article 1, 1st Protocol ECHR.

[30] See e.g. *Lithgow* v. *UK*, para. 122; *James* v. *UK*, para. 46; *Former King of Greece and Others* v. *Greece*, para. 87; *Broniowski* v. *Poland*, paras. 149, 162; *Jahn* v. *Germany*, para. 91. See

being regulated can be a deference-increasing factor, although the exact role that consensus plays in the court's decision-making is not always clear.[31] Generally speaking, the ECtHR will accept the state's assessment that the measure's objective serves the public interest in property cases unless that assessment is considered to be 'manifestly without reasonable foundation'.[32] In some cases, the ECtHR appears to give the benefit of the doubt to states in terms of the *bona fides* of the regulatory objective,[33] and has rarely found that the state's objective was manifestly without reasonable foundation.[34] Again, many of the policy areas that have arisen in property cases are familiar to international investment law.[35] They include infrastructure development and town and country planning,[36] protection of cultural and artistic heritage,[37] prevention of tax evasion[38] and smuggling,[39] environmental protection,[40] macroeconomic and fiscal policy[41] including with respect to banking and financial crises[42] and the

---

Mountfield, 'Regulatory Expropriations in Europe', p. 146; Çoban, *Protection of Property Rights*, pp. 180, 202–3; Van Dijk, van Hoof, Van Rijn and Zwaak, *Theory and Practice of the European Convention on Human Rights* (2006) 889–90; Gerards, 'Margin of Appreciation', p. 110.

[31] See Legg, *Margin of Appreciation*, pp. 116–20; Wildhaber, Hjartarson and Donnelly, 'No Consensus on Consensus? The Practice of the European Court of Human Rights' (2011) 33 *Human Rights Law Journal* 248.

[32] For example, *Mellacher and Others* v. *Austria*, para. 45; *Spadea and Scalabrino* v. *Italy*, para. 29; *Broniowski* v. *Poland*, para. 149; *Hentrich* v. *France*, para. 39; *James* v. *UK*, para. 46. See Van Dijk et al., *Theory and Practice of the European Convention*, pp. 880–1; Mountfield, 'Regulatory Expropriations in Europe', pp. 140–1; Çoban, *Protection of Property Rights*, pp. 202–4.

[33] For example, *Holy Monasteries* v. *Greece*, para. 69; *Former King of Greece* v. *Greece*, para. 88; *Allan Jacobsson* v. *Sweden*, para. 63; *N.K.M.* v. *Hungary*, para. 59. See Çoban, *Protection of Property Rights*, pp. 202–4; Van Dijk et al., *Theory and Practice of the European Convention*, pp. 880, 888–9.

[34] But see e.g. *Darby* v. *Sweden*, paras. 33–4 (discriminatory objective); *Tkachevy* v. *Russia*, para. 50 (direct expropriation of property for commercial purposes).

[35] See, e.g. as well as the abovementioned investment cases, *Feldman* v. *Mexico* and *EDF (Services) Limited* v. *Romania* (smuggling); *CMS* v. *Argentina*, *Enron* v. *Argentina* and *Sempra* v. *Argentina* (economic policy/crisis); *Alex Genin, Eastern Credit Limited, Inc. and A.S. Baltoil* v. *Estonia*, and *Saluka* v. *Czech Republic* (banking regulation).

[36] *Sporrong and Lönnroth* v. *Sweden*, para. 69; *Allan Jacobsson* v. *Sweden*, para. 57; *Hamer* v. *Belgium*, para. 78.

[37] *Beyeler* v. *Italy*, paras. 112–13.   [38] *Hentrich* v. *France*, para. 39.

[39] *Air Canada* v. *UK*, para. 42.

[40] *Pine Valley Developments Ltd and Others* v. *Ireland*, para. 57.

[41] For example, *Hentrich* v. *France*, para. 39; *Gasus Dosier-und Fordertechnik GmbH* v. *Netherlands*, para. 60; *National & Provincial Building Society, Leeds Permanent Building Society and Yorkshire Building Society* v. *UK*, para. 80.

[42] *Grainger and Others* v. *UK*, paras. 39, 42.

question of the existence of a public emergency or whether authorities are acting to protect national security or public order.[43]

Several provisions of the WTO agreements specify permissible objectives for domestic measures, whether in terms of exceptions or positive obligations.[44] The general exceptions provisions in GATT and GATS permit WTO members to promulgate measures directed at certain policy objectives that would otherwise be inconsistent with WTO rules, including the protection of public morals and human health, the conservation of exhaustible natural resources and securing compliance with otherwise WTO-compliant laws or regulations.[45] The TBT Agreement permits WTO members to maintain technical regulations directed at a non-exhaustive list of legitimate objectives including national security and the protection of human health and the environment, and the SPS Agreement permits members to adopt measures to protect human, animal or plant life or health.[46]

WTO tribunals have repeatedly emphasized the autonomy of WTO members to set their own regulatory objectives and the appropriate level of achievement of those objectives.[47] The Appellate Body has expressly stated that it will not examine the 'level of protection' (i.e. the desired level of achievement) directed towards an objective, and in no case has a WTO tribunal explicitly determined that a measure's objective or level of protection is illegitimate or unimportant.[48] WTO tribunals have not articulated why it might not be appropriate to employ a strict standard of review in this assessment, and, in practice, have never undertaken more than a superficial analysis of the importance of a particular regulatory objective nor elucidated criteria with which to evaluate them, except by

[43] See e.g. *Brannigan and McBride* v. *UK*, para. 43; *Aksoy* v. *Turkey*, para. 68 (existence of emergency situation); *Leander* v. *Sweden*, para. 59 (whether measures were taken with respect to legitimize national security objectives).

[44] The inquiry into whether the objective of a challenged measure is permissible is usually a relatively straightforward factual determination, involving analyzing the text, design and regulatory context of the measure along with any statements of legislatures or officials: see Appellate Body Reports, *Japan-Taxes on Alcoholic Beverages*, 26; *Australia-Measures Affecting the Importation of Apples from New Zealand*, para. 173; Panel Report, *US-Gambling*, paras. 6.481–6.487.

[45] Article XX GATT; Article XIV GATS.

[46] Article 5.6 and Annex A(5) SPS Agreement; Article 2.2 TBT Agreement.

[47] Appellate Body Reports, *EC-Hormones*, paras. 124, 187; *Korea-Beef*, para. 176; *EC-Asbestos*, paras. 168, 178; Panel Report, *US-Measures Affecting the Cross Border Supply of Gambling and Betting Services*, paras. 6.461–6.474.

[48] See Appellate Body Reports, *EC-Asbestos*, para. 168; *Brazil-Measures Affecting Imports of Retreaded Tyres*, para. 210 (but see the discussion of the *Korea-Beef* case, below).

some references to the common interests of members.[49] At times, WTO tribunals appear to give the benefit of the doubt to a government in terms of whether its objective falls within the relevant category.[50] Apart from objectives clearly falling with the exceptions (such as the protection of human health), other objectives found to be legitimate by WTO tribunals include protection of the environment,[51] protection of tax revenue,[52] the prevention of fraud and money laundering and the regulation of gambling[53] – again, all policy areas that have also arisen in investor-state arbitration.[54]

3.3   Suitability: the connection between a measure and its objective

The suitability stage of proportionality analysis tests the rationality of the connection between a measure and its objective. This stage is generally regarded as undemanding even when unmodified by deference, in part because courts and tribunals employing proportionality analysis subsequently analyze the necessity of a measure: a potential, partial or inefficient realization of the purpose of the measure is likely to suffice.[55] In some cases, the government may be required to establish the suitability of the measure without concrete evidence, such as the predicted efficacy of a measure or the unsuitability of measures proposed by the claimant as part of the necessity test.[56] These matters cannot be proven in the

---

[49] For example, Appellate Body Report, *Korea-Beef,* para. 162.

[50] For example, Panel Report, *China-Measures Affecting Trading Rights and Distribution Services for Certain Publications and Audiovisual Entertainment Products,* para. 7.763, where the panel accepted that China's censorship regime was an expression of public morals and that China's measures could be examined under Article XX(a) GATT and *US-Gasoline,* where the Appellate Body accepted that measures adopted to protect clean air came within the purview of 'exhaustible natural resources' in terms of Article XX(g) GATT.

[51] Appellate Body Reports, *US-Import Prohibition of Certain Shrimp and Shrimp Products,* para. 129 and *Brazil-Tyres,* para. 179.

[52] Appellate Body Report, *Dominican Republic-Measures Affecting the Importation and Internal Sale of Cigarettes,* para. 59.

[53] Appellate Body Reports, *Korea-Beef,* paras. 153, 158; *US-Measures Affecting the Cross Border Supply of Gambling and Betting Services,* para. 313.

[54] See, as well as the abovementioned investment cases, *Thunderbird* v. *Mexico* (gambling regulation).

[55] See e.g. Jans, 'Proportionality Revisited', p. 244; Bermann, 'Proportionality and Subsidiarity', pp. 75, 80.

[56] Christoffersen, *Fair Balance: Proportionality, Subsidiarity and Primarity in the European Convention on Human Rights* (2009) 176.

ordinary sense, but must be established on the basis of inference.[57] A court or tribunal can afford deference in these and other circumstances of uncertainty by examining whether the measure could be expected to be effective in future, by lowering the standard of proof, or by requiring the claimant to show that the measure was not capable of achieving its aims and that this was readily foreseeable by the authorities.[58]

The CJEU, ECtHR and WTO tribunals all apply an undemanding test to this stage of proportionality analysis. The CJEU does not appear to scrutinize the effectiveness of a measure with a great deal of rigour, and will only find a measure to be unsuitable in circumstances where it is completely ineffective at achieving its objective.[59] It has stated that partial fulfilment of a measure's objective would meet the criterion of suitability.[60] The CJEU appears to take this approach on the basis that in many cases, institutional limitations make it poorly equipped to make this assessment, particularly in complex policy areas.[61]

In ECHR law, the concept of suitability is largely subsumed within the concept of necessity.[62] Although the ECtHR has, in the context of other ECHR rights, affirmed that states have a margin of appreciation with respect to this assessment,[63] it does not appear to have made any particular pronouncements on the requirement of suitability in the context of the right to property. However, in relation to the right to privacy (to which it usually applies a stricter standard of review), the ECtHR has stated that in cases concerning 'complex issues of environmental and economic policy', a government need not establish 'comprehensive and measurable data . . . in relation to each and every aspect of the matter to be decided'.[64] Rather, the authorities need only demonstrate that they have undertaken 'appropriate investigations and studies', and the level of information required in this respect will be dependent on the circumstances of the case.[65] The ECtHR has occasionally found that a measure does not comply with this stage of

---

[57] Christoffersen, *Fair Balance*, p. 176.

[58] Jans, 'Proportionality Revisited', pp. 243–4; Gerards, 'Margin of Appreciation', pp. 88–9.

[59] See Schwarze, *European Administrative Law* (2006) 856–7; Case C-434/04, *Ahokainen and Leppik* v. *Virallinen Syyttäjä*, Opinion of Advocate-General Maduro, para. 24: 'The question to be determined in applying the suitability test is whether the measure has any benefits at all for the legitimate interests on which the member State relies.'

[60] For example, Cases C-434/04, *Ahokainen*, para. 39; C-67/98, *Questore di Verona* v. *Diego Zenatti*, paras. 36–7.

[61] See Gerards, 'Margin of Appreciation', p. 85.

[62] See Christoffersen, *Fair Balance*, pp. 163–5.

[63] For example, *Handyside* v. *UK*, para. 48.   [64] *Hatton and Others* v. *UK*, para. 128.

[65] For example, *Fadeyeva* v. *Russia*, para. 128.

analysis,[66] but the research has not identified any such case in the context of the right to property.

Compared to the jurisprudence of the CJEU and ECtHR, WTO law in this area is more complex. Like the ECtHR case law, the distinction between suitability and necessity can be somewhat blurred, with WTO tribunals generally taking a fairly flexible approach to this stage of review.[67] In the context of the general exceptions provisions containing a necessity test, the Appellate Body has held that the suitability requirement falls closer to the concept of 'indispensible' than 'make a contribution to' and that the greater the impact of the measure on international trade, the correspondingly more stringent the suitability requirement, implying a relatively strict approach to the standard of review.[68] In practice, however, WTO tribunals have deferred to governments' assessments as to the suitability of a measure[69] or found a measure to be suitable where its capacity to achieve its objective is uncertain.[70] In *Brazil-Tyres*, the Appellate Body held that where the measure (in this case, a ban on the import of used tyres for environmental reasons) was novel or part of a package of interrelated measures, the government could establish the suitability of the measure in terms of its capacity to achieve its objective in future through quantitative projections or qualitative reasoning, remarking that the effectiveness of a given measure might only be able to be discerned with the passage of time.[71] The approach taken by WTO tribunals in this area recognizes the

---

[66] For example, *Sabou and Pircalab* v. *Romania*, paras. 46–9; *Znamenskaya* v. *Russia*, paras. 28–31; *B and L* v. *UK*, paras. 37–8.

[67] The permissible objectives with the nexus requirement of 'necessary' are the protection of public morals (XX(a) GATT/XIV(a) GATS); and human, animal or plant life or health (XX(b)/XIV(b)); securing compliance with laws or regulations not otherwise inconsistent with WTO agreements (XX(d)/XIV(c)); and restricting exports of domestic materials in relation to a governmental stabilization plan (XX(i)). Additionally, XX(j) GATT refers to measures 'essential to the acquisition or distribution of products in general or local short supply'. This provision appears to function as a strict test of necessity, but has not been litigated in the WTO context.

[68] Appellate Body Reports, *Korea-Beef*, paras. 161–3; *Brazil-Tyres*, para. 210.

[69] Panel Report, *US-Gambling*, paras. 6.499–6.521. See Lovric, *Deference to the Legislature*, p. 94. WTO tribunals have relied on statutory language, legislative history and statements made by agencies and officials in this determination, see e.g. Appellate Body Report, *US-Gambling*, para. 304.

[70] Appellate Body Report, *Mexico-Soft Drinks*, para. 74.

[71] Appellate Body Report, *Brazil-Tyres*, para. 151. It has been suggested that following *Brazil-Tyres* all that is required in this context is that the measure be plausibly connected to its objective: see McGrady, 'Necessity Exceptions in WTO Law: Retreaded Tyres, Regulatory Purpose and Cumulative Regulatory Measures' (2009) 12 *Journal of International Economic*

practical advantages of a flexible approach to the standard of review in situations of empirical uncertainty.

The test applied under the other general exceptions depends on the text of the provision.[72] For example, the Appellate Body has held that the requirement in that a measure be 'related to' the conservation of exhaustible natural resources will be met where the measure is substantially related to or primarily aimed at its objective,[73] is 'reasonably related' to its objective, and is not 'disproportionately wide in its scope and reach'.[74] WTO tribunals apply a similar test under the TBT Agreement to that applied to the necessity-based general exceptions, whereby a technical regulation will meet the suitability requirement where it 'partially achieves' its objective.[75] WTO tribunals also appear to take a flexible approach to suitability under the necessity test in the SPS Agreement.[76]

A measure that survives scrutiny against one of the enumerated paragraphs of the general exceptions in GATT and GATS will subsequently be examined under the introductory paragraph of the provision (chapeau) to determine whether the measure has been 'applied in a manner which would constitute a means of arbitrary or unjustifiable discrimination between countries where the same conditions prevail, or a disguised restriction on international trade'.[77] This analysis acts as a second-stage

---

Law 153, 166–8; McGrady, *Trade and Public Health: The WTO, Tobacco, Alcohol and Diet* (2010) 148, 160–4; Lovric, *Deference to the Legislature*, p. 149.

[72] These are 'relating to' the importations or exportations of gold or silver, the products of prison labour and the conservation of exhaustible natural resources (XX(c), (e) and (g) GATT); 'imposed for' the protection of national treasures of artistic, historic or archaeological value (XX(f) GATT); 'in pursuance of' obligations under certain intergovernmental commodity agreements (XX(h) GATT); 'involving' restrictions on exports of domestic materials in certain circumstances (Article XX(i) GATT) and 'aimed at' ensuring the equitable or effective imposition or collection of direct taxes (XIV(d) GATS).

[73] Appellate Body Reports, *US-Gasoline*, pp. 18–19, 21.

[74] Appellate Body Report, *US-Shrimp*, para. 141.

[75] Article 2.2 TBT Agreement. See Appellate Body Reports, *US-Measures Concerning the Importation, Marketing and Sale of Tuna and Tuna Products ('US-Tuna II')*, paras. 129, 315, 318; *US-Certain Country of Origin Labelling (COOL) Requirements ('US-COOL')*, para. 468.

[76] Article 5.6 SPS Agreement. See also Appellate Body Report, *EC-Hormones*, para. 528. Additionally, Article 5.1 requires that WTO members base their SPS measures on a risk assessment, which requires that there be 'a rational relationship' between the measure and the risk assessment (Appellate Body Report, *EC-Hormones*, para. 193).

[77] 'Disguised restriction' includes measures which, though not discriminatory, 'conceal the pursuit of trade-restrictive objectives': Appellate Body Report, *US-Gasoline*, p. 25, or that have dual proper and improper purposes: Bartels, 'The Chapeau of the General Exceptions in the WTO GATT and GATS Agreements' (2015) 109 *American Journal*

suitability test that can identify situations where the WTO member's ostensible objective was not its true objective, where there are gaps in the application of a measure in situations in which it should logically have been applied, and situations where there is no explanation for the differential treatment or rational relationship to the measure's objective.[78] There are also indications that WTO tribunals have applied a necessity test under the chapeau to the exceptions with a less stringent nexus requirement, because some tribunals have discussed available alternative measures in this context.[79]

3.4 Necessity: the least-restrictive means reasonably available

In determining whether a measure is necessary, an adjudicator must attempt to determine whether alternative measures would be capable of achieving the objective and be feasible in the circumstances. Compared to courts and tribunals, governments will frequently have more complete information as to the various trade-offs that were made in arriving at a measure and the true costs of alternative measures.[80] Governments may also, as noted in Chapter 2, have special expertise with respect to the relevant policy area, or greater capacity to apprehend the social implications of various regulatory options. This suggests that a deferential approach to necessity testing is appropriate in circumstances where there is uncertainty in relation to the availability, feasibility or potential effectiveness of alternative measures.[81]

---

of International Law 95, 123. That a measure's effect is to protect domestic producers does not inevitably mean that it is a disguised restriction: see Panel Report, *EC-Asbestos*, paras. 8.236, 8.239.

[78] Ortino, *Basic Legal Instruments*, pp. 193–4, 201; Bown and Trachtman, '*Brazil–Measures Affecting Imports of Retreaded Tyres*: A Balancing Act' (2009) 8 *World Trade Review* 85, 87; Vranes, *Trade and the Environment: Fundamental Issues in International Law, WTO Law, and Legal Theory* (2009) 281. See Appellate Body Reports, *US-Shrimp*, paras. 165, 177–81; *Brazil-Tyres*, paras. 215, 225–7; *US-Gambling*, paras. 367–72; *EC-Measures Prohibiting the Importation and Marketing of Seal* Products, para. 5.306.

[79] For example, Appellate Body Reports, *US-Gasoline*, p. 24; *US-Shrimp*, paras. 163, 165, 166, 171; *EC-Seal Products*, para. 5.320; Panel Report, *Argentina-Measures Affecting the Export of Bovine Hides and the Import of Finished Leather*, para. 11.324. See Neumann and Türk, 'Necessity Revisited', pp. 229–320; Qin, 'Defining Non-Discrimination Under the Law of the World Trade Organization' (2005) 23 *Boston University International Law Journal* 215, 267–70.

[80] See Jans, 'Proportionality Revisited', p. 241; Rivers, 'Variable Intensity of Review', p. 171; Rivers, 'Second Law of Balancing', p. 185; Barak, *Proportionality*, p. 321.

[81] Brady, *Proportionality and Deference*, p. 68.

Some legal systems also permit additional factors to be taken into consideration in determining the necessity of a measure, whereby a government may select a measure other than the least-restrictive alternative where there are good reasons for not adopting it, such as significant administrative complexities or fiscal implications, or where the adoption of the least-restrictive alternative would result in harm to other rights or interests.[82] Other legal systems place strong emphasis on the requirement that any alternative measure should be equally as effective at achieving the objective as the challenged measure. Alternatively, a court or tribunal might characterize the necessity test as a strict least-restrictive means test, but apply the test in a deferential way by having regard to the expertise of primary decision-makers in determining the existence of alternative measures.

Like the suitability stage of proportionality analysis, the necessity stage may require proof of matters on the basis of inference.[83] In reviewing hypothetical alternative measures proposed by claimants, adjudicators review measures *de novo*, as alternative measures will most likely be untested.[84] In this respect, the standard of review operates in relation to the standard of proof in terms of establishing that alternative measures would be unfeasible or ineffective, rather than deference to national authorities' actual knowledge and experience in relation to these matters. An adjudicator might calibrate the standard of proof by determining whether a government had a reasonable basis for its conclusion that the measure selected was the least-restrictive means available to achieve the objective.[85]

The CJEU generally reviews the necessity of an argued derogation or mandatory requirement fairly strictly, which acts as a check on protectionism – a central concern in the context of the single market. The degree of scrutiny that it applies to a measure will, however, depend on the circumstances: the CJEU will be more likely to accept a government's assertions as to the necessity of a measure where the measure is in a sensitive policy area, one in which there is no European consensus,

[82] For example, Neumann and Türk, 'Necessity Revisited', pp. 210–11, 214–17; Çoban, *Protection of Property Rights*, pp. 202–3; Andenas and Zleptnig, 'Proportionality: WTO Law in Comparative Perspective', pp. 392–3; Kavanagh, 'Deference or Defiance?', p. 191; Elliott, 'Proportionality and Deference', pp. 277–8. See also Matthews and Stone Sweet, 'All Things in Proportion?', p. 107.
[83] Christoffersen, *Fair Balance*, p. 176.   [84] I am grateful to Lorand Bartels for this point.
[85] See e.g. Çoban, *Protection of Property Rights*, pp. 202–3; Andenas and Zleptnig, 'Proportionality: WTO Law in Comparative Perspective', pp. 392–3.

or one where national authorities have exclusive competence.[86] This approach is taken even where other member states have less restrictive measures in place, the rationale being the desirability of avoiding a 'race to the bottom' in the regulatory area.[87] The CJEU has also held that the desirability of general and simple rules and the avoidance of high administrative costs may justify a more flexible approach to necessity testing. In *Trailers*, for example, it held that although it was possible to envisage alternatives to a ban on trailers being towed by motorcycles for safety reasons (such as banning their use only in particularly dangerous areas), the Italian government should not be denied the option of 'general and simple rules which will be easily understood and applied by drivers and easily managed and supervised by the competent authorities'.[88]

In some cases, the CJEU has required member states to discharge the necessity test procedurally by demonstrating that alternative measures had been investigated, and has found governments in breach for failing to conduct such an analysis.[89] In *Commission* v. *Austria (Air Quality)*, for example, the CJEU held that a measure instituting a traffic ban on a motorway with the aim of reducing emissions was an unjustifiable restriction on free movement because the authorities had not inquired into the availability of other measures such as speed limits and levying a toll on heavy vehicles. Moreover, the means selected was overly restrictive in light of uncertainty over whether there was sufficient rail capacity for transportation of goods across borders.[90]

The approach taken by the ECtHR to least-restrictive means analysis depends on the right at issue. The ECtHR does not apply a strict necessity

---

[86] de Búrca, 'The Principle of Proportionality in EC Law', p. 126; Jans, 'Proportionality Revisited', pp. 245, 247; Ortino, *Basic Legal Instruments*, p. 433; Tridimas, *The General Principles of EU Law*, p. 214; Gerards, 'Margin of Appreciation', p. 91. For example, Cases 174/82, *Officier van Justitie* v. *Sandoz BV*, paras. 18–19; C-124/97, *Markku Juhani Läärä, Cotswold Microsystems Ltd and Oy Transatlantic Software Ltd* v. *Kihlakunnansyyttäjä (Jyväskylä) and Suomen valtio (Finnish State)*; Joined Cases C-171/07 and C-172/07, *Apothekerkammer des Saarlandes and others and Helga Neumann-Seiwert* v. *Saarland and Ministerium für Justiz, Gesundheit und Soziales*, paras. 53–7. See also Case C-89/09, *Commission* v. *France (Medical Laboratories)*, paras. 88–9.

[87] For example, Case 384/93, *Alpine Investments BV* v. *Minister van Financiën*, paras. 50–5. See also Case C-108/96, *Criminal Proceedings against Dennis Mac Quen and Others*, paras. 33–4. See Jans, 'Proportionality Revisited', p. 247; Tridimas, *The General Principles of EU Law*, p. 214.

[88] Case C-110/05, *Commission* v. *Italy (Trailers)*, para. 67.

[89] See Schueler, 'Proportionality Principle in Environmental Law', pp. 231, 238.

[90] Case C-320/03, *Commission* v. *Austria (Air Quality)*, paras. 87–91.

test in relation to the right to property, and has stated that it is not its role to 'say whether the legislation represented the best solution for dealing with the problem or whether the legislative discretion should have been exercised in another way'.[91] By contrast, in circumstances where the ECtHR applies a narrow margin of appreciation (such as in relation to the right to privacy), it generally applies a stricter necessity test.[92] This difference in approaches reflects the perspective that the protection of property rights carries lesser normative force (or social importance) than the protection of other ECHR rights.[93]

In relation to the right to property, provided that the measure falls within a margin of reasonable alternatives, the availability of other means to achieve an objective will not definitively render a particular measure unlawful, but rather is taken into account in the ECtHR's overall assessment of proportionality.[94] In this respect, the ECtHR's approach differs from the orthodox understanding of proportionality analysis as a sequentially staged test, which means that its reasoning is not always clear. A measure will not generally fail the necessity test unless its impact is particularly harsh and other measures are clearly available.[95] Like the CJEU, the ECtHR has also adopted a procedural approach to necessity testing in some cases. In areas where a wide margin is applicable, the ECtHR will be less likely to find a measure to lack proportionality in circumstances where authorities have carefully assessed and decided the case.[96]

WTO tribunals undertake least-restrictive means analysis in relation to the necessity-based general exceptions and under the necessity tests set out in the SPS and TBT Agreements. They are generally relatively deferential in this respect, seemingly in recognition of their lack of institutional

---

[91] For example, *James* v. *UK*, para. 51; *Mellacher* v. *Austria*, para. 53; *Tre Traktörer AB* v. *Sweden*, para. 69.

[92] For example, *Connors* v. *UK*, para. 94. See Gerards, 'Margin of Appreciation', p. 106.

[93] See e.g. Emberland, *The Human Rights of Companies: Exploring the Structure of ECHR Protection* (2006), pp. 192–3; Greer, *Achievements, Problems and Prospects*, p. 210.

[94] See e.g. *Hentrich* v. *France*, paras. 47–9; *Capital Bank AD* v. *Bulgaria*, paras. 137–8. See Christoffersen, *Fair Balance*, pp. 67–76 and Brems and Lavrysen, '"A Sledgehammer to Crack a Nut"', p. 141, describing the ECtHR's approach as a 'horizontal' proportionality inquiry, in contrast to the vertical (sequentially staged) approach undertaken by other bodies such as the CJEU.

[95] See e.g. Arai-Takahashi, *Margin of Appreciation and Proportionality*, pp. 155, 159; Gerards, 'Margin of Appreciation', p. 105.

[96] For example, *Maurice* v. *France*, paras. 118–24; *Evans* v. *UK*, paras. 86–7, 91–2. See Gerards, 'Margin of Appreciation', pp. 105–6. The ECtHR has also applied a procedural test in privacy cases: see Brems and Lavrysen, '"A Sledgehammer to Crack a Nut"', pp. 156–7.

competence and expertise compared to national decision-makers.[97] In the context of the general exceptions, the Appellate Body has held that a measure will be necessary to achieve its objective unless there is a less restrictive measure 'reasonably available' to the WTO member. To be reasonably available, the WTO member must be capable of adopting the measure, the measure must not impose an undue burden on the government such as prohibitive costs or substantial technical difficulties, and the measure must achieve the member's chosen level of protection.[98] The Appellate Body has never fully explained what is meant by an 'undue burden' in this context. Although it has been argued that this determination involves a form of cost-benefit analysis whereby the cost to trade of the challenged measure is balanced against the extra costs that the government would incur by adopting an alternative measure, this is not apparent from the case law.[99]

The Appellate Body has interpreted the necessity test under the TBT Agreement in a similar manner to its approach to the general exceptions, requiring alternative measures to be reasonably available and as effective at achieving the objective of the challenged measure.[100] In *US-Tuna II*, for example, a labelling regime only permitted tuna products to display a 'dolphin-safe' label only where certain conditions relating to the method of harvesting were met, with the dual aims of protecting dolphins and providing consumer information. The Appellate Body found that an alternative labelling regime proposed by Mexico, although less restrictive of trade, would achieve the objectives of the challenged measure to a lesser degree than the challenged measure because it would permit more tuna that had been harvested in conditions adversely affecting dolphins to be labelled as dolphin-safe.[101]

In contrast to the necessity tests under GATT, GATS and the TBT Agreement, the necessity test set out in the SPS Agreement is more permissive. This is due to the text of the necessity test in the SPS Agreement,

---

[97] For example, Panel Report, *Brazil-Measures Affecting Imports of Retreaded Tyres*, para. 7.207. See Lovric, *Deference to the Legislature*, pp. 152–5.

[98] See GATT Panel Report, *US-Section 337 of the Tariff Act of 1930*, para. 5.26; Appellate Body Reports, *Korea-Beef*, para. 166; *US-Gambling*, para. 308.

[99] See Regan, 'The Meaning of "Necessary" in GATT Article XX and GATS Article XIV: The Myth of Cost–Benefit Balancing' (2007) 6 *World Trade Review* 347, 349, cf. Mitchell and Henckels, 'Variations on a Theme', p. 134.

[100] Articles 2.2 TBT Agreement. See Appellate Body Reports, *US-Tuna II*, para. 320; *US-Certain Country of Origin Labelling (COOL) Requirements*, para. 376.

[101] Appellate Body Report, *US-Tuna II*, paras. 329–30.

which provides that any alternative measure must be 'significantly less restrictive' of trade, while achieving the respondent's level of protection against risks to health, and expressly stipulates that the technical and economic feasibility of alternative measures must be taken into account in determining their availability.[102]

3.5   Proportionality *stricto sensu*: weighing and balancing the competing interests

As explained in Chapter 2, the proportionality *stricto sensu* stage of proportionality analysis – being a type of value judgement – is considered to be a highly intrusive technique, permitting adjudicators to substitute their judgment in relation to whether the importance of avoiding harm to the protected right or interest outweighs the importance of achieving the objective. This stage of proportionality analysis may be especially controversial in the international and supranational legal contexts, because adjudicators cannot rely on the fact that they are embedded within the local community as a means to bolster their adjudicative legitimacy. Where a court or tribunal affords deference in relation to this stage of analysis, it does so in most circumstances due to the normative uncertainty inherent in weighing and balancing competing interests.[103] In some cases, however, this stage may also attract empirical deference, where there is uncertainty as to the level of achievement of (or detriment to) the public interest that is to be weighed against the level of interference with the right or interest.[104]

The CJEU appears to be cognizant of the legitimacy concerns arising in relation to this stage of review, although its jurisprudence is inconsistent and somewhat ambiguous in this respect.[105] It gives the impression of being more reluctant to engage in the proportionality *stricto sensu* stage in areas where there is no European harmonization or consensus, but

---

[102] Articles 2.2 and 5.6 and Annex A(5) SPS Agreement. Also, the level of protection sought to be achieved by an SPS measure is 'deemed' by the WTO member itself, rather than being objectively verified by the tribunal, which gives the responding government more leeway in relation to the least-restrictive means test in terms of the determination of whether an alternative measure would achieve the level of protection sought by the government: Appellate Body Report, *Australia-Salmon*, paras. 203–4; McGrady, *Trade and Public Health*, pp. 192–3.

[103] Brady, *Proportionality and Deference*, p. 151.

[104] See Brady, *Proportionality and Deference*, p. 152.

[105] Jans, 'Proportionality Revisited', p. 239.

will be more willing to undertake this analysis where the matter concerns an area where there is a degree of consensus between member states or where EU law has already elucidated a common level of protection in respect of the issue.[106] In most cases, however, the CJEU has conflated the proportionality *stricto sensu* with least-restrictive means analysis. It has done so by finding that an alternative measure would achieve the objective in circumstances where the alternative would be less effective at achieving the objective, thereby implicitly holding that the government's level of achievement of the objective was unreasonably high.[107] The CJEU aims to avoid the perception of judicial overreach by adopting this approach, but this elision of the two stages is somewhat deceptive because frequently value-oriented considerations are buried in the factual inquiry into the necessity of the measure.[108]

Commentators have been able to identify only one case in which the CJEU explicitly employed the proportionality *stricto sensu* stage in finding that a measure was an unlawful interference with free movement. In *Commission v. Denmark (Bottles)*, concerning a scheme requiring certain beverages to be sold in approved reusable containers, the CJEU took the view that the authorities had set their level of environmental protection too high, requiring that it be lowered to what the CJEU considered to be a more reasonable level.[109] The CJEU is not so reticent, however, to engage in the proportionality *stricto sensu* stage in order to find that a national measure complies with the requirement of proportionality.[110]

---

[106] See Emiliou, *The Principle of Proportionality in European Law: A Comparative Study* (1996) 250–1; Jans, 'Proportionality Revisited', p. 249; Tridimas, *The General Principles of EU Law*, p. 208. The CJEU has also remitted cases to national courts for consideration of proportionality on the basis that they are better equipped to engage in such a value judgement: see Tridimas, 'Proportionality in Community Law: Searching for the Appropriate Standard of Scrutiny' in Ellis (ed.), *The Principle of Proportionality in the Laws of Europe* (1999) 65, 79–80; Pirker, *Proportionality Analysis and Judicial Review*, pp. 272–3.

[107] For example, Cases C-120/78, *Cassis de Dijon*, paras. 10–14; C-40/82, *Commission v. UK (Poultry)*, paras. 41–4; C-112/00, *Eugen Schmidberger, Internationale Transporte und Planzügev. Republik Österreich*, paras. 84–93. See Ortino, *Basic Legal Instruments*, pp. 418–19, 431–3, 471; Craig, *EU Administrative Law*, pp. 601–4.

[108] See Jans, 'Proportionality Revisited', pp. 242, 248; Bermann, 'Proportionality and Subsidiarity', p. 82; Ortino, *Basic Legal Instruments*, pp. 421, 433, 472.

[109] Case C-302/86, *Commission v. Denmark (Bottles)*, paras. 20–1. See also Case C-169/89, *Criminal proceedings against Gourmetterie Van den Burg*, Opinion of Advocate-General Van Gerven, para. 10.

[110] See e.g. Case C-169/91, *Council of the City of Stoke-on-Trent and Norwich City Council v. B & Q Plc*, paras. 11, 15–17; Cases C-1/90 and C-176/90, *Aragonesa de Publicidad v. Departamento de Sanidad*, paras. 16–18; C-112/00, *Schmidberger*, paras. 81–94.

In *Stoke-on-Trent*, for example, the CJEU held that the restrictive effects of a law limiting Sunday trading were not excessive in relation to the aim pursued bearing in mind that national socio-cultural characteristics influence legislative choices, and indicating that it would be loath to interfere with local determinations of societal needs.[111]

The ECtHR also appears to be highly aware of legitimacy concerns arising from the proportionality *stricto sensu* stage.[112] In the context of the right to property, the ECtHR has stated that there must be a 'reasonable relationship of proportionality' between the challenged measure and its objective or a 'fair balance' between the public interest pursued by the measure and the degree of interference with the right, and that a measure will lack proportionality only where the claimant bears an 'individual and excessive burden'.[113] The case law has not clearly established when the circumstances will give rise to a finding of a lack of proportionality on this basis.[114] The concept of 'individual and excessive burden' does not appear to relate to whether the measure is directed towards a certain individual or is generally applicable in nature. However, the ECtHR is more willing to hold a measure to be proportionate in relation to general or complex measures that affect a large number of property owners, on the basis that a finding of lack of proportionality would place a significant fiscal burden on the state.[115] In particular, the ECtHR appears to take the position that commercial enterprises should bear the risk of changes in regulatory policy, because the government would otherwise function as insurer to commercial entities for what would normally be regarded

---

[111] Case C-169/91, *Stoke-on-Trent*, paras. 11, 15–17.

[112] See Rivers, 'Second Law of Balancing', p. 178; Legg, *Margin of Appreciation*, pp. 86–8.

[113] For example, *Sporrong* v. *Sweden*, para. 73; *N.K.M.* v. *Hungary*, paras. 71–2; *Stefanetti* v. *Italy*, para. 66; *Gladysheva* v. *Russia*, para. 82; *Richet and Le Ber* v. *France*, para. 124. See Freeman, 'Regulatory Expropriation Under NAFTA Chapter 11', p. 201; Ratner, 'Regulatory Takings in Institutional Context', p. 498.

[114] Freeman, 'Regulatory Expropriation Under NAFTA Chapter 11', p. 195; Van Dijk et al., *Theory and Practice of the European Convention on Human Rights*, p. 876; Perkams, 'The Concept of Indirect Expropriation in Comparative Public Law–Searching for Light in the Dark' in Schill (ed.), *International Investment Law and Comparative Public Law* (2010) 107, 117, 121.

[115] Freeman, 'Regulatory Expropriation Under NAFTA Chapter 11', p. 195; Kriebaum, 'Regulatory Takings', pp. 740, 742–3. See also De Sena, 'Economic and Non-Economic Values in the Case Law of the European Court of Human Rights', in Dupuy, Petersmann and Francioni (eds.), *Human Rights in International Investment Law and Arbitration* (2009) 208, 215–16.

as commercial risks.[116] The effect of the application of a wide margin of appreciation to all stages of proportionality analysis in property cases is that states have very broad discretion to interfere with property in the public interest. These cases include broad, general reforms to a country's political or economic system;[117] measures directed at infrastructure development, town planning and environmental protection;[118] and issues of domestic political importance, such as achieving social justice through land reform.[119]

In practice, the ECtHR will only find that the fair balance is upset where a measure's effect on the applicant's property rights is 'manifestly disproportionate'.[120] Examples of cases where the ECtHR has found a violation include where property was requisitioned by the state for use as public offices and subject to a long-term lease without fair compensation[121] and a widespread practice of *de facto* expropriation whereby the authorities occupied land without a formal transfer of ownership and could irreversibly change the prospective use of the property.[122] In *Sporrong*, for example, the ECtHR held that the measures (expropriation permits and prohibitions on construction in relation to the applicants' properties, which had been in place for 23 years and 25 years in relation to one of the applicants) were in breach of the right to property. The applicants were forbidden to erect new structures on their land and the value of the land depreciated over the period that the permits were in place, making it difficult to sell or lease the land or obtain a mortgage over it; moreover, the law gave the applicants no opportunity to object or to claim compensation.[123] It should also be noted that in some cases (not

---

[116] See Mountfield, 'Regulatory Expropriations in Europe', pp. 147–8; Harris, O'Boyle, Bates and Buckley, *Law of the European Convention on Human Rights* (2014) 895.

[117] *Jahn* v. *Germany*, paras. 93–5, 113–17.

[118] *Allan Jacobsson* v. *Sweden*, paras. 60–4; *Fredin* v. *Sweden*, paras. 48, 51–5; *Pine Valley* v. *Ireland*, paras. 57, 59.

[119] For example, *James* v. *UK*, para. 69; *J.A. Pye (Oxford) Ltd and J.A. Pye (Oxford) Land Ltd.* v. *UK*, paras. 75–85.

[120] For example, *Lithgow* v. *UK*, para. 122. See e.g. Greer, *The Margin of Appreciation*, p. 13; Arai-Takahashi, *Margin of Appreciation and Proportionality*, pp. 154, 157, 164; Van Dijk et al., *Theory and Practice of the European Convention on Human Rights*, pp. 888–9.

[121] *Fleri Soler and Camilleri* v. *Malta*, paras. 68–80.

[122] *Sarica and Dilaver* v. *Turkey*, paras. 43–52.

[123] *Sporrong and Lönnroth* v. *Sweden*, paras. 58, 73. See also *Chassagnou* v. *France*, paras. 82–5; *Immobilaire Saffi* v. *Italy*, paras. 54–9; *Hutten-Czapska* v. *Poland*, paras. 223–5; *Saliba* v. *Malta*, paras. 63–7; *Lindheim* v. *Norway*, paras. 119–34.

restricted to property) the ECtHR has held that failure of national authorities to undertake a proportionality assessment will render the measure unlawful.[124]

WTO tribunals have not (with one possible exception) engaged in proportionality *stricto sensu* testing.[125] The possible exception is the *Korea-Beef* case, where the Appellate Body, determining the necessity of a measure requiring that domestic and imported beef be sold in separate stores, restated Korea's level of protection against fraudulent labelling of imported beef from one that 'totally eliminates' fraud to one that 'considerably reduces' fraud.[126] The Appellate Body then found that other measures were reasonably available that would considerably reduce fraud, whereas those measures would likely not have achieved the government's original objective of total elimination of fraud.[127] It is arguable that the Appellate Body implicitly held that the importance of Korea's regulatory objective was outweighed by the importance of avoiding discrimination against imports, because the total elimination of fraud would have required an import ban.

More generally, the Appellate Body has stated that panels must assess the importance of the interests or values furthered by the measure's objective as part of the overall inquiry into whether the measure satisfies the requirements of the exception.[128] One reading of WTO case law in light of this statement is that the greater the importance ascribed to a measure's objective by a WTO tribunal, the less strictly the tribunal will scrutinize the suitability and necessity of a measure, and the greater the level of interference with trade it will permit implies a form of balancing between the importance of the objective and the degree of interference with trade.[129] However, there is no clear evidence of proportionality *stricto sensu* analysis taking place in the decided cases. Rather, it appears that the greater the importance of the objective as assessed by the tribunal, the more leeway it will permit with respect to the degree of contribution between the

---

[124] For example, *Dickson* v. *UK*, para. 85.

[125] See Ortino, *Basic Legal Instruments*, pp. 207–8; Marceau and Trachtman, 'Domestic Regulation of Goods', pp. 25, 50–1; Weiler, 'Comment: *Brazil–Measures Affecting Imports of Retreaded Tyres*' (2009) 8 *World Trade Review* 137, 140–1.

[126] In terms of Article XX(d) GATT ('necessary to secure compliance with laws or regulations which are not inconsistent with GATT, including measures relating to the prevention of deceptive practices').

[127] Appellate Body Report, *Korea-Beef*, paras. 178–80.

[128] See e.g. Appellate Body Reports, *Korea-Beef*, para. 162; *US-Gambling*, para. 306; *Brazil–Tyres*, para. 158.

[129] Regan, 'The Meaning of "Necessary"', pp. 352–3.

measure and its objective and the less significance it will attribute to the measure's trade-restrictiveness.[130]

The reluctance of WTO tribunals to engage in proportionality *stricto sensu* review may be explained both by the Appellate Body's strict emphasis on textual interpretation – at least in the first few years following its inception[131] – and by the institutional position of WTO tribunals in comparison to the CJEU and ECtHR, whose greater embeddedness in the European polity may explain their more expansive approach to textually similar provisions. In any event, the prevailing view among commentators appears to be that WTO tribunals should not undertake proportionality *stricto sensu* analysis. Their concerns include that WTO tribunals do not enjoy democratic legitimacy and are not embedded in national communities, making them poorly situated to make decisions regarding matters of local concern, and that is it inappropriate to engage in proportionality *stricto sensu* review in the context of a diverse worldwide (rather than regional) membership.[132]

3.6 Conclusion

This chapter has elaborated on the crucial connection between proportionality and deference by examining the approaches of the CJEU, the ECtHR and WTO tribunals. These bodies employ deference to varying degrees when undertaking proportionality analysis in order to deal with the sensitivities inherent in evaluating the legitimacy of governmental policy objectives, the practicalities of determining the suitability of measures

---

[130] Regan, 'The Meaning of "Necessary"', pp. 352–3.

[131] See e.g. Howse, 'Adjudicative Legitimacy and Treaty Interpretation', pp. 35, 51–6; Weiler, 'The Rule of Lawyers and the Ethos of Diplomats: Reflections on the Internal and External Legitimacy of WTO Dispute Settlement' (2002) 13 *American Review of International Arbitration* 177, 195; cf. Van Damme, *Treaty Interpretation by the WTO Appellate Body* (2009) 221–35.

[132] See Desmedt, 'Proportionality in WTO Law' (2001) *Journal of International Economic Law* 441, 480; Neumann and Türk, 'Necessity Revisited', pp. 232–3; Ortino, *Basic Legal Instruments*, p. 472; Regan, 'The Meaning of "Necessary"', pp. 349, 366; Van Den Bossche, 'Looking for Proportionality in WTO Law' (2008) 35 *Legal Issues of Economic Integration* 283, 284; Shaffer, 'A Structural Approach to WTO Jurisprudence: Why Institutional Choice Lies at the Centre of the GMO Case' (2008) 41 *New York University Journal of International Law and Politics* 1, 60; Du, 'Autonomy in Setting Appropriate Level of Protection under the WTO Law: Rhetoric or Reality?' (2010) 13 *Journal of International Economic Law* 1077, 1101; Shaffer and Trachtman, 'Interpretation and Institutional Choice at the WTO', pp. 143–4; Lang, *World Trade Law after Neoliberalism: Reimagining the Global Economic Order* (2011) 314.

and whether alternatives are available and, in some cases, the question of weighing the importance of the measure against the importance of avoiding harm to private rights or interests. These bodies afford a measure of deference to governments on the basis of the need to avoid intruding into matters of national competence and sensitivity, respecting the discretion of primary decision-makers, and based on more practical reasons relating to adjudicators' technical and evidential constraints.

The approaches taken by the CJEU, ECtHR and WTO tribunals to proportionality and deference are not always consistent or coherent, and in some cases regime-specific considerations animate their approaches. Nevertheless, the approaches of these jurisdictions demonstrate that proportionality analysis need not be approached in an intrusive manner and that the technique can be used sensitively to mediate between national autonomy and the regime's primary norm in a manner that pays due respect to the roles and relative capacities of primary decision-makers in situations of normative and empirical uncertainty. In other words, proportionality analysis permits variable intensity of review, depending on the particular issues that require consideration by the tribunal. The approaches demonstrated by these courts and tribunals may lessen concerns that proportionality analysis invariably results in a stringent review of measures and/or unrestrained value judgements. This, in turn, may assuage concerns about the potential for proportionality analysis to perpetuate unwarranted incursions into regulatory autonomy in the context of international investment law. Arguably, concerns about the potential for proportionality analysis to give overly broad discretion to arbitrators and the negative impact that this discretion may have on regulatory autonomy can be accommodated by way of the standard of review as it relates to the various stages of proportionality analysis. With these considerations in mind, Chapters 4 and 5 assess how investment tribunals have approached the method and standard of review in determining state liability in regulatory disputes.

4

Methods of review employed by investment tribunals in regulatory disputes

4.1 Introduction

As foreshadowed in Chapter 1, an increasing number of investment tribunals have referred to the concepts of balancing and proportionality in recent years. However, no tribunal has explicitly employed proportionality analysis in the sense of identifying and applying its discrete analytical stages in the same manner as have the CJEU, ECtHR and WTO tribunals. Investment tribunals have more frequently relied on the ideas inherent in the proportionality assessment rather than using its terminology, or have discussed and applied some of the elements of proportionality analysis but not others.

This chapter and Chapter 5 examine investment tribunals' approaches to the method and standard of review in regulatory disputes in relation to fair and equitable treatment and arbitrary measures clauses, indirect expropriation, non-discrimination and treaty exceptions. Apart from cases where tribunals have not taken into account the state's reasons for its actions, which constitute a minority of the decided cases, tribunals have adopted a range of approaches to the applicable method of review, and the substantial inconsistencies in tribunals' approaches mean that at this is time it is difficult to predict how a tribunal will decide a given regulatory dispute in any of these areas of law. These areas are introduced below, with a primer on the various ways in which investment tribunals have taken into account the host state's regulatory purpose in determining liability, followed by a more substantial elaboration of the methods of review they have adopted.

4.2   The areas of international investment law that are the focus of this study

4.2.1   *Fair and equitable treatment*

The obligation to accord fair and equitable treatment appears in most investment treaties, and is the most frequently invoked and most successfully argued standard of investment protection.[1] However, there is a lack of consensus among states, arbitrators and commentators as to the normative content of the obligation, due in part to the vague nature of the concepts of 'fair' and 'equitable'.[2] As noted in the Introduction, the combination of vaguely drafted standards of investment protection and an absence of any appeal mechanism increases the discretion available to arbitrators. Many tribunal decisions are open to the criticism that cases have been decided according to the arbitrators' own opinions as to what might be fair and equitable, rather than through the application of a legal standard that has normative content.[3]

Nevertheless, investment tribunal decisions on the content of fair and equitable treatment have increasingly converged around a number of elements.[4] Most significantly from the perspective of potential limitations on the rights of states to regulate and take other action in the public interest is that many tribunals have held that adjudicating a fair and equitable treatment claim permits them to engage in substantive review of the content of changes to laws and policies and administrative decisions affecting foreign investors. A small number of tribunals have found (and some authors have argued) that proportionality is itself a principle of fair and equitable treatment (i.e. a general obligation that states must act in a proportionate manner towards foreign investors), but these tribunals and

---

[1] Newcombe and Paradell, *Law and Practice of Investment Treaties* (2009) 255; Dolzer and Schreuer, *Principles of International Investment Law* (2012) 130; UNCTAD, *Fair and Equitable Treatment*, p. 1; Bonnitcha, *Substantive Protection under Investment Treaties*, p. 144.

[2] For example, Schill, 'Fair and Equitable Treatment, the Rule of Law, and Comparative Public Law' in Schill (ed.), *International Investment Law and Comparative Public Law* (2010) 151–7; Kläger, *Fair and Equitable Treatment*, pp. 3, 87.

[3] Schill, 'Fair and Equitable Treatment', p. 157; Kläger, *Fair and Equitable Treatment*, pp. 86–7; Paparinskis, *The International Minimum Standard*, p. 116.

[4] Other obligations that are regarded as elements of fair and equitable treatment are prohibitions on arbitrary, unreasonable or discriminatory treatment, harassment and coercion; obligations of due process by administrators and in judicial proceedings; and obligations of good faith and transparency in dealings with investors. See Kläger, *Fair and Equitable Treatment*, pp. 117–18; Dolzer and Schreuer, *Principles of International Investment Law*, pp. 145–60.

authors have not further elaborated on the content of proportionality as an independent norm of fair and equitable treatment or its relationship to the more substantive obligations that come within the concept.[5]

This chapter also discusses certain cases involving the determination of liability in terms of 'arbitrary or discriminatory measures'[6] and 'unreasonable or discriminatory measures' clauses, which are contained in some investment treaties.[7] Tribunals do not appear to attach significance to the differences in terminology in terms of arbitrariness or unreasonableness, instead using the terms synonymously.[8] Investment tribunals have suggested that these concepts overlap in the sense that conduct that is arbitrary, unreasonable or discriminatory will also breach fair and equitable treatment (and vice versa), and many tribunals have analyzed these provisions together with their analysis of fair and equitable treatment.[9]

4.2.1.1 Legitimate expectations and substantive review

Tribunals have increasingly used the doctrine of legitimate expectations as the organizing principle for substantive review.[10] Investment tribunals have found that a claimant holds a legitimate expectation in the stability of the legal environment or the consistency of government conduct in

---

[5] For example, *MTD* v. *Chile*, Award, para. 109; *El Paso* v. *Argentina*, Award, para. 373. See also *Occidental* v. *Ecuador (No 2)*, Award, para. 452 (discussed further in Section 4.3 of this chapter). See Waibel, 'Opening Pandora's Box: Sovereign Bonds in International Arbitration' (2007) 101 *American Journal of International Law* 711, 750; Kingsbury and Schill, 'Investor-State Arbitration as Governance', p. 16; Schill, 'Fair and Equitable Treatment', p. 160; Kläger, *Fair and Equitable Treatment*, pp. 118–19.

[6] For example, Article II(2)(b) Argentina-US BIT; Article II(3)(b) Ecuador-US BIT; Article II(2)(b) US-Romania BIT.

[7] For example, Article 10(1) Energy Charter Treaty; Article 2(2) Hong Kong-Australia BIT; Article 3(3) Croatia-Oman BIT; Article 4(1) Mauritius-Switzerland BIT. Less frequently, treaties prohibit measures that are 'arbitrary and discriminatory' (e.g. Article 10(1) Energy Charter Treaty; Article 2(2) Hong Kong-Australia BIT; Article 3(3) Croatia-Oman BIT; Article 4(1) Switzerland-Mauritius BIT) or 'unreasonable and discriminatory' (e.g. Article II (3)(b) US-Albania BIT; Article II (3)(b) US-Jordan BIT). See Newcombe and Paradell, *Law and Practice of Investment Treaties*, pp. 298–9.

[8] Schreuer, *The ICSID Convention*, p. 183; Kläger, *Fair and Equitable Treatment*, p. 289.

[9] For example, *CMS* v. *Argentina*, Award, para. 290; *MTD* v. *Chile*, Award, para. 196; *Saluka* v. *Czech Republic*, Partial Award, para. 465, but see e.g. *LG&E* v. *Argentina*, Liability, para. 163; *Azurix* v. *Argentina*, Award, paras. 385–93 (holding that the two obligations are separate). See Heiskanen, 'Arbitrary and Unreasonable Measures' in Reinisch (ed.), *Standards of Investment Protection* (2008) 87, 89–100; Stone, 'Arbitrariness, the Fair and Equitable Treatment Standard, and the International Law of Investment' (2012) 25 *Leiden Journal of International Law* 77, 90–2 (with further references).

[10] Bonnitcha, *Substantive Protection under Investment Treaties*, p. 211.

a variety of situations.[11] Earlier tribunals found that the claimant had a legitimate expectation in remarkably broad circumstances, such as where the state had made no specific commitments to the claimant[12] or where the tribunal discerned such commitments from general legislation.[13] The prevalent approach taken by tribunals in the past few years, however, has narrowed the circumstances in which a legitimate expectations claim can be made, by requiring that there be a specific and enforceable legal right vested in the claimant[14] or that the government had made specific representations or assurances to the claimant.[15] In later cases, many tribunals have found the state's conduct insufficiently specific to give rise to a legitimate expectation.[16] However, even where tribunals have taken a restrictive approach to the concept of legitimate expectations, they have, in some cases, gone on to substantively review regulatory changes or other

---

[11] See Potestà, 'Legitimate Expectations in Investment Treaty Law: Understanding the Roots and the Limits of a Controversial Concept' (2013) 28 *ICSID Review* 88, 100–19; Bonnitcha, *Substantive Protection under Investment Treaties*, pp. 170–89 (with further references).

[12] For example, *Tecmed* v. *Mexico*, Award, para. 154; *MTD* v. *Chile*, Award, paras. 104, 114–15, 163–6. By comparison, in ECHR law a legitimate expectation in the stability of the applicable legal framework and consistency in administrative decision-making in relation to the right to property can be recognized even in the absence of representations or assurances made by government, see e.g. Wildhaber, 'The Protection of Legitimate Expectations in European Human Rights Law' in Monti, Prinz von und zu Liechtenstein, Versterdorf, Westbrook and Wildhaber (eds.), *Economic Law and Justice in Times of Globalisation: Festschrift for Carl Baudenbacher* (2007) 253, 261–3; Kriebaum, 'Regulatory Takings: Balancing the Interests of the Investor and the State' (2007) 8 *Journal of World Investment and Trade* 734; Perkams, 'The Concept of Indirect Expropriation in Comparative Public Law – Searching for Light in the Dark' in Schill (ed.), *International Investment Law and Comparative Public Law* (2010) 107. Legitimate expectations are also a feature of EU law, but only in relation to acts by EU institutions and by member states pursuant to EU rules. Review of the conduct taken under EU rules has a different dimension to review of national measures, and the CJEU is generally more deferential in its review, see e.g. Craig, *EU Administrative Law*, pp. 549–89.

[13] For example (discussed further below), *CMS* v. *Argentina*, Award, para. 277; *Enron* v. *Argentina*, Award, para. 264; *Sempra* v. *Argentina*, Award, para. 303; *National Grid Plc* v. *Argentina*, Award, paras. 176–9.

[14] *LG&E* v. *Argentina*, Liability, paras. 130–9; *BG Group Plc.* v. *Argentina*, Final Award, para. 308. See Bonnitcha, *Substantive Protection under Investment Treaties*, pp. 170–5.

[15] See e.g. Potestà, 'Legitimate Expectations in Investment Treaty Law', pp. 105–10; Bonnitcha, *Substantive Protection under Investment Treaties*, pp. 176–9 (with further references).

[16] For example, *Frontier Petroleum Services* v. *Czech Republic*, Final Award, paras. 76, 455, 465, 468; *White Industries Australia Limited* v. *India*, Final Award, paras. 5.2.6, 10.3.17; *PSEG* v. *Turkey*, Award, paras. 241, 243.

government conduct affecting the claimant for reasonableness, arbitrariness or proportionality.[17]

The general theme emerging from the fair and equitable treatment cases is that tribunals frequently require a state to justify its actions (legislative or policy changes or departures from previous decisions, representations or assurances) on the basis of public policy, whether through the framework of legitimate expectations or in terms of a more general form of substantive review. To be sure, a degree of stability in laws and policies and consistency in administrative conduct are important considerations for foreign investors, particularly in relation to longer-term investments with high sunk costs where exit or divestment is difficult. However, depending on the approach that a tribunal takes to the question of whether the treatment of the investor or investment is justifiable, this interpretation of fair and equitable treatment may substantively restrict the ability of a government to act to promote public welfare by holding it liable to compensate a foreign investor for changes to general laws or policies or for other actions such as refusing or revoking a licence or permit. In this respect, the approach taken by a tribunal to the method and standard of review is crucial.

4.2.1.2 Resiling from legitimate expectations, amending legislation or changing a course of conduct

Tribunals have adopted a variety of approaches to the circumstances in which a state may lawfully amend the regulatory framework or act inconsistently with a prior decision, representation or assurance. Some tribunals disregarded the state's reasons for its actions, holding that the state was obliged to maintain a stable regulatory environment or to refrain from acting inconsistently with previous decisions regardless of the circumstances. This approach can be traced to the *Occidental (No 1)* award in 2004, where the tribunal held that the government had, by denying the claimant's applications for reimbursements on value-added tax due to a change in tax policy, violated an obligation 'not to alter the legal and business environment in which the investment had been made'.[18]

---

[17] For example, *Glamis v. US*, Award, paras. 621–2. See also e.g. *Separate Opinions of Arbitrator Nikken in InterAgua v. Argentina*, Liability, paras. 26–7, 32–4, 42; *AWG v. Argentina*, Liability, paras. 26–7, 32–4, 42.

[18] *Occidental Exploration and Production Co.* v. *Ecuador (Occidental v. Ecuador (No 1))*, paras. 191, 196. See also *Duke Energy Electroquil Partners & Electroquil S.A.* v. *Ecuador*, Award, paras. 338–40, 355 (although the tribunal found on the facts that there had been no relevant changes to the legal framework affecting the claimant); *MTD v. Chile*, Award,

The early cases against Argentina by foreign investors in the energy sector in relation to its emergency measures are also examples of this approach. In *CMS, Enron* and *Sempra*, the claimants argued that the enactment of the emergency laws had breached previous commitments made by Argentina as to the stability of the regulatory framework governing the utilities sectors. The tribunals found that in implementing a regulatory framework to attract investors to the utilities sectors, Argentina had made specific commitments to investors that had engendered legitimate expectations in the stability of the legal framework governing their investments that it could not lawfully resile from.[19] This approach did not take into account the state's reasons for its actions in determining whether it was possible to take action interfering with these claimants' investments; as such, it has significant implications for regulatory autonomy.[20]

More commonly, however, tribunals have held that any changes to laws and policies or inconsistent administrative treatment of investors must be justifiable on the basis of public policy, thereby envisaging a balance between the protection of investments and the autonomy of host states to act in the public interest.[21] This is where methods of review such as

paras. 104, 114–15, 163–6 (government not permitted to act inconsistently with prior administrative decision regardless of policy considerations underlying change of course of conduct).

[19] *CMS* v. *Argentina*, Award, para. 274; *Enron* v. *Argentina*, Award, paras. 264, 266, 268; *Sempra* v. *Argentina*, Award, para. 298.

[20] For example, Muchlinski, *Multinational Enterprises and the Law* (2007) 635–7; Sornarajah, *The International Law on Foreign Investment* (2010) 355; Sornarajah, 'Evolution or Revolution in International Investment Arbitration? The Descent into Normlessness' in Brown and Miles (eds.), *Evolution in Investment Treaty Law and Arbitration* (2011) 631, 651.

[21] Many commentators have made this observation in relation to fair and equitable treatment: see Muchlinski, *Multinational Enterprises and the Law*, pp. 635–7; Behrens, 'Towards the Constitutionalization of International Investment Protection' (2007) 45 *Archiv des Völkerrechts* 153; Montt, *State Liability in Investment Treaty Arbitration* (2007) 366; Kingsbury and Schill, 'Investor-State Arbitration as Governance', p. 48; Schill, 'Fair and Equitable Treatment', p. 158; Kingsbury and Schill, 'Public Law Concepts to Balance Investors' Rights with State Regulatory Actions in the Public Interest – The Concept of Proportionality' in Schill (ed.), *International Investment Law and Comparative Public Law* (2010) 96; Stone Sweet, 'Investor-State Arbitration: Proportionality's New Frontier' (2010) 4 *Law and Ethics of Human Rights* 62; Kläger, *Fair and Equitable Treatment*, p. 123; Radi, 'Realizing Human Rights in Investment Treaty Arbitration: A Perspective from Within the International Investment Law Toolbox' (2012) 37 *North Carolina Journal of International Law and Commercial Regulation* 1166. See also, in relation to the concept of fairness more generally as requiring a balance of interests, Franck, *Fairness in International Law and Institutions*, pp. 16–18; Kläger, *Fair and Equitable Treatment*, p. 151.

proportionality analysis can play a role. Tribunals have adopted several different methods of review in determining liability when undertaking a substantive review of host state conduct or determining a legitimate expectations claim. Several tribunals have employed proportionality analysis (or one or more of its component stages) in their assessment of such claims, or have adverted to the principle of proportionality. Others have assessed the 'reasonableness' of the measure, or have determined whether the measure was 'arbitrary.' Their approaches are discussed later in this chapter.

4.2.2   Indirect expropriation

Prohibitions on uncompensated direct and indirect expropriations also appear in almost every investment treaty.[22] The vast majority of investment treaties contain provisions reflecting customary international law of expropriation: an expropriation will be lawful provided that it is effectuated for a public purpose, is not arbitrary or discriminatory in its effect, follows principles of due process and is properly compensated.[23] Direct expropriations involve transfer of title to the state, and are less likely to be the subject of contemporary investment disputes. Alleged indirect expropriations – measures that significantly affect the value of the investment or that result in the effective loss of the investor's enjoyment of or control over their property[24] – have more frequently been the subject of investment disputes in recent years.[25]

Not every significant interference with an investment will amount to an indirect expropriation. The customary international law doctrine of police powers permits states to regulate or take other actions significantly affecting an investment without liability where the measure pursues a legitimate public welfare objective.[26] However, investment treaties

---

[22] UNCTAD, *Expropriation: A Sequel* (2012) 5.

[23] See e.g. Reinisch, 'Expropriation' in Muchlinski, Ortino and Schreuer (eds.), *The Oxford Handbook on International Investment Law* (2008) 407, 422, 426–7; Crawford, *Brownlie's Principles of Public International Law* (2012) 620–6; UNCTAD, *Expropriation*, p. xii.

[24] See Crawford, *Public International Law*, p. 621.

[25] See Reinisch, 'Expropriation', p. 409; Yannaca-Small, 'Indirect Expropriation and the Right to Regulate: How to Draw the Line?' in Yannaca-Small (ed.), *Arbitration Under International Investment Agreements: A Guide to the Key Issues* (2010) 445, 446; Dolzer and Schreuer, *Principles of International Investment Law*, p. 101.

[26] See e.g. *Feldman* v. *Mexico*, Merits, para. 103; *Saluka* v. *Czech Republic*, Partial Award, para. 262; *Azurix* v. *Argentina*, Award, para. 310. See also American Law Institute, *Restatement of the Law Third, Foreign Relations of the United States*, Volume 1 (1987), section 712(g); Article 10(5), Harvard Law School, Draft Convention on the International Responsibility

generally do not provide any guidance to arbitrators as to the circumstances in which a measure will be considered to be an indirect expropriation or an exercise of police powers, and customary international law is unclear in this respect. This area of law is characterized by a relatively small number of disputes combined with significant incoherence in methodological approaches.

Arbitrators' approaches to determining indirect expropriation claims can be grouped into three categories. The first category focuses only on the effect of the measure on the investment and not the state's reasons for its actions.[27] In other words, this approach does not recognize the police powers doctrine and leaves states vulnerable to successful claims in relation to any measures significantly impacting on foreign investments. In *Metalclad*, for example, the authorities refused to renew an operating permit for a hazardous waste facility on environmental grounds. The authorities also issued a decree declaring the land a conservation area for the protection of rare cacti, precluding the operation of the facility. The tribunal found both the refusal of the permit and the enactment of the conservation decree to be expropriatory. It held that the authorities had acted *ultra vires* domestic law by denying the permit on the basis of the adverse environmental effects of the facility and the geological unsuitability of the landfill site – a finding that was subject to heavy criticism.[28] The tribunal did not refer to the fact that the claimant had dumped large amounts of waste at the site without authorization and that the authorities had previously refused applications by the claimant to construct a facility at that site.[29] In relation to the conservation decree, the tribunal held that it was not required to consider the government's

---

of States for Injuries to Aliens (1961); Article 3, notes 1, 4(a) and (b) OECD Draft Convention on the Protection of Foreign Property (1967); Kriebaum, 'Regulatory Takings', pp. 726–7; Dolzer and Schreuer, *Principles of International Investment Law*, pp. 120–3; UNCTAD, *Expropriation*, p. 79.

[27] For example, *Metalclad v. Mexico*, Award, paras. 106–11; *Biloune v. Ghana*, Jurisdiction and Liability, p. 209; *Compañía de Aguas del Aconquija S.A. and Vivendi Universal v. Argentine Republic*, Award, para. 7.5.21; *BG v. Argentina*, Final Award, para. 268; *Siemens v. Argentina*, Award, para. 270; *Marion Unglaube and Reinhard Unglaube v. Costa Rica*, Award, paras. 202–23. See Bonnitcha, *Substantive Protection under Investment Treaties*, pp. 247–55.

[28] *Metalclad v. Mexico*, Award, para. 106. See e.g. Schneiderman, *Constitutionalizing Economic Globalization* (2008) 82–6; Montt, *State Liability in Investment Treaty Arbitration*, pp. 325, 336.

[29] See the Canadian court's decision (determining Mexico's application to set aside the award) *Mexico v. Metalclad Corporation* (2001), 14 BLR (3d) 285, 89 BCLR (3d) 359, 2001 BCSC 664, paras. 5–6.

objective when determining whether an expropriation had taken place.[30] More recently, the *Unglaube* tribunal took this approach in determining whether measures establishing a conservation reserve for endangered sea turtles (which placed controls on the use of the claimants' land) were expropriatory. The tribunal, while making a lengthy statement as to the importance of wildlife conservation, held that the importance of the state's objective in promulgating environmental policy did not affect its determination of whether the measures amounted to an expropriation.[31]

The second approach to determining indirect expropriation claims is to exempt any non-discriminatory measure directed to a public welfare objective from the scope of an expropriation.[32] This approach is also regarded by many as unsatisfactory, because the criteria used to determine the existence of a lawful expropriation are the same criteria used to determine whether the measure is an exercise of police powers or an expropriation.[33] The *Saluka* case is an example of this approach. The tribunal, determining a challenge to a decision to place the claimant's bank into involuntary administration, held that though the investment was 'eviscerated', the challenged measures were taken to stabilize the banking system in light of the claimant's failure to maintain the required capital adequacy ratios, were 'aimed at the maintenance of public order' or 'general welfare,' and were therefore not expropriatory.[34]

The third approach, which is becoming increasingly prevalent, entails taking both purpose and effect of the measure into consideration, or, in other words, both state and investor interests.[35] Many newly concluded

---

[30] *Metalclad* v. *Mexico*, Award, paras. 106–11.

[31] *Unglaube* v. *Costa Rica*, Award, paras. 202–23. This case contained elements of direct and indirect expropriation.

[32] See e.g. *Saluka* v. *Czech Republic*, Partial Award, paras. 254–65, 275–6; Bonnitcha, *Substantive Protection under Investment Treaties*, pp. 256–60 (with further references). Other tribunals that appear to support this approach, though finding that the impact of the measure on the claimant was insufficiently severe to ground a finding of expropriation, are *Methanex* v. *US*, Final Award, Part IV, Chapter D, paras. 15–16; *Chemtura* v. *Canada*, Award, para. 266; *AWG* v. *Argentina*, Liability, paras. 139–40; *Renée Rose Levy de Levi* v. *Republic of Peru*, Award, para. 475; *Spyridon Roussalis* v. *Romania*, Award, para. 663.

[33] See Higgins, 'The Taking of Property by the State: Recent Developments in International Law' (1982) 176 *Recueil des Cours* 267, 331; Mostafa, 'The Sole Effects Doctrine, Police Powers and Indirect Expropriation under International Law' (2008) 15 *Australian International Law Journal* 267, 273–4; *Pope and Talbot* v. *Canada*, Merits, para. 99.

[34] *Saluka* v. *Czech Republic*, Partial Award, paras. 254–65, 275–6.

[35] Fortier and Drymer, 'Indirect Expropriation in the Law of International Investment: I Know It When I See It, or *Caveat Investor*' (2004) 19 *ICSID Review* 293, 300, 313; McLachlan, Shore and Weiniger, *International Investment Arbitration: Substantive Principles*

investment treaties adopt this approach, obliging tribunals to take into account both the measure's purpose and effect.[36] However, most investment treaties provide no guidance in this respect. Several more recent tribunals have adopted or indicated support for proportionality-based methodologies in this determination, but their approaches have been less than clear in this respect. This chapter will later examine tribunals' methodologies in more detail.

4.2.3   Non-discrimination

Non-discrimination is another core obligation of international investment law. The concept covers both *de jure* discrimination (discrimination that is enshrined in a law or policy) and *de facto* discrimination (a facially neutral measure with a discriminatory effect, such as affecting only foreign investors, affecting greater numbers of foreign than domestic investors, or imposing requirements that are more difficult for foreign investors to comply with).[37] Most discrimination claims in investor-state arbitration relate to alleged *de facto* discrimination.[38]

Investment treaties typically contain provisions on national treatment, obliging states to accord treatment to foreign investors that is no less favourable than that provided to domestic investors in like circumstances,[39] and most-favoured nation treatment, extending this

---

(2007) 298, 302; Kriebaum, 'Regulatory Takings', pp. 724–9; UNCTAD, *Expropriation*, pp. 76–8; Bonnitcha, *Substantive Protection under Investment Treaties*, pp. 260–71.

[36] See e.g. Article 6 and Annex B(4)(b) 2012 US Model BIT; Article 13 and Annex B.13(1) Canada Model FIPA; Article 14(1) Australia-New Zealand Closer Economic Relations Investment Protocol; Annex 3 India-Singapore CEPA. To date, only one tribunal has applied this type of treaty provision, but did not make findings on the character and purpose of the measure, finding that the interference with the investment was insufficient to ground a successful claim: *Railroad Development Corporation* v. *Republic of Guatemala*, Award, paras. 92, 110, 151–2. See Bonnitcha, *Substantive Protection under Investment Treaties*, pp. 268–9.

[37] See e.g. Bjorklund, 'The National Treatment Obligation' in Yannaca-Small (ed.), *Arbitration Under International Investment Agreements: A Guide to the Key Issues* (2010) 411.

[38] Bjorklund, 'The National Treatment Obligation', pp. 419–20.

[39] Many treaties use the term 'like circumstances', whereas others refer to concepts including 'same circumstances', 'like situations', 'comparable situations' or 'similar situations'. These differences in wording do not appear to affect the way in which this analysis is conducted, see UNCTAD, *National Treatment* (1999) 14–15; Diebold, 'Standards of Non-discrimination in International Economic Law' (2011) 60 *International and Comparative Law Quarterly* 831, 835. Moreover, some treaties do not explicitly refer to likeness, see e.g. Article 10(7), Energy Charter Treaty.

protection (and others) to investors of third states.[40] Fair and equitable treatment is also understood to encompass an obligation of non-discrimination, particularly in relation to treaties that contain no separate injunction against discrimination, though some treaties specifically prohibit discrimination in the same provision as the fair and equitable treatment clause.[41]

The obligations of non-discrimination are, like fair and equitable treatment and indirect expropriation, also normatively vague. Treaty provisions are almost invariably silent as to the purpose and scope of the obligations of non-discrimination and how *bona fide* measures taken with legitimate objectives should be analyzed for breach. There are several major issues on which the decided cases are divided in terms of the applicable legal test for liability. The approaches taken by tribunals in relation to these issues all have implications for regulatory autonomy in terms of the breadth of the obligation. First, there is disagreement about whether the obligations of non-discrimination prohibit only intentional discrimination or whether they also prohibit measures with legitimate objectives that incidentally place an unjustifiably greater burden on foreign investors.[42] Second, tribunals have not taken a uniform approach to the analytical stage at which they take into account the objective of a challenged measure, whether as part of the like circumstances inquiry[43] or as part of the justification for differential treatment of foreign and domestic investors that have been found to be in like circumstances.[44] Third, there is

---

[40] Investors have challenged administrative treatment by state authorities for breach of most-favoured nation treatment in three known cases (*Parkerings* v. *Lithuania*, Award; *Bayindir Insaat Turizm Ticaret Ve Sanayi A.S.* v. *Islamic Republic of Pakistan*, Award; *Apotex Holdings Inc. and Apotex Inc.* v. *US*, Award), but no known cases involve legislative or other regulatory measures. Most cases involving claims of breach of most-favoured nation treatment have involved claimants seeking to rely on favourable procedural provisions from other investment treaties to which the host state is also a party. Most-favoured nation treatment is not discussed further except to the extent that the obligation interacts with other obligations of non-discrimination.

[41] For example, Article II(2) US-Romania BIT. Non-discrimination is also a requirement for a lawful expropriation: UNCTAD, *Expropriation*, p. 1 and for the exercise of police powers: American Law Institute, *Restatement of the Law Third*, Volume 1, Section 712 g.

[42] This issue is discussed further in Chapter 6.

[43] For example, *SD Myers* v. *Canada*, Partial Award, para. 250; *Pope and Talbot* v. *Canada*, Merits, paras. 76–79; *Cargill, Incorporated* v. *Mexico*, Award, paras. 193–201 (all national treatment). See Newcombe and Paradell, *Law and Practice of Investment Treaties*, pp. 162–3; Kinnear, Bjorklund and Hannaford, *Investment Disputes Under NAFTA: An Annotated Guide to NAFTA Chapter 11* (2006) 1102–25–1102.26.

[44] For example, *Feldman* v. *Mexico*, Merits, para. 182; (national treatment); *Parkerings* v. *Lithuania*, Award, paras. 375, 392, 396 (most-favoured nation treatment); *SAUR*

a lack of consensus on whether the concept of like circumstances requires the claimant to be in a competitive relationship with a domestic investor or investors,[45] which affects the breadth of the group of cases that come under scrutiny for possible breach. Fourth, tribunals have not adopted a consistent test to determine whether greater numbers of investors are adversely affected in terms of the concept of 'less favourable treatment'.[46] These issues also make it difficult to draw any firm conclusions about the normative content of the obligations of non-discrimination, apart from a general consensus among tribunals and commentators that states may rely on policy reasons to differentiate between otherwise similarly situated domestic and foreign investors – which gives rise to the issue of the appropriate method of review.[47]

A small minority of tribunals appears to have taken the position that differential treatment causing detriment or disadvantage to a foreign investor is never permissible, meaning that a state will not be able to rely on a legitimate objective to justify its actions and avoid liability. In *Occidental (No 1)*, the tribunal found that foreign exporters of oil were in like circumstances to domestic exporters of other products such as seafood and flowers in relation to eligibility for refunds of value-added taxes, yet oil producers received less favourable treatment, which amounted to a breach of national treatment.[48] However, the tribunal did not permit the

International SA v. *Argentina*, Jurisdiction and Liability, para. 486 (fair and equitable treatment); *Genin* v. *Estonia*, Award, para. 368; (discriminatory measures); *Consortium RFCC* v. *Morocco*, Award, para. 74 (fair and equitable treatment and national treatment). See also Newcombe and Paradell, *Law and Practice of Investment Treaties*, p. 163.

[45] This issue has arisen mainly in relation to national treatment, where the vast majority of tribunals have held that there must be a competitive relationship between the claimant and any comparable domestic investor or investors. See Kurtz, 'Use and Abuse of WTO Law' (arguing that a competitive relationship is essential), cf. e.g. DiMascio and Pauwelyn, 'Nondiscrimination in Trade and Investment Treaties: Worlds Apart or Different Sides of the Same Coin?' (2008) 102 *American Journal of International Law* 48, 81–9; Bjorklund, 'The National Treatment Obligation', p. 422 (arguing that national treatment in the context of international investment law should protect foreign investors where foreign and domestic investors both face sufficiently similar regulatory circumstances but differentiated rights or obligations regardless of the sector or sectors they operate in).

[46] In particular, whether only a single affected investor would suffice for a finding of breach or whether a pool of foreign investors should be compared with domestic counterparts: see Kurtz, 'The Merits and Limits of Comparativism', pp. 266–72.

[47] This approach is also prevalent in international human rights law, see e.g. McKean, 'The Meaning of Discrimination in International and Municipal Law' (1970) 44 *British Yearbook of International Law* 177, 178, 185–6; Vierdag, *The Concept of Discrimination in International Law: With Special Reference to Human Rights* (1973) 48–65; Shaw, *International Law*, pp. 286–9.

[48] *Occidental* v. *Ecuador (No 1)*, paras. 173, 177.

state to plead a justification for the differential treatment, even though it found that the government had not acted with a discriminatory motive.[49]

In the vast majority of cases, however, tribunals have held that governments may draw distinctions between foreign and domestic investors or investments provided that the differential treatment is taken in pursuance of a legitimate objective. In this respect, a tribunal must determine whether the objective pursued by the measure is non-discriminatory, and then interrogate the connection between that objective and the challenged measure. Most tribunals have not articulated the nature of the required nexus between a measure and its objective so as to avoid a finding of breach (and thus the applicable method of review), but those that have done so have used either a suitability or necessity test. The approach adopted by a tribunal does not appear to have any bearing on the type of discrimination claim or the point at which the purpose of the measure is examined. No tribunal has engaged in proportionality *stricto sensu* testing in the determination of a discrimination claim. Tribunals' approaches are discussed later in this chapter.

4.2.4 Treaty exceptions

Treaty exceptions (also known as non-precluded measures clauses or derogation clauses) permit a government to take action directed at a particular regulatory objective that would otherwise be inconsistent with the state's substantive treaty obligations. Exception clauses fulfil a similar function to the general exceptions contained in the WTO agreements, the derogation clauses in the TFEU, and certain ECHR provisions. In 2011, it was estimated that some form of exception appeared in approximately 10 per cent of investment treaties.[50] This type of provision is, however, becoming more common in recently concluded treaties, suggesting that states are concerned that investment tribunals have paid insufficient attention to the right to regulate in terms of substantive obligations contained in investment treaties.[51]

---

[49] See *Occidental* v. *Ecuador (No 1)*, para. 177. It is arguable that the *Corn Products* v. *Mexico* tribunal took a similar position (Award, paras. 137, 142), commenting that '[Discrimination] does not cease to be discrimination . . . because it is undertaken to achieve a laudable goal or because the achievement of that goal can be described as necessary.'

[50] Alvarez and Brink, 'Revisiting the Necessity Defense: *Continental Casualty* v. *Argentina*' in Sauvant (ed.), *Yearbook on International Investment Law and Policy 2010–2011* (2011) 319, 357.

[51] Spears, 'The Quest for Policy Space in a New Generation of International Investment Agreements' (2010) 13 *Journal of International Economic Law* 1037, 1043–4.

Unlike provisions on fair and equitable treatment, expropriation and discrimination, the permissible policy objectives and the required nexus between a derogating measure and its objective are set out in the text of the exception clause itself. In this respect, states will be constrained in terms of the circumstances in which they will be able to rely on the clause in order to escape liability. Commonly occurring objectives are essential security and public order,[52] public health,[53] public morals,[54] conservation of natural resources[55] and prudential measures taken with respect to the financial system.[56] Treaty provisions contain a range of formulations of the nexus requirement, including 'necessary for',[57] 'proportional to',[58] 'related to',[59] 'directed to',[60] 'for',[61] 'designed and applied'[62] or 'appropriate to'[63] further the one of the permissible objectives.[64] To be clear, treaties containing an exception clause with a less onerous method of review than necessity testing (such as 'related to') must be interpreted on their own terms, which will preclude the use of proportionality analysis. However, all of the decided cases to date have involved an exception clause permitting 'necessary' actions (discussed below).

4.3   The methods of review

The above discussion demonstrates that in each of these areas of law, investment tribunals are in need of a workable methodology by which to determine state liability in regulatory disputes. This section discusses the methods of review that tribunals have adopted in the determination of regulatory disputes in these areas.

---

[52] For example, Article XI, Argentina-US BIT.
[53] For example, Article 11(3), Mauritius-Switzerland BIT.
[54] For example, Article X(1), US-Egypt BIT.
[55] For example, Annex I, Article III (2)(c), Canada-Uruguay BIT.
[56] For example, Annex I, Article III (3)(c), Canada-Uruguay BIT.
[57] For example, Article XI, Argentina-US BIT.
[58] For example, Article 8, Colombia Model BIT (2007).
[59] For example, Article 10(4), Canada Model FIPA (2004).
[60] For example, Article 11, New Zealand-China FTA.
[61] For example, Article 12(2), Croatia-India BIT.
[62] For example, Article 22(1), COMESA Investment Agreement.
[63] For example, Article 22(1), COMESA Investment Agreement.
[64] The provisions also differ in their scope: some (e.g. Article XI, Argentina-US BIT and Article 200, New Zealand-China FTA) apply to all substantive investor protections, whereas others (e.g. Article 11(2), UK-India BIT) apply only to non-discriminatory measures.

4.3.1 Full proportionality analysis and the dangers of substitutionary review

To date, the only investment decision involving full proportionality analysis did not arise in the context of a typical regulatory dispute involving legislative or policy changes, or a straightforward administrative decision affecting a foreign investor. Nevertheless, the *Occidental (No 2)* decision, in which the tribunal engaged with the necessity and proportionality *stricto sensu* stages of proportionality analysis, deserves attention because it highlights some of the problems that can arise where a tribunal substitutes its own view for that of the state in undertaking proportionality analysis without consideration of the appropriate standard of review. This case also sets the scene for a discussion of the relevance of the standard of review to proportionality analysis in the context of international investment law, and the circumstances in which proportionality analysis will be an appropriate method of review.

The *Occidental (No 2)* claim concerned a contract for the exploration and exploitation of hydrocarbons in the Ecuadorian Amazon. The contract provided that Occidental could only transfer or assign contractual rights under certain conditions and that in the event that those rights were transferred or assigned without authorization, the government could terminate the contract and require the investor to return the contracted areas and equipment.[65] Occidental sold a 40 per cent share of the concession without such authorization, and the government exercised its contractual rights by issuing a decree terminating the contract. The terms of the contract appeared clear with respect to the state's rights and did not appear to envisage a role for proportionality analysis.[66] However, the decree referred to the legislation governing the sector rather than the contract itself, a point which the tribunal relied on as empowering it to employ proportionality analysis to determine liability on the basis that Ecuadorian law in force at the time provided that 'laws shall establish due proportionality between offences and penalties'.[67]

---

[65] *Occidental Petroleum Corporation and Occidental Exploration and Production Company* v. *Ecuador*, Award, paras. 105, 119–21 (*Occidental* v. *Ecuador (No 2)*).

[66] See Sabahi and Duggal, '*Occidental Petroleum* v. *Ecuador* (2012): Observations on Proportionality, Assessment of Damages and Contributory Fault' (2013) 28 *ICSID Review* 279, 282.

[67] *Occidental* v. *Ecuador (No 2)*, paras. 397, 417–23; Article 24(3), Constitution of the Republic of Ecuador (1998) (repealed). See Sabahi and Duggal, '*Occidental Petroleum* v. *Ecuador*', pp. 281–2.

Ecuador argued that the tribunal should not undertake proportionality analysis because the terms of the contract itself were clear and the law on proportionality did not apply, or alternatively that its actions were proportionate.[68] However, the tribunal held that the law on proportionality applied to all administrative and legal proceedings and not just criminal offences, and that the issuance of the decree was an administrative (rather than private law) decision.[69] Moreover, it held that the principle of proportionality was applicable to the state's actions under Ecuadorian law, international investment law and customary international law.[70] According to the tribunal, the exercise of discretion by the authorities in relation to the contractual breach was required to 'bear a proportionate relationship to the violation which is being addressed and its consequences' and that in this context, proportionality analysis would entail 'balancing the interests of the State against those of the individual'.[71]

The tribunal determined that the government was acting with the objectives of punishment and general deterrence, appearing to accept that these objectives were legitimate reasons for acting and that the state's actions were suitable to that aim.[72] However, the tribunal considered it relevant that there was substantial community opposition to Occidental's actions and that a previous successful investment treaty claim by Occidental (*Occidental (No 1)*, discussed above) had caused opposition to the claimant's presence in Ecuador among political figures and within civil society, which it appeared to view as a negative influence on the government's actions.[73] The tribunal then went on to assess whether alternative courses of action were available to the state, finding that the government could have imposed a transfer fee on the claimant or could have required the transferee to enter into a new contract that would be more favourable to the state.[74] Although these alternatives were permitted by the regulatory regime, they did not appear to be directed at, let alone equally effective at, achieving the state's objectives. Rather, these alternatives were rights that the state could have exercised when determining whether to authorize the transfer.[75]

---

[68] *Occidental* v. *Ecuador (No 2)*, paras. 393–52.
[69] *Occidental* v. *Ecuador (No 2)*, paras. 398–401.
[70] *Occidental* v. *Ecuador (No 2)*, para. 452.
[71] *Occidental* v. *Ecuador (No 2)*, para. 417.   [72] *Occidental* v. *Ecuador (No 2)*, para. 414.
[73] *Occidental* v. *Ecuador (No 2)*, paras. 181, 196, 442.
[74] *Occidental* v. *Ecuador (No 2)*, paras. 428–36.
[75] Fuentes, 'Proportionality Analysis and Disproportionate Damages: *Occidental Petroleum Corporation and Occidental Exploration and Production Company* v. *The Republic of Ecuador*' (2015) 16 *Journal of World Investment and Trade* 315, 322–3.

The tribunal also undertook a form of proportionality *stricto sensu* analysis. It balanced the degree of harm to the claimant's interests against the degree of harm to the state caused by the claimant's actions, rather than taking the orthodox approach of balancing the importance of achieving the state's objective against the importance of avoiding harm to the claimant's interests. The tribunal found that the breach of contract was insufficiently serious to justify the penalty because the state had not suffered harm and, in the view of the tribunal, the government would likely have approved the transfer had approval been sought.[76] The tribunal then concluded that the quantum of the loss suffered by the claimant was out of proportion to the wrongdoing and 'the importance and effectiveness' of the objective.[77]

In the context of the review of a penalty or sanction, proportionality analysis functions as a test for excessiveness in terms of an individual case rather than as a test of the proportionality of a general policy objective, because a penalty may be held to be disproportionate without undermining the law or policy itself.[78] Arguably, in cases where the regulatory regime prescribes or permits proportionality analysis to be used in the determination of the lawfulness of an administrative sanction, courts and tribunals might have less reason for granting deference to governments because the adjudicator's decision does not impugn the underlying policy – and the body that ordered the sanction is usually permitted to take the decision again, guided by the court or the tribunal's ruling.[79] As such, engaging in proportionality analysis might be regarded as less likely to undermine regulatory autonomy, because the annulment of a single act through levying a penalty does not call into question the general regulatory scheme. However, this would depend on proportionality analysis being permitted (or not precluded) by the law in question.

Even assuming that proportionality analysis was an appropriate method of review in this case, the tribunal mischaracterized the government's objective. Although one aim of a system of sanctions such as the regime at issue in this case is to address any actual harm to the state's interest arising from the contractual breach, the requirement of prior authorization for the transfer of the claimants' contractual rights had two further significant objectives that the tribunal did not properly

---

[76] *Occidental v. Ecuador (No 2)*, paras. 445–6.
[77] *Occidental v. Ecuador (No 2)*, paras. 450–5.
[78] Craig, *EU Administrative Law*, pp. 611–14 (in relation to the proportionality of penalties and financial burdens levied by EU authorities); Craig, *Administrative Law* (2012) 659.
[79] See Craig, *EU Administrative Law*, pp. 611–14.

take into account. First, the requirement was a means for the state to exercise control over the parties that can exercise rights of exploitation of natural resources; exploitation may have significant consequences for the state's economy and the environment that the state may seek to avoid or mitigate.[80] Second, this requirement allows the state to assess any other relevant strategic and political considerations in terms of the identity of the transferee.[81] These additional objectives make the relevant interest of the state in terms of proportionality analysis a broader consideration than actual harm caused to the state through the claimant's actions.[82]

Apart from the contested issue of whether Ecuadorian law in fact permitted the tribunal to embark on proportionality analysis in the first place in relation to contractual breaches,[83] the tribunal's approach may also be criticized for taking a strict approach to the standard of review by mischaracterizing and undermining the importance of the regulatory objective, taking an approach to necessity that did not consider whether alternatives would have been as effective at achieving the objective, and undertaking its own proportionality *stricto sensu* test without regard to the desirability of an institutionally sensitive approach to the standard of review. Yet, perhaps the most significant aspect of the decision is that the tribunal made several statements to the effect that a duty to act proportionately was a norm of general international law and customary international law. The decision suggests that arbitrators have broad scope to rule on the proportionality of measures as a general principle applicable to all state obligations under an investment treaty, a conclusion that no other investment tribunal has thus far reached and that is questionable in this case in light of the clear terms of the contract.[84]

---

[80] The tribunal acknowledged this objective, but did not appear to take it into account: *Occidental* v. *Ecuador (No 2)*, para. 446.

[81] See *Occidental* v. *Ecuador (No 2)*, para. 395; Fuentes, 'Proportionality Analysis and Disproportionate Damages', p. 322.

[82] Fuentes, 'Proportionality Analysis and Disproportionate Damages', p. 322.

[83] See Sabahi and Duggal, '*Occidental Petroleum* v. *Ecuador*', p. 282.

[84] See Peterson, 'Liability Ruling in *Oxy* v. *Ecuador* Arbitration Puts Spotlight on Need for States to Mete Out Treatment that is Proportionate' (2012) *Investment Arbitration Reporter*. The limits of proportionality analysis as a method of review in investor-state arbitration are discussed further in Chapter 6. At the time of publication, the award was subject to an application for annulment. The annulment decision may shed some light on the source and scope of the obligation of proportionality in this area or in international investment law more generally.

4.3.2   Least-restrictive means analysis as the limit of review

More frequently, investment tribunals have employed a form of proportionality analysis that involves undertaking least-restrictive means analysis but not the proportionality *stricto sensu* stage of review. Tribunals have taken this approach in cases decided under the exception clause in the Argentina-US BIT, where the provision expressly refers to necessity, as well as in relation to fair and equitable treatment, national treatment and arbitrary measures clauses.

4.3.2.1   The Argentina-US BIT security exception

Article XI of the Argentina-US BIT permits a state party to take 'measures necessary for the maintenance of public order, the fulfillment of its obligations with respect to the maintenance or restoration of international peace or security, or the protection of its own essential security interests'. The cases in this area all involved challenges by US investors to Argentina's emergency measures adopted in relation to its 2001–2002 economic crisis, in which tribunals had found Argentina in breach of fair and equitable treatment.[85] In these cases, Argentina sought to rely on Article XI and mounted a separate defence based on the customary international law defence of necessity. Tribunals adopted varying interpretations of what the concept of 'necessary' required in these circumstances.

4.3.2.1.1   Early tribunals: conflating the requirements of Article XI with the customary plea of necessity   There are some superficial similarities between exception clauses such as Article XI and the prerequisites for invocation of the customary plea: both forms of analysis require the identification of a legitimate objective and the analysis of whether the challenged measure is necessary to achieve that objective. However, in the context of exception clauses, the test of necessity functions as a primary rule: successful invocation of the clause means that there will be no breach of the treaty and no state liability at international law.[86] The customary

---

[85] *CMS* v. *Argentina*, Award, paras. 273–81; *Enron* v. *Argentina*, Award, paras. 264–8; *Sempra* v. *Argentina*, Award, paras. 303–4; *LG&E* v. *Argentina*, Liability, paras. 132–9; *Continental* v. *Argentina*, Award, paras. 255–58, 261.

[86] See e.g. *CMS* v. *Argentina*, Annulment, para. 146; but see e.g. Schill, 'International Investment Law and the Host State's Power to Handle Economic Crises – Comment on the ICSID Decision in *LG&E* v. *Argentina*' (2007) 24 *Journal of International Arbitration* 265, 286; Desierto, 'Necessity and "Supplementary Means of Interpretation" for Non-Precluded Measures in Bilateral Investment Treaties' (2010) 31 *University of Pennsylvania Journal of International Law* 827, 875–82, 890–2, 899; Sloane, 'On the Use and Abuse of Necessity

plea of necessity, however, may be invoked only where a breach of an international obligation has been established according to the rules of the particular regime, and operates as a secondary rule to determine whether this wrongfulness is precluded.[87]

The first three tribunals to determine claims involving Article XI (*CMS, Enron* and *Sempra*) conflated the treaty exception with the requirements of the customary plea.[88] The *CMS* tribunal found that Argentina could not rely on the customary plea and purported to rely on Article XI to confirm this interpretation, whereas the *Enron* and *Sempra* tribunals both held that Article XI was 'inseparable' from the customary plea with respect to the definition of necessity and the preconditions for its operation,[89] and that these requirements had not been made out.

These tribunals all relied on the International Law Commission's Draft Articles on the Responsibility of States for Internationally Wrongful Acts ('ILC Articles'), which detail the circumstances in which the wrongfulness of conduct under international law may be precluded. Article 25 of the ILC Articles provides that the plea of necessity may only be invoked to excuse the wrongfulness of a breach of the state's international obligations where, *inter alia*, that act is 'the only way for the State to safeguard an essential interest against a grave and imminent peril'. The term 'grave and imminent peril' has traditionally been understood as a very stringent requirement relating to the continued existence of the state,[90] and the ILC has stated that 'the interest relied on must outweigh all other considerations'.[91] The Commentary to the ILC Articles also provides that 'any conduct going

---

in the Law of State Responsibility' (2012) 106 *American Journal of International Law* 447, 510 (arguing that Article XI and similarly worded provisions in other treaties are relevant not to liability but to the question of the quantum of compensation payable).

[87] See e.g. Reinisch, 'Necessity in Investment Arbitration' (2010) 41 *Netherlands Yearbook of International Law* 137, 148–9, 156.

[88] See Kurtz, 'Adjudging the Exceptional', pp. 341–51 (discussing these tribunals' methodologies).

[89] *CMS* v. *Argentina*, Award, paras. 320–4, 329, 355–6, 374; *Sempra* v. *Argentina*, Award, paras. 376, 388; *Enron* v. *Argentina*, Award, para. 334.

[90] See McNair, *International Law Opinions*, Volume 2 (1956) 232; International Law Commission, *Yearbook of the International Law Commission 1980*, Volume II, Part One (1982). However, Roberto Ago (former ILC Special Rapporteur on State Responsibility) opined that the concept covers, in theory, a broad range of circumstances ranging from the political or economic survival of a state to the continued functioning of essential services and the preservation of the environment: *Yearbook of the International Law Commission 1980*, Volume II, Part Two (1982) 14, 19; *Yearbook of the International Law Commission 2001*, Volume II, Part Two (2007) 83.

[91] Commentary to the ILC Articles, p. 84.

beyond what is strictly necessary for the purpose will not be covered',[92] and the ICJ has applied the customary plea stringently.[93]

Following this stringent approach, the *CMS* tribunal held that Argentina could not invoke the protection of Article XI because the crisis had not resulted in 'total economic and social collapse',[94] and the *Enron* and *Sempra* tribunals held that Argentina had not demonstrated that 'the very existence of the state and its independence' were threatened by the crisis.[95] These tribunals also held that the measures were not 'the only way' for Argentina to safeguard its interests. The *CMS* tribunal proposed a range of measures that it considered were available to Argentina, but did not analyze whether these measures would have been feasible and effective in the circumstances, stating that 'which of these policy alternatives would have been better is a decision beyond the scope of the Tribunal's task, which is to establish whether there was only one way or various ways and thus whether the requirements for the preclusion of wrongfulness have or have not been met'.[96] The *Sempra* and *Enron* tribunals appeared to accept alternative measures put forward by the claimants at face value without scrutinizing whether these measures were actually available to Argentina in the circumstances.[97] These tribunals both appeared to point to the insurmountable nature of the necessity test in this context, stating that there were always a number of approaches available to a government in the context of an economic crisis. However, these observations did not affect their determination of the issue.[98]

Each of these decisions was subject to an application for annulment. The *CMS* annulment committee held that Article XI and the customary plea were 'substantively different' and should be addressed separately, but did not annul the award because in its view this error did not rise to a manifest excess of powers for the purpose of exercising the power of annulment under the ICSID Convention (although the committee

---

[92] Commentary to ILC Articles, p. 83, para. 14.

[93] *Gabčíkovo-Nagymaros (Hungary v. Slovakia)*, para. 55; Legal Consequences of the Construction of a Wall in the Occupied Palestinian Territory, Advisory Opinion, para. 140. See also Crawford, *The International Law Commission's Articles on State Responsibility*, p. 183.

[94] *CMS* v. *Argentina*, Award, paras. 322, 355.

[95] *Enron* v. *Argentina*, Award, paras. 306–7; *Sempra* v. *Argentina*, Award, paras. 348–9.

[96] *CMS* v. *Argentina*, Award, para. 323.

[97] *Sempra* v. *Argentina*, Award, paras. 339, 351; *Enron* v. *Argentina*, Award, paras. 300, 309.

[98] *Enron* v. *Argentina*, Award, para. 308; *Sempra* v. *Argentina*, Award, para. 350.

noted that, had it been acting as a court of appeal, it would have reconsidered the award on that basis).[99] The *Sempra* decision was later annulled due to the tribunal's failure to consider the applicability of Article XI,[100] and the *Enron* decision was annulled for failing to properly apply the Article 25 and Article XI tests.[101]

4.3.2.1.2   *LG&E* v. *Argentina*: a more flexible approach to the concept of 'necessary'.   The *LG&E* tribunal was the first tribunal to examine Article XI independently of the customary plea following the *CMS* annulment decision. The tribunal held that responding to the economic crisis fell within both the permissible objectives of protecting the state's essential security interests and public order, noting the political upheaval, disorder and high rates of poverty and unemployment in Argentina during the crisis.[102] The tribunal held that a suite of 'across-the-board solutions' was necessary to address the crisis, appearing to accept that the measures formed an interdependent package that was itself a suitable response to it (but not separately analyzing the suitability of each individual measure).[103] This approach can be likened to the Appellate Body's decision in *Brazil-Tyres*, in which the Appellate Body afforded a measure of deference in relation to whether individual measures in a package of inter-related measures would be effective at achieving the objective.[104] Although some commentators have argued that the *LG&E* tribunal's approach was overly deferential, because it would permit measures to pass muster even if they were wholly ineffective at arresting the crisis, arguably the tribunal required that the package of measures as a whole was capable of achieving the objective.[105]

In relation to whether the challenged measures were necessary to achieve their objectives, the *LG&E* tribunal stated that although a

---

[99] *CMS* v. *Argentina*, Annulment, paras. 129, 350. Article 52(1) ICSID Convention sets out the permissible grounds for the annulment of awards; manifest excess of powers is the only substantive legal basis upon which an award can be annulled.

[100] *Sempra Energy International* v. *Argentina*, Annulment, paras. 208–9.

[101] *Enron* v. *Argentina*, Annulment, paras. 355–95, 400–7.

[102] *LG&E* v. *Argentina*, Liability, paras. 231, 237–9, 251, 257.

[103] *LG&E* v. *Argentina*, Liability, paras. 239–42, 257.

[104] Appellate Body Report, *Brazil–Tyres*, para. 211. See Mitchell and Henckels, 'Variations on a Theme', p. 131.

[105] Binder and Reinisch, 'Economic Emergency Powers: A Comparative Law Perspective' in Schill (ed.), *International Investment Law and Comparative Public Law* (2010) 503, 511; Kurtz, 'Adjudging the Exceptional', p. 356; Reinisch, 'Necessity in Investment Arbitration', p. 154.

government might have several options at its disposal, it would regard any 'legitimate' measure as necessary.[106] The tribunal also took into account the situation of urgency and evidence that Argentina had considered the interests of foreign investors and had determined that they could not be excluded from the emergency measures.[107] This latter consideration appeared to function as a procedural justification: Argentina could establish that the measures were necessary by demonstrating that it had taken the interests of foreign investors into account in designing the measures.[108] The tribunal concluded that the measures were necessary to avert the crisis and thus to protect Argentina's essential security interests.[109]

The *LG&E* tribunal permitted Argentina broad discretion to formulate its policy response to the crisis. Granting a government the flexibility to respond to a crisis in a situation of significant empirical uncertainty without liability reflects the deferential postures adopted by other courts and tribunals in similar situations. However, the tribunal's approach to least-restrictive means analysis may be criticized for lacking analytical rigour, for referring to the 'legitimacy' and 'reasonableness' of the measures without detailed explication, failing to perform least-restrictive means analysis in the orthodox sense, and not articulating its reasons for affording deference.[110] As such, though this approach was far more supportive of regulatory autonomy than earlier tribunals' interpretations of the clause, it does not provide a high degree of certainty for states or investors as to when a measure will be lawful in terms of the exception clause.

4.3.2.1.3 *Continental* v. *Argentina*: the influence of WTO jurisprudence

The *Continental* award is the most recent decision to determine the necessity of Argentina's emergency measures under Article XI of the Argentina-US BIT.[111] Unlike the earlier cases involving Article XI brought

---

[106] *LG&E* v. *Argentina*, Liability, paras. 239–40.
[107] *LG&E* v. *Argentina*, Liability, para. 241.
[108] Mitchell and Henckels, 'Variations on a Theme', p. 112.
[109] However, the tribunal concluded that Argentina could rely on Article XI only during the acute period of the crisis: *LG&E* v. *Argentina*, Liability, paras. 228–9.
[110] See Mitchell and Henckels, 'Variations on a Theme', p. 113. The decision is also criticized for its cursory approach to finding that Argentina could successfully invoke the customary plea, applying similar reasoning as it had used in relation to Article XI (at paras. 245, 257–8): see Waibel, 'Two Worlds of Necessity in ICSID Arbitration: *CMS* and *LG&E*' (2007) 20 *Leiden Journal of International Law* 637, 646; Kurtz, 'Adjudging the Exceptional', pp. 355–6; Sloane, 'On the Use and Abuse of Necessity', p. 501.
[111] At the time of publication, only one further tribunal had considered Article XI (*El Paso* v. *Argentina*, Award) but did not directly consider the question of necessity on the

by investors in the energy sector, the claimant was an insurance company that maintained a portfolio of investments in Argentina including cash deposits, treasury bills and government bonds. Continental claimed that as a result of the emergency measures, its investments had significantly diminished in value, which amounted to a breach of fair and equitable treatment under the BIT. The tribunal did not definitively conclude that the pesification of the economy and related measures were in breach of fair and equitable treatment, but held that as far these measures could be considered to be in breach of Argentina's obligations, Article XI would apply to preclude liability.[112] Like the *LG&E* tribunal, the *Continental* tribunal permitted far greater autonomy to Argentina in crafting its legislative response to the crisis within the framework of Article XI than earlier cases. However, the *Continental* tribunal, presided over by a former chairperson of the WTO Appellate Body,[113] adopted a more structured approach to determining whether the measures were necessary to achieve their objective than the *LG&E* tribunal, referring extensively to the Appellate Body's approach to necessity testing under the general exceptions to the WTO agreements.

As indicated in Chapter 3, international and supranational courts and tribunals generally are reluctant to engage in substantive review of whether a challenged measure has been adopted in order to protect sensitive national interests such as the existence of an emergency situation or a matter engaging national security concerns. Treaty parties have in some circumstances specifically indicated that this should be the case. For example, the security exceptions in Article XXI(b) GATT and Article XIV *bis* GATS are self-judging, permitting a government to determine for itself the existence of preconditions to derogating from their obligations subject only to review for whether the state has invoked the clause in good faith.[114] Recent investment treaties concluded by the United States

---

basis that Argentina had contributed to endangering its essential security interests (at paras. 555, 615). In this respect, the tribunal appeared to conflate the requirements of Article XI with those of the customary plea, which preclude the invocation of the plea of necessity where the state has 'contributed to the situation of necessity': see ILC Articles, p. 84m para. 20; *Gabčíkovo-Nagymaros* (*Hungary* v. *Slovakia*), para. 57. Arbitrator Stern, however, dissented on this point, and also held that the measures were 'a suitable means to overcome the chaos' and 'were necessary to prevent the crisis from resulting in anarchy and social disintegration': *El Paso* v. *Argentina*, Award, paras. 667–70. Other tribunals have considered the applicability of the customary plea of necessity in relation to claims under other treaties that do not contain an exception clause.

[112] *Continental* v. *Argentina*, Award, para. 262.   [113] Professor Giorgio Sacerdoti.

[114] These provisions, however, restrict the meaning of essential security interests to war and military-related issues. They have not been litigated in the WTO context.

also contain self-judging security exceptions, no doubt influenced by the Argentina decisions.[115] But even where an exception clause is not self-judging, courts and tribunals typically are reluctant to substitute their judgment in relation to whether there is an emergency situation or one engaging security or public order concerns. The approaches of these bodies to the question whether a state is legitimately acting in furtherance of the public interest in these circumstances suggest that it is appropriate that investment arbitrators afford a measure of deference in the determination of whether this aspect of a treaty exception has been made out.

The *Continental* tribunal followed this approach, citing the ECHR case of *Jahn*, in which the ECtHR held that national authorities were better placed to determine whether measures interfering with property rights were in the public interest because of their 'direct knowledge of their society and its needs'.[116]

In relation to the suitability of the measures, the tribunal stated that it would determine whether the measures had 'contributed materially' to achieving their objectives.[117] Although this stipulation appeared to set a relatively high threshold for the criterion of suitability, it did not affect the tribunal's conclusions as to the legality of the measures, as the tribunal found that they had been effective at arresting the crisis.[118] The tribunal also noted the Appellate Body's remark in *Brazil-Tyres* to the effect that in some cases, it might be possible to evaluate the efficacy of measures only after a period of time had passed since their introduction, suggesting that the full effect of the emergency measures on Argentina's economic recovery was yet to be determined.[119] However, in a departure from this generally deferential approach, the tribunal also saw fit to ask whether Argentina could have adopted different economic policies at an earlier point in time that would have avoided or prevented the crisis situation and therefore precluded the adoption of the challenged measures.[120] Yet, the tribunal concluded that states were 'basically free to adopt economic and monetary policies of their choice' and stated that it would not engage in substitutionary review of those policies.[121] The tribunal also noted

---

[115] For example, Article 22(2)(b) Australia–US FTA.

[116] *Jahn* v. *Germany*, para. 91; *Continental* v. *Argentina*, Award, paras. 178, 181.

[117] *Continental* v. *Argentina*, Award, para. 196.

[118] *Continental* v. *Argentina*, Award, paras. 196–7, 214, 232.

[119] Continental v. Argentina, Award, para. 197, citing Appellate Body Report, *Brazil-Tyres*, para. 151.

[120] *Continental* v. *Argentina*, Award, para. 198. See Kurtz, 'Adjudging the Exceptional', p. 369; Kingsbury and Schill, 'Public Law Concepts', pp. 75, 101–2.

[121] *Continental* v. *Argentina*, Award, para. 227.

that Argentina's previous economic policies has been recommended by the International Monetary Fund and had received its financial support along with the political support of the United States.[122]

In addressing whether alternative measures were available to Argentina, the tribunal took an expressly deferential approach. It emphasized that given the circumstances of the crisis, it would afford 'a certain deference' and 'a margin of discretion and appreciation' and refrain from substituting its view as to the merits of Argentina's decisions.[123] Following WTO jurisprudence, the tribunal held that any alternatives would have to be equally effective at achieving the objective.[124] In relation to the devaluation of the peso and related measures, it held that alternative measures proposed by the claimant would have been impractical and ineffective at arresting the crisis and were therefore not true alternatives.[125] The tribunal's findings as to the necessity of the other measures were less clear: the tribunal held that the suspension of payments and the default and rescheduling of government financial instruments were 'reasonably necessary', and appeared to implicitly find that the pesification of the US dollar-denominated contracts and deposits was also necessary.[126] The tribunal's explicit references to deference in this context go further than WTO case law, which has not gone so far as to adopt an explicitly deferential posture. This approach might, however, be explained by two factors: the nature of the circumstances in which the measures were adopted, which bear no precedent in WTO law, and a perceived need on the part of the tribunal to distance itself from the earlier awards that took a strict approach to Article XI and/or that found breaches of fair and equitable treatment in relation to the same measures.

The tribunal concluded that in general, the measures were 'applied in a reasonable and proportionate way' and that Argentina had 'struck an appropriate balance' between trying to respect its international obligations and its responsibility to its own population.[127] It remarked that Argentina had made reasonable attempts to comply with its obligations to investors, and noted the divergence of expert opinion in relation to what Argentina could have done to prevent the crisis.[128] The tribunal

---

[122] *Continental* v. *Argentina*, Award, para. 235.
[123] *Continental* v. *Argentina*, Award, paras. 181, 198–9, 233.
[124] *Continental* v. *Argentina*, Award, para. 198.
[125] *Continental* v. *Argentina*, Award, paras. 208–10, 230.
[126] *Continental* v. *Argentina*, Award, paras. 217, 219.
[127] *Continental* v. *Argentina*, Award, paras. 227, 232.
[128] *Continental* v. *Argentina*, Award, para. 227.

also stressed that the concept of proportionality did not require that 'every sacrifice can properly be imposed on a country's people in order to . . . ensure full respect towards international obligations in the financial sphere'.[129] Although the tribunal hinted at the concept of balancing state and investor interests, it did not actually engage in the proportionality *stricto sensu* stage.

The *Continental* decision has attracted criticism for explicitly relying on WTO case law in determining the necessity of Argentina's emergency measures. Critics argue that the exception clause should be read as affirming the content of the customary plea of necessity and that the *Continental* tribunal paid insufficient regard to the contextual and textual differences between the WTO agreements and the Argentina-US BIT.[130] However, it has convincingly been argued that the conflation of the customary plea with the necessity test in the exception clause cannot be sustained.[131] Moreover, although institutional differences must be acknowledged, the textual similarities between exception clauses such as Article XI and the general exceptions in the WTO agreements indicate that it is legitimate for investment tribunals to look to how WTO tribunals – and, indeed, other legal systems – approach the applicable method and standard of review in interpreting similar concepts.[132]

The *Continental* decision has also been criticized for not providing a comprehensive representation of how necessity testing operates in the context of the WTO agreements' general exceptions. In particular, the tribunal did not discuss the relevance of the chapeaux to the general

---

[129] *Continental* v. *Argentina*, Award, para. 227.

[130] See Alvarez and Khamsi, 'The Argentine Crisis and Foreign Investors: A Glimpse into the Heart of the Investment Regime' in Sauvant (ed.), *Yearbook on International Investment Law and Policy 2008–2009* (2009) 379, 427–35; Desierto, 'Necessity and "Supplementary Means of Interpretation"', pp. 875–6, 882–95, 931; Alvarez and Brink, 'Revisiting the Necessity Defense', pp. 334–8; Desierto, *Necessity and National Emergency Clauses: Sovereignty in Modern Treaty Interpretation* (2012) 221–226; Alvarez, 'Beware: Boundary Crossings', pp. 28–36.

[131] Kurtz, 'Adjudging the Exceptional', pp. 341–51.

[132] A point made emphatically by Sacerdoti: Sacerdoti, 'BIT Protections and Economic Crises: Limits to Their Coverage, the Impact of Multilateral Financial Regulation and the Defence of Necessity' (2013) 28 *ICSID Review* 351, 382; Sacerdoti, 'The Application of BITs in Time of Economic Crisis: Limits to Their Coverage, Necessity and the Relevance of WTO Law' in Sacerdoti (ed.), *General Interests of Host States in International Investment Law* (2014) 3, 20; Sacerdoti, 'Trade and Investment Law: Institutional Differences and Substantive Similarities' (2014) 9 *Jerusalem Review of Legal Studies* 1, 10. See also Stone Sweet and della Cananea, 'General Principles of Law', pp. 937–8.

exceptions in relation to its analysis of how WTO tribunals approach the concept of necessity.[133] As discussed in Chapter 3, WTO tribunals assess all measures sought to be justified in terms of the general exceptions against the chapeau in order to determine whether a measure has been 'applied in a manner which would constitute a means of arbitrary or unjustifiable discrimination between countries where the same conditions prevail' or whether it amounts to 'a disguised restriction on international trade'.[134] Alvarez and his collaborators argue that WTO tribunals give more leeway to states in their analysis of whether a measure is necessary under the relevant policy exception than is appropriate to the context of investment treaty exceptions such as Article XI, because WTO tribunals subsequently scrutinize the measure in terms of the chapeau.[135] While this is an interesting supposition, these authors have not provided any evidence that this occurs.[136] In any event, the Appellate Body has emphasized that a similarly structured test for necessity applies under the TBT Agreements, which does not contain chapeau-like language as part of the necessity test.[137]

To be sure, the *Continental* tribunal can be criticized for not clearly articulating the reasons for its comparative approach or explaining why the standard of review it adopted was appropriate to the circumstances.[138] However, these critiques do not take into account the similar manner in which other international and supranational courts and tribunals undertake least-restrictive means analysis in the context of similarly structured provisions permitting derogations and exceptions from the legal regime's norm. As Chapter 3 has explained in detail, the CJEU and ECtHR also employ least-restrictive means analysis in a more flexible way in the context of determining whether conduct derogating from protection of the

---

[133] Desierto, 'Necessity and "Supplementary Means of Interpretation"', pp. 875–76; Alvarez and Brink, 'Revisiting the Necessity Defense', pp. 325, 335–52.

[134] See the chapeaux to Article XX GATS and Article XIV GATS.

[135] Alvarez and Khamsi, 'The Argentine Crisis and Foreign Investors', p. 441; Alvarez and Brink, 'Revisiting the Necessity Defense', p. 346; Alvarez, 'Beware: Boundary Crossings', pp. 32–3.

[136] Mitchell and Henckels, 'Variations on a Theme', p. 137. Sacerdoti, 'BIT Protections and Economic Crises', p. 382.

[137] Appellate Body Report, *US-Tuna II*, para. 330 (although chapeau-like language does appear in the preamble to the TBT Agreement). See Mitchell and Henckels, 'Variations on a Theme', p. 137. See also Sacerdoti, 'BIT Protections and Economic Crises', p. 382 (arguing that the chapeau is relevant to the application rather than the design of the measure), but see Bartels, 'The Chapeau of the General Exceptions', pp. 98–101.

[138] See Burke-White and von Staden, 'Private Litigation', p. 299.

regime's primary norm or conduct limiting rights or other interests may be justified.

4.3.2.2   Substantive obligations

Several tribunals have employed least-restrictive means testing in the context of substantive obligations. In these cases, arbitrators have undertaken necessity testing in the determination of liability where the treaty text does not provide guidance as to how state and investor interests should be taken into account.

4.3.2.2.1   Early approaches: *Pope and Talbot* v. *Canada* and *SD Myers* v. *Canada*

The first known example of an investment tribunal applying least-restrictive analysis was the *Pope and Talbot* decision. The claim involved challenges to a number of regulatory measures adopted to implement the Canada-US Softwood Lumber Agreement, including export fees on lumber and various export quotas allocated to lumber producers, re-manufacturers of lumber products and new entrants into the industry. These measures had negatively affected the claimant and other operators in certain provinces.[139]

The tribunal applied a type of suitability test to most of the measures, finding them to be 'reasonably related' to the objective of avoiding the threat of imposition of countervailing duties by the United States in relation to those provinces[140] or a 'reasonable response' to the circumstances and the need to implement the Agreement.[141] However, the tribunal applied a necessity test in the determination of whether a fee levied on exports of lumber exceeding an export quota complied with fair and equitable treatment, briefly noting that though the government might have selected an alternative measure, the tribunal would not substitute its judgment for that of the authorities.[142] The tribunal also analysed an alternative measure in relation to a quota for new entrants to the industry, finding that it would have been ineffective at achieving its objective

---

[139] *Pope and Talbot* v. *Canada*, Merits, paras. 121–41.

[140] *Pope and Talbot* v. *Canada*, Merits, paras. 78, 81, 87, 93 (fair and equitable treatment). However, in relation to an audit of the claimant's records after it had filed the notice of arbitration, the tribunal held that Canada's failure to justify the need for the measure to achieve its objective (lack of suitability) amounted to a breach of fair and equitable treatment (at paras. 172–3).

[141] *Pope and Talbot* v. *Canada*, Merits, paras. 123, 125, 128 (national treatment).

[142] *Pope and Talbot* v. *Canada*, Merits, para. 155. See also Montt, *State Liability in Investment Treaty Arbitration*, p. 159.

and was not therefore a true alternative.[143] This approach suggested an understanding on the part of the tribunal that governments – rather than adjudicators – may be best placed to engage in regulatory design in complex areas of public policy.

The *SD Myers* tribunal subsequently employed a necessity test in the context of an alleged breach of national treatment. The Canadian government had placed a ban on the export of a toxic substance (PCB), with the effect that the claimant (a US-based disposal provider) was no longer able to export PCB for disposal within the US. Canada argued that the purpose of the measure was to implement its international obligations under the Basel Convention, which obliges states to take appropriate measures to minimize the transboundary movement of hazardous waste.[144] However, the record of parliamentary proceedings showed that the minister responsible for the legislation had stated that it was 'the position of the government that the handling of PCBs should be done in Canada by Canadians'.[145] The tribunal therefore found that the primary purpose of the ban was to protect the domestic hazardous waste remediation industry, but that this objective was nevertheless consistent with the Convention.[146]

However, the tribunal held that where an objective could be achieved 'through a variety of equally effective and reasonable means', a government was 'obliged to adopt the alternative that is most consistent with open trade'.[147] The tribunal applied the exception clause in Chapter 3 of NAFTA (trade in goods), which provides that parties may adopt or maintain export restrictions in certain circumstances provided they are consistent with, *inter alia*, Article XX(g) GATT ('relating to the conservation of exhaustible natural resources').[148] While stating that it did not have an 'open-ended mandate to second-guess government decision-making', the tribunal ultimately found that the measure was not necessary as the government could have given preferential treatment to the domestic industry through subsidies or government procurement, which were

---

[143] *Pope and Talbot* v. *Canada*, Merits, para. 121.

[144] *Pope and Talbot* v. *Canada*, Merits, para. 121.

[145] *SD Myers* v. *Canada*, Partial Award, para. 16.

[146] Article 4(2)(d) Basel Convention on the Control of Transboundary Movements of Hazardous Wastes and Their Disposal obliges states to take appropriate measures to '[ensure] that the transboundary movement of hazardous wastes and other wastes is reduced to the minimum.' See *SD Myers* v. *Canada*, Partial Award, paras. 162–95, 255.

[147] *SD Myers* v. *Canada*, Partial Award, paras. 195, 215, 221, 255.

[148] Article XX(g) does not contain a necessity test itself, but is subject to the requirements of the chapeau to Article XX. The tribunal justified its approach by stating that like the WTO agreements, NAFTA's chapters formed a 'single undertaking': *SD Myers* v. *Canada*, Partial Award, para. 292; Article 315, NAFTA.

both specifically permitted by NAFTA's investment chapter, and that these alternatives would have been equally effective at achieving the measure's objective.[149] The tribunal also remarked that the challenged measure would not have satisfied the requirements of the chapeau to Article XX GATT, but did not elaborate further – though this finding presumably related to the protectionist purpose of the measure.[150] The tribunal also concluded that the measure breached fair and equitable treatment.[151]

The *SD Myers* tribunal's approach is a relatively straightforward way of undertaking necessity testing, which reflected WTO jurisprudence at the time the award was rendered in that the tribunal referred to the need for alternative measures to be equally effective and reasonably available.[152] The decision has, however, been criticized for not appearing to properly explore whether the alternatives were, in fact, less restrictive of the investor's invests in the sense that subsidies and government procurement policies may have significantly affected foreign investors.[153]

4.3.2.2.2 *Methanex* v. *US* and *Chemtura* v. *Canada*: reliance on scientific expertise

Two tribunals have reviewed primary decision-makers' consideration of alternative measures rather than conducting their own analysis, both in the context of measures based on scientific evidence.

The claimant in *Methanex* was a manufacturer of methanol, an ingredient in the gasoline additive MTBE, which had been banned by the Californian government. The claimant alleged that the ban had been effected for protectionist rather than health and environmental reasons, targeting foreign producers of methanol with the intention of favouring domestic producers of ethanol, a competing product. Reviewing the scientific evidence that the government had relied on in deciding to ban MTBE, the tribunal found that the expert report took a 'serious, objective and scientific approach to a complex problem' and was subjected 'to public hearings, testimony and peer-review', and that the ban was motivated by an 'honest belief, held in good faith and on reasonable scientific grounds'.[154]

The tribunal noted that the authorities had undertaken a cost-benefit analysis in relation to non-oxygenated, ethanol-oxygenated and MTBE-oxygenated formulations of gasoline, which had concluded that

---

[149] *SD Myers* v. *Canada*, Partial Award, para. 195. Article 1108(7), NAFTA exempts these forms of support from the national treatment obligation.
[150] *SD Myers* v. *Canada*, Partial Award, para. 298.
[151] *SD Myers* v. *Canada*, Partial Award, para. 266.
[152] *SD Myers* v. *Canada*, Partial Award, paras. 195, 215, 221.
[153] See Kläger, *Fair and Equitable Treatment*, p. 241.
[154] *Methanex* v. *US*, Final Award, Part III, Chapter A, paras. 101–2.

retaining the MTBE formulation would create the highest costs of treating contaminated water supplies and result in the poorest air quality of all the three options.[155] The tribunal also noted that the expert report had examined alternatives to the ban such as phasing out the use of MTBE.[156] In this respect, the authorities' consideration of alternative measures appeared to satisfy the tribunal in the sense of discharging a procedural obligation, though it is not altogether clear the role that this consideration played in the determination of liability.

In *Chemtura*, the claimant challenged a Canadian ban on the planting of canola seeds treated with lindane, a pesticide, and a decision to cancel the claimant's product registrations for the pesticide.[157] The claimant argued, *inter alia*, that there was an insufficient scientific basis for the measure, but the tribunal found that the measure was adopted in good faith following a scientific review and to give effect to Canada's obligations under multilateral environmental agreements.[158] The tribunal referred to an alternative measure proposed by the claimant (a phase-out rather than a product ban), but found that that this option had been offered to the claimant and the claimant had refused.[159] The fact that many other states had also banned the substance supported the tribunal's findings as to the suitability of the measure and, implicitly, its necessity.[160]

4.3.2.2.3 *Glamis* v. *US*: least-restrictive means analysis required by domestic law   The *Glamis* tribunal also relied on the authorities' consideration of alternative measures in the determination of a fair and equitable treatment claim. The claim involved challenges to legislative and administrative measures adopted by federal and state governments in relation to cultural and environmental concerns associated with mining.

The claimant challenged the denial of an application for a mining permit, a delay in approving a related mining project and the manner in which a cultural review of the proposed mining site was carried out. The

---

[155] *Methanex* v. *US*, Final Award, Part III, Chapter A, para. 13.
[156] *Methanex* v. *US*, Final Award, Part III, Chapter A, para. 15–16. The tribunal concluded that the measure bore no 'legally significant connection' to the claimant as the methanol it produced could be used for other purposes, and therefore that the measures were not adopted 'relating to' the claimant for the purpose of jurisdiction under Article 1101 NAFTA: *Methanex* v. *US*, Final Award, Part V, Chapter E, para. 22.
[157] *Chemtura* v. *Canada*, Award, para. 93.
[158] *Chemtura* v. *Canada*, Award, paras. 135–53.
[159] *Chemtura* v. *Canada*, Award, paras. 181–2, 192.
[160] *Chemtura* v. *Canada*, Award, para. 135.

history of these decisions was convoluted. Federal legislation required that the primary decision-maker, when determining whether to approve a mining permit or to impose mitigation measures in relation to a project, consider 'reasonable alternatives' and select a 'preferred alternative', taking into account several criteria including the environmental implications of each alternative.[161] Governmental policy documents defined 'reasonable alternatives' as those that were 'technically and economically practical or feasible and that [met] the purpose and need of the proposed action'.[162] The decision-maker was required to select a 'preferred alternative' on the basis of the environmental implications of each alternative and 'other factors which influence the decision or are required under another statutory authority'.[163] The preferred alternative had to 'fulfill [the agency's] statutory mission and responsibilities, while giving consideration to economic, environmental, technical, and other factors'. State legislation also required that the decision-maker consider feasible alternatives or mitigation measures in terms of their impact on the environment; projects with significant environmental impacts were permitted to proceed if economic, social, or other conditions made any alternatives unfeasible.[164]

The permit application related to the area that was culturally significant to the Quechan Nation. Initially, the authorities had selected the claimant's proposed project as the preferred alternative, with additional mitigation and environmental conditions.[165] A revised decision, however, noted that the proposed project – including an alternative that required complete backfilling of all open pits – would have an unavoidable impact on the cultural activities and sites of the Quechan, but that further mitigation measures to better protect the religious and cultural sites would render this the preferred alternative.[166] Subsequently, the government received a legal opinion advising that it could lawfully deny approval of the project, and the federal authorities decided that this was the preferred alternative.[167] This decision triggered an obligation under state legislation for the agency to select an alternative that was the next best option for the environment, and the agency accordingly decided to approve the project with mitigation measures.[168] However, federal authorities subsequently issued a decision to deny the approval for the project on the basis that available mitigation measures did not go far enough to protect the

---

[161] *Glamis* v. *US*, Award, para. 64.   [162] *Glamis* v. *US*, Award, para. 64.
[163] *Glamis* v. *US*, Award, para. 64.   [164] *Glamis* v. *US*, Award, para. 70.
[165] *Glamis* v. *US*, Award, para. 99.   [166] *Glamis* v. *US*, Award, paras. 109–10.
[167] *Glamis* v. *US*, Award, paras. 145, 149.   [168] *Glamis* v. *US*, Award, para. 151.

cultural sites.[169] The claimant then initiated domestic legal proceedings, at which point the decision was rescinded.[170] The state agency was in the process of reassessing the project when the claimant initiated the NAFTA proceeding.[171]

At the outset, the tribunal held that under the customary international law minimum standard of treatment (the threshold for liability under NAFTA's fair and equitable treatment clause),[172] a breach would only be established where government conduct (new legislation or administrative decision-making) was 'manifestly arbitrary'.[173] Several investment tribunals have held that a breach of fair and equitable treatment requires arbitrary conduct,[174] but the modifier 'manifest' signalled that any mistreatment of the claimant would have to reach an especially high level of severity in order to establish a breach.[175] Stating that mere disagreement with the actions of government would not suffice for a finding of breach, the tribunal cautioned that it would be improper 'to supplant its own judgment of underlying factual material . . . for that of a qualified domestic agency' or 'to delve into the details of and justifications for domestic law' in determining the appropriateness of administrative decisions.[176]

The tribunal then reviewed the authorities' approach to determining the necessity of the measure. Although the analysis of alternative measures principally had an environmental focus, the authorities had also considered the claimant's interests in determining whether the proposed mitigation measures would be economically feasible in the circumstances.[177] The tribunal did not make any pronouncements on the merits of the authorities' approach to selecting a preferred alternative, but nor did it find that the authorities had acted in a manifestly arbitrary way.

The tribunal took a similarly restrained approach to its review of the challenged legislation, but more explicitly engaged with proportionality considerations.[178] The legislation required operators to backfill open pit

---

[169] *Glamis* v. *US*, Award, paras. 153–5.   [170] *Glamis* v. *US*, Award, paras. 156–9.
[171] *Glamis* v. *US*, Award, paras. 160–5.   [172] This issue is discussed further in Chapter 6.
[173] *Glamis* v. *US*, Award, para. 803.   [174] See Section 4.3.4.4 below.
[175] See also *Thunderbird* v. *Mexico*, Award, para. 197: 'As to the . . . alleged manifest arbitrariness in administration . . . the Tribunal cannot find sufficient evidence on the record establishing that the SEGOB proceedings were arbitrary or unfair, let alone so manifestly arbitrary or unfair as to violate the minimum standard of treatment.'
[176] *Glamis* v. *US*, Award, paras. 625, 762, 779.
[177] *Glamis* v. *US*, Award, paras. 133, 138, 140.
[178] *Glamis* v. *US*, Award, paras. 621–2. The tribunal held that a claim for legitimate expectations could not be made in the absence of specific conduct taken to induce an investment.

mines in certain circumstances, and placed greater regulatory controls on mining sites where cultural artefacts were uncovered in the process of mining. The tribunal indicated that it would not strictly scrutinize the objective of the measure, stating that its role in this respect was only to determine 'whether or not there was a manifest lack of reasons for the legislation'.[179] With respect to the connection between the measure and its objective (suitability), the tribunal noted the government's 'sufficient good faith belief that there was a reasonable connection between the harm and the proposed remedy', and found the legislation 'reasonably drafted to address its objectives' and 'rationally related to its stated purpose'.[180] Although the tribunal did not undertake necessity testing itself, it referred in its decision to similar processes undertaken by primary decision-makers. Prior to promulgating the new legislation, the authorities had considered alternative legislative options (such as exempting open pit mines from the requirements of backfilling and recontouring in certain circumstances), but had found that the option pursued was 'necessary for the immediate preservation of the public general welfare'.[181]

The tribunal concluded that the legislation appeared to reflect a compromise between the interests of various parties, stating that it would respect the legislature's attempt to arrive at a measure that appropriately balanced the needs of different constituencies where it was apparent that those interests had been taken into account.[182] The tribunal also noted the legislature's attempt to balance the various interests at stake in other federal legislation that was applicable to the matter[183] and in relation to policies promulgated under that legislation.[184] Although this approach does not appear to envisage an explicit role for the proportionality *stricto sensu* stage of proportionality analysis, it suggests that a deferential approach would be indicated where the government could demonstrate that it had taken into account the interests of affected stakeholders in designing the measure. The tribunal's decision reflects an understanding of the normative desirability of governments (rather than adjudicators) having primary responsibility for promulgating measures that deal with the competing interests of stakeholders in sensitive policy areas.

---

[179] *Glamis* v. *US*, Award, paras. 803, 805, 817.
[180] *Glamis* v. *US*, Award, paras. 803, 805, 816–17.
[181] *Glamis* v. *US*, Award, para. 181, citing a report of the State Mining and Geology Board.
[182] *Glamis* v. *US*, Award, paras. 803–5.
[183] *Glamis* v. *US*, Award, paras. 41–3.   [184] *Glamis* v. *US*, Award, para. 48.

4.3.2.2.4 *UPS* v. *Canada*: the most efficient option?   Least-restrictive means analysis has also been employed in a very deferential manner by a tribunal in the context of alleged discrimination. In *UPS*, a US courier company challenged a regime of postal subsidies granted to Canadian newspaper and magazine publishers electing to use Canada Post (a state enterprise) to deliver their publications.[185] Canada argued that the measure was covered by the cultural industries carve-out in NAFTA and that the NAFTA rules on the treatment of foreign investors were not applicable to the measure.[186] The tribunal agreed, but nevertheless went on to determine whether national treatment would otherwise have been breached by the measure.[187]

The government argued that the objective of the regime was to ensure the accessibility of Canadian publications so as to sustain the domestic publishing industry and strengthen cultural identity.[188] The government also submitted that it had considered alternative options but had rejected them, because Canada Post had a statutory obligation of nationwide delivery and could guarantee that the publications could be delivered throughout Canada and because the government had been able to negotiate favourable contractual terms with it.[189] The tribunal accepted the argument that the measure was 'the most efficient means' of achieving the objective, but arguably did not embark on full consideration of the alternative proposed by the claimant whereby several firms would deliver periodicals to different parts of Canada, even though the claimant had adduced evidence that Canadian publishers would have preferred a choice of delivery vendors.[190] In any case, the question of efficiency is a separate issue to the question of necessity: efficiency entails comparing the costs and benefits of alternative measures, while a necessity test entails comparing the restrictive impact of the challenged measure and its alternatives on the right or interest at stake – though a court or tribunal may permit

---

[185] *United Parcel Service of America Inc.* v. *Canada*, Award, paras. 151–3.

[186] Article 2106 and Annex 2106 NAFTA provide that measures taken by the US and Canada with respect to cultural industries are exclusively governed by the Canada-US FTA and that Chapter 11 NAFTA does not apply (though the other state party is permitted to retaliate by taking measures of equivalent commercial effect).

[187] *UPS* v. *Canada*, Award, paras. 137–8.

[188] *UPS* v. *Canada*, Award, Separate Statement of Arbitrator Cass, paras. 9, 131.

[189] *UPS* v. *Canada*, Award, para. 165.

[190] See *UPS* v. *Canada*, Award, paras. 165, 173–81 and Separate Statement of Arbitrator Cass, paras. 115, 119. See also the criticism levelled at the majority decision in Kurtz, 'The Merits and Limits of Comparativism', p. 276.

a government to adopt an alternative that is not the least restrictive to avoid an undue fiscal burden.[191]

4.3.2.2.5 *InterAgua* v. *Argentina* and *AWG* v. *Argentina*: the relevance of the crisis situation

Arbitrators have not always been appropriately deferential in the determination of a measure's necessity. The *InterAgua* and *AWG* claims concerned a number of actions by Argentine provincial authorities taken during the economic crisis to ensure the population's access to the water supply. Following the onset of the crisis, the consumer price of drinking water and sewerage services was set to rise to a level that was unaffordable to most of the population. The provincial authorities froze tariffs for these services with the aim of ensuring the population's continuing access to water, but in a manner that was inconsistent with the governing legal framework and the concession contracts.[192]

The tribunals both found that the national and provincial governments had 'deliberately and actively' engendered the claimants' legitimate expectations in the stability of the tariff framework through actions including entering investment treaties, adopting laws and regulations in the utilities sectors, and entering into concession contracts with foreign investors.[193] Although they referred to the need to balance 'the legitimate and reasonable expectations of the claimants' with 'Argentina's right to regulate the provision of a vital public service', both tribunals found that the authorities could have implemented 'tariff increases for other consumers while applying a social tariff or a subsidy to the poor', which would have impacted less on the claimants' interests.[194] This alternative was permitted

---

[191] See Brems and Lavrysen, "'A Sledgehammer to Crack a Nut'", pp. 144–5.

[192] *Suez, Sociedad General de Aguas de Barcelona S.A., and InterAgua Servicios Integrales del Agua S.A.* v. *Argentina*, Liability, para. 217; *Suez, Sociedad General de Aguas de Barcelona S.A., and Vivendi Universal S.A. and AWG* v. *Argentina*, Liability, para. 237. The government's emergency law permitted authorities to renegotiate public service contracts on the basis of criteria including 'the interests of the consumers and the accessibility of services': *InterAgua* v. *Argentina*, Liability, para. 43; *AWG* v. *Argentina*, Liability, para. 44.

[193] *InterAgua* v. *Argentina*, Liability, paras. 208–14; *AWG* v. *Argentina*, Liability, paras. 227–34.

[194] *InterAgua* v. *Argentina*, Award, para. 215; *AWG* v. *Argentina*, Liability, para. 235. The tribunal also found breaches of fair and equitable treatment in relation to the actions of the authorities in forcing renegotiations of the concession and unilaterally terminating the concession: *InterAgua* v. *Argentina*, Liability, paras. 217–28; *AWG* v. *Argentina*, Liability, paras. 237–48.

by the regulatory framework, but obliged the authorities to compensate the concessionaires for any resulting reduction in revenue.[195] It is arguable that the tribunal did not take into account whether this alternative was reasonably available to the government in the circumstances of the crisis – both in terms the government's institutional capacity to design and implement the scheme and the availability of revenue to compensate the claimant.[196] At the very least, these tribunals could have considered these issues more explicitly.

The Separate Opinions rendered by Arbitrator Nikken in both cases appeared to acknowledge this issue. Arbitrator Nikken opined that fair and equitable treatment would be breached only where new laws and policies were not 'reasonably justifiable by public policies', and stated that the role of a tribunal should be to determine whether a measure was 'within the range of decisions that any reasonable government could have adopted under the same circumstances'.[197] In this respect, Arbitrator Nikken suggested that tribunals should take a much more flexible approach to the determination of liability – at least in the context of an economic crisis. Arbitrator Nikken's statements also indicate concern with the competence of tribunals to evaluate the feasibility of alternative measures, particularly in the context of economic policy and crisis situations. Arbitrator Nikken concluded that the measures were not themselves outside the range of decisions open to Argentina during the crisis period, but the fact that the measures had remained in place after the acute period of crisis rendered them in breach of fair and equitable treatment from that point in time.[198] This is a more flexible approach to least-restrictive means testing that is redolent of the *LG&E* decision, which suggests that states should have the discretion to select a measure from a range of reasonable alternatives in a crisis situation.

4.3.3   *Proportionality* stricto sensu *without necessity testing*

Other tribunals have employed the proportionality *stricto sensu* stage of proportionality analysis without full consideration of its prior analytical

---

[195] *InterAgua* v. *Argentina*, Award, para. 215; *AWG* v. *Argentina*, Liability, para. 111.

[196] Although it is not clear whether this was argued by Argentina.

[197] Separate Opinions of Arbitrator Nikken in *InterAgua* v. *Argentina*, Liability, paras. 26–7, 32–4, 42; *AWG* v. *Argentina*, Liability, paras. 26–7, 32–4, 42.

[198] Separate Opinions of Arbitrator Nikken in *InterAgua* v. *Argentina*, Liability, para. 43; *AWG* v. *Argentina*, Liability, para. 43.

stages, particularly the necessity of the measure at issue. This is problematic. Proportionality analysis is generally understood to entail a sequence of successively more stringent tests. This analytical structure is designed to minimize an adjudicator's interference with value judgements inherent in the state's policy-making process, because the stages of suitability and necessity are questions of fact that should be determined before an adjudicator embarks on the more value-laden proportionality *stricto sensu* stage. Engaging in proportionality *stricto sensu* review without prior factual inquiries into the way the measure is targeted gives arbitrators extremely broad discretion to decide the case according to value judgement. This may be problematic not only for governments, but also for claimants. From the perspective of a claimant, a finding that a measure is proportionate without a determination that it is rationally connected to its objective and necessary to achieve that objective could result in a finding that a measure is lawful even where it is ineffective at achieving its objective or where there are less restrictive measures reasonably available to the government.

4.3.3.1 *Tecmed* v. *Mexico*: proportionality *stricto sensu* test favoured the claimant

The *Tecmed* case exemplifies these difficulties. Although the case is regarded by some as a methodologically sound approach to proportionality analysis in the context of indirect expropriation,[199] this book argues that the decision exemplifies a flawed methodology and an overly strict approach to the standard of review.

The claim related to the operation of a hazardous waste disposal facility by the claimant in a rapidly expanding urban area of Mexico. The claimant had failed to comply with conditions of the operating permit by exceeding the facility's capacity and by processing and storing toxic waste. Open trucks full of waste had been driven through an adjacent residential area, and community opposition to the facility had been mounting.[200] Responding to these concerns, the authorities entered into an agreement with the claimant to relocate the facility, but subsequently refused to renew the facility's operating permit and ordered the claimant to cease

---

[199] Schill, 'Revisiting a Landmark: Indirect Expropriation and Fair and Equitable Treatment in the ICSID Case *Tecmed*' (2006) 3 *Transnational Dispute Management*, 10–13; Kingsbury and Schill, 'Investor-State Arbitration as Governance', pp. 43–6; Kingsbury and Schill, 'Public Law Concepts', pp. 91–4.

[200] *Tecmed* v. *Mexico*, Award, paras. 43, 99, 107–10, 135.

operations immediately.[201] The site could not be used for other purposes due to the accumulation of hazardous material.[202] The claimant argued that the authorities' actions amounted to an indirect expropriation and a breach of fair and equitable treatment.[203]

The tribunal held that the relevant legal test for whether the authorities' actions amounted to an indirect expropriation was whether the conduct of the authorities was 'proportional to the public interest . . . and to the protection legally granted to investments'.[204] It also stated that the impact of the authorities' actions on the investment would play a central role in determining the question of proportionality.[205] The tribunal quoted from a passage of the ECtHR's judgment in *James* to the effect that the measure would lack proportionality if the claimant bore an 'individual and excessive burden', and referred to the need for a 'reasonable relationship of proportionality' between the objective and its impact on the claimant.[206] It stated that it would determine whether the authorities' actions were 'reasonable with respect to their goals', and that it would afford 'due deference' to the government in terms of determining which policy objectives to pursue and the measures adopted to achieve those objectives.[207] The tribunal remarked that it was 'indisputable' that states could exercise their 'sovereign powers' without liability – but cautioned that measures could be expropriatory even if taken for legitimate reasons such as environmental protection, if the impact of the measure on the investment outweighed the importance of the objective.[208]

The value that a court or tribunal ascribes to a measure's objective in undertaking proportionality analysis can have a significant impact on the outcome of the case. If a court or tribunal finds that the challenged measure does not pursue a legitimate objective, the measure will be unlawful and the court or tribunal will not proceed to the other stages of proportionality analysis. If the objective is regarded as having low importance and is subsequently directly balanced against the impact on the right or interest through the proportionality *stricto sensu* stage, it is likely that the

---

[201] *Tecmed* v. *Mexico*, Award, paras. 44, 60, 99, 110.

[202] *Tecmed* v. *Mexico*, Award, para. 117.

[203] The tribunal's approach to fair and equitable treatment is discussed in Section 4.3.4.1.

[204] *Tecmed* v. *Mexico*, Award, para. 122.

[205] *Tecmed* v. *Mexico*, Award, para. 122.   [206] *Tecmed* v. *Mexico*, Award, para. 122.

[207] *Tecmed* v. *Mexico*, Award, para. 122. The tribunal also cited similar passages from the ECtHR cases, *Matos e Silva, Lda. and Others* v. *Portugal*, para. 92 and *Mellacher* v. *Austria*, para. 48.

[208] *Tecmed* v. *Mexico*, Award, paras. 119, 121.

outcome will be that the state has unjustifiably interfered with the right or interest.

Mexico had argued that the authorities had acted with the objective of protecting the environment and public health. The tribunal, however, discerned that the government's true purpose was to respond to 'socio-political difficulties' arising from community pressure on government caused by the location of the site (and implied that this was a questionable motivation) rather than to address the breaches of the permit or for environmental reasons more generally.[209] The tribunal emphasized in several passages that there was no evidence that the operation of the facility had seriously harmed the environment or public health, concluding that responding to community concerns could not justify the authorities' actions.[210]

In its evaluation of the importance of the authorities' objective, the tribunal did not appear to seriously consider what might have motivated the community opposition; namely, the possibility of risks to health and the environment emerging over time given the landfill's urban location and the increasing population in the area. Although it indicated that it would take a deferential approach to its assessment of the authorities' objective, the tribunal did not appear to actually turn its mind to the question of deference, even when confronted with a situation of normative uncertainty: the importance of responding to community concerns about a planning decision involving potential risks to the environment and public health. Having discounted the state's purpose and implied that nothing less than an emergency situation could outweigh the importance of avoiding the interference with the investment, the tribunal concluded that there had been an expropriation.

Notably, the tribunal did not examine the necessity of the state's actions in terms of whether there were other measures available to achieve the objective that might have lessened the impact on the claimant, though it briefly noted that 'all the infringements committed were either remediable or remediated or subject to minor penalties'.[211] In particular, the tribunal did not consider whether, bearing in mind the community opposition to the landfill and the agreement to locate it, the authorities could have (for example) expedited new permits and other approvals or agreed to pay a greater amount of the costs of relocation. To be sure, the authorities'

---

[209] *Tecmed* v. *Mexico*, Award, paras. 97, 99, 123–40.
[210] *Tecmed* v. *Mexico*, Award, paras. 118, 124, 127–8, 130–9, 145–7.
[211] *Tecmed* v. *Mexico*, Award, para. 148.

conduct appears to have lacked due process; however, the tribunal's decision is problematic for second-guessing the importance of the authorities' motivations and conducting proportionality analysis in a methodologically problematic way. The decision lends itself to concerns of subjectivity, failure to assess relevant considerations, and lack of appreciation for the context of the decisions taken. Furthermore, the tribunal's reliance on ECtHR cases was selective and, as a result, misleading.

4.3.3.2   Subsequent cases: proportionality *stricto sensu* test favoured the state

This methodology has persisted in subsequent cases, although not to the detriment of host states. The *EDF (Romania)* claim concerned a challenge to legislation that revoked licences to operate duty-free stores in airports, including stores owned by the claimant. The tribunal also adopted language from ECtHR case law, stating that fair and equitable treatment required that there be 'a reasonable relationship of proportionality between the means employed and the aim sought to be realized' and that proportionality would be lacking if the claimant bore 'an individual and excessive burden'.[212] The tribunal held that the measure's objective (to combat smuggling involving airports and duty-free sales and to combat corruption in customs and border security) was legitimate and found that the measure impacted only on a small proportion of the investor's business operations, causing a relatively small amount of economic loss. This articulation of the strength of the competing interests was the basis for its implicit finding that the importance of combating corruption outweighed the impact on the investment.[213] However, the tribunal did not refer to the suitability of the measure (in terms of its likely effectiveness in addressing smuggling and corruption) or to alternative measures that would have impacted less on the claimant's operations, such as greater regulatory controls.[214]

The *Total* tribunal also employed a proportionality *stricto sensu* test in the determination of whether Argentina's emergency measures complied with fair and equitable treatment. In relation to the generally applicable legislation, the tribunal stated that it would balance the right to regulate in

---

[212] *EDF* v. *Romania*, Award, para. 293. However, the tribunal did suggest (at paras. 217–20) that legitimate expectations arising from specific promises or representations as to the stability of the legal framework would be binding on a government and could not be departed from.

[213] *EDF* v. *Romania*, Award, paras. 179, 293–4.

[214] See Kläger, *Fair and Equitable Treatment*, pp. 244–5.

the public interest and the importance and urgency of the objective against the severity of the measures' impact on the claimant's investment 'in the light of a standard of reasonableness and proportionality'.[215] Applying this test, it held that the pesification of the Argentine economy and related measures had a legitimate aim (attempting to avert a complete collapse of the economy), were 'within the monetary sovereignty of the State', were taken in good faith and were proportionate to the aim.[216] The general nature of the legislation and the emergency context of its enactment appeared crucial to the tribunal's conclusion.

The tribunal did not refer to suitability or necessity in this assessment, though it later referred to Argentina's evidence as to the lack of any reasonable alternatives in its consideration of the customary plea in determining whether breaches could be excused on account of a state of necessity.[217] The tribunal also adverted to a proportionality test in the context of determining whether these measures were expropriatory, stating that 'legitimate, proportionate, reasonable and non-discriminatory' measures would not give rise to liability,[218] and concluding that the pesification of the economy was 'a *bona fide* regulatory measure of general application, which was reasonable in light of Argentina's economic and monetary emergency and proportionate to the aim of facing such an emergency'.[219]

The *Total* tribunal found, however, that several other regulatory measures were unsuitable to achieve their objectives. For example, in relation to a measure which altered the way that electricity prices were set, the tribunal appeared to approve of the regulatory objective (to promote economic stability and access to essential services), but held that the measures were '[incompatible] with the criteria of economic rationality [and the]

---

[215] *Total* v. *Argentina*, Award, paras. 122–3, 162, 309, citing *Saluka* v. *Czech Republic*, Partial Award, paras. 305–6; *Genin* v. *Estonia*, Award, para. 348.

[216] *Total* v. *Argentina*, Award, paras. 163–5, 309, 429.

[217] *Total* v. *Argentina*, Award, para. 223, finding that Argentina could not rely on the customary plea in part because it could not demonstrate that its actions were 'the only way' for it to safeguard its essential interests. Van Harten criticizes the *Total* and *EDF* (*Argentina*) tribunals for failing to follow the *Continental* tribunal's more deferential approach to necessity testing (Van Harten, *Sovereign Choices and Sovereign Constraints*, pp. 67–8). Yet, these claims were not determined under the Argentina-US BIT but rather were analyzed in terms of the customary plea. Although an argument can be made that a less stringent approach to the 'only way' requirement may be appropriate in some areas where a state of necessity arises, it seems unlikely that the analysis undertaken by the *Continental* tribunal under Article XI is (or should be) transposable to the context of the customary plea.

[218] *Total* v. *Argentina*, Award, para. 197.   [219] *Total* v. *Argentina*, Award, para. 197.

public interest', because the set prices neither adequately remunerated the claimant nor allowed for reasonable profit, had led to a substantial increase in consumption with resulting power failures, and had resulted in Argentina having to import electricity to satisfy consumer demand.[220] The tribunal also found that Argentina had breached fair and equitable treatment by failing to raise gas tariffs since the crisis had abated and by failing to pay receivables due to the claimant.[221] The circumstances indicated that the government had not acted in good faith due to the period of time that had elapsed since the crisis.

The *Saluka* tribunal also adverted to a proportionality *stricto sensu* test without consideration of the necessity of the challenged measures. The claimant, the owner of a formerly state-owned bank, argued that the introduction of new prudential regulations had negatively affected its investment and had violated its legitimate expectations in the stability of the regulatory environment. The tribunal stated that it would balance the state's right to regulate against the claimant's legitimate expectations in order to determine whether there had been a breach of fair and equitable treatment.[222] However, the tribunal found that the claimant did not hold a legitimate expectation in regulatory stability given the context of the Czech Republic's preparation for accession to the EU, which required the government to reform prudential and other banking regulations. This meant that the claimant had no recognizable interest to be balanced against the interest of the state in achieving the regulatory objective.[223]

The tribunal's decision-making in relation to fair and equitable treatment was inconsistent, as it did not advert to a proportionality test in relation to the other measures it reviewed.[224] Also, in relation to a treaty provision prohibiting unreasonable and discriminatory measures, the tribunal held that the concept of reasonableness had the same normative content as fair and equitable treatment but then applied a suitability test, requiring only that the measures bear 'a reasonable relationship to some

---

[220] *Total* v. *Argentina*, Award, paras. 325–35 (referring to fair and equitable treatment being 'objectively breached' rather than in terms of frustration of legitimate expectations).

[221] *Total* v. *Argentina*, Award, paras. 166–75, 336–8.

[222] *Saluka* v. *Czech Republic*, Partial Award, para. 306.

[223] *Saluka* v. *Czech Republic*, Partial Award, para. 354–60.

[224] The findings of breach were based on the differential treatment of the claimant without justification (discussed further in Chapter 5) (paras. 327–47); frustration of the investor's attempts to negotiate (para. 407); failure to deal with the claimant even-handedly (para. 408); inconsistency in communicating with the claimant (paras. 417–19); lack of transparency in negotiations (para. 420); and refusal to adequately negotiate with the claimant (para. 426).

rational policy'.[225] It appeared that the tribunal viewed the proportionality test as only applicable to legitimate expectations claims and not other forms of substantive review of government conduct. Arguably, the tribunal could have employed a more consistent methodology in relation to all of these measures, as there is no reason why a tribunal should employ different forms of analysis under the same standard of protection and related obligations. In particular, proportionality analysis can also be used to identify measures that are taken with impermissible objectives, as well as measures that fall outside a broad understanding of suitability and necessity. Whether the claim is viewed through the lens of legitimate expectations or based on a general principle of stability in the regulatory environment or consistency in government conduct would not seem to be relevant to the question of how to determine liability, given that legitimate expectations are regarded as an element of fair and equitable treatment.[226] In any case, the context of the measures' adoption suggests that the government would have prevailed in relation to substantive review.

4.3.3.3 Other references to proportionality and balancing in the decided cases

Several other tribunals and tribunal members issuing separate opinions have referred to the concept of a balance of interests, referred more specifically to proportionality as the relevant method of review, or have concluded that a measure is proportionate without further elaboration.[227]

---

[225] *Saluka* v. *Czech Republic*, Partial Award, para. 460.

[226] By comparison, the ECtHR employs proportionality analysis in the determination of legitimate expectations claims using its general approach to the right to property, e.g. *Pine Valley* v. *Ireland*, para. 51; *Veselinski* v. *"The former Yugoslav Republic of Macedonia"*, paras. 80–1; *Djidrovski* v. *"The former Yugoslav Republic of Macedonia"*, paras. 85–6. See also e.g. *Former King of Greece* v. *Greece*, para. 98 (legitimate expectations outweighed by the public interest). See Wildhaber, 'The Protection of Legitimate Expectations in European Human Rights Law', pp. 261–2.

[227] As well as the cases discussed below, see the brief references to proportionality and balancing in *AIG Capital Partners, Inc and CJSC Tema Real Estate Co Ltd* v. *Kazakhstan*, Award, p. 52; *Azurix* v. *Argentina*, Award, paras. 310–12; *Fireman's Fund Insurance Company* v. *Mexico*, Award, para. 176(j); *Archer* v. *Mexico*, Award, para. 250; *Corn Products* v. *Mexico*, Award, para. 87; *InterAgua* v. *Argentina*, Liability, paras. 147–8; *Les Laboratoires Servier, S.A.A., Biofarma, S.A.S., Arts et Techniques du Progrès S.A.S.* v. *Poland*, Final Award, paras. 399–400, 404, 569, 575; *Inmaris Perestroika Sailing Maritime Services GmbH and Others* v. *Ukraine*, Award, para. 303; *Deutsche Bank AG* v. *Sri Lanka*, Award, para. 522; *Vigotop* v. *Hungary*, Award, para. 631 (expropriation); *MTD* v. *Chile*, Award, para. 109; *MCI Power Group LC and New Turbine, Inc* v. *Ecuador*, Award, para. 278; *Limited Liability*

For example, the *Arif* tribunal remarked that the determination of a fair and equitable treatment claim 'involves a balancing exercise that might involve taking into account the host State's legitimate right subsequently to regulate domestic matters in the public interest'.[228] In *Thunderbird*, Arbitrator Wälde similarly referred to the need to balance the investor's legitimate expectations against 'an equally legitimate public interest in preserving a large "regulatory space" in particular in the field of gambling regulation' and 'the need for flexibility in public policy'.[229] In *LG&E*, the tribunal stated that it would balance 'the degree of the measure's interference with the right of ownership' against 'the power of the State to adopt its policies' and take into account 'the context within which a measure was adopted and the state's purpose' in the determination of an indirect expropriation claim.[230] The *El Paso* tribunal indicated a relatively high threshold for a finding of expropriation, holding that regulatory measures would only be expropriatory where they were 'arbitrary, discriminatory, disproportionate or otherwise unfair', appearing to characterize a lack of proportionality as something close to bad faith and suggesting a wide margin of appreciation was applicable.[231] The *Continental* tribunal similarly stated that regulations adopted in the public interest would not be expropriatory provided that they did 'not affect property in an intolerable, discriminatory or disproportionate manner'.[232]

Company *Amto* v. *Ukraine*, Award, para. 99; *Parkerings* v. *Lithuania*, Award, paras. 368, 371; *Joseph Charles Lemire* v. *Ukraine*, Jurisdiction and Liability, para. 285; *Vivendi* v. *Argentina*, Liability, paras. 7.4.18, 7.4.26; *Paushok* v. *Mongolia*, Jurisdiction and Liability, para. 299; *Jan Oostergetel and Theodora Laurentius* v. *Slovak Republic*, Final Award, para. 224; *Toto* v. *Lebanon*, Award, para. 165; Separate Opinions of Arbitrator Nikken in *AWG* v. *Argentina*, Liability, paras. 37, 42 and *InterAgua* v. *Argentina*, Liability, paras. 37, 42; *Apotex* v. *US*, Award, para. 9.48; *Gold Reserve Inc.* v. *Venezuela*, Award, para. 595; *Mamidoil* v. *Albania*, Award, paras. 614–22, 723–4, 731–4 (fair and equitable treatment); *SAUR* v. *Argentina*, Jurisdiction and Liability, paras. 330–2; *Levy de Levi* v. *Peru*, Award, paras. 329, 332, 342, 479, 482–3 (fair and equitable treatment and expropriation); *SD Myers* v. *Canada*, Partial Award, para. 252 (national treatment); *AES Summit Generation Limited and AES-Tisza Erömü Kft* v. *Hungary*, Award, para. 10.3.36; and *LG&E* v. *Argentina*, Liability, para. 158 (unreasonable or discriminatory measures). See also *Pantechniki SA Contractors and Engineers (Greece)* v. *Albania*, Award, paras. 76–7 (full protection and security).

[228] *Franck Charles Arif* v. *Moldova*, Award, paras. 536–7, citing *Saluka* v. *Czech Republic*, Partial Award, para. 305 (internal punctuation omitted).

[229] *Thunderbird* v. *Mexico*, Separate Opinion of Arbitrator Wälde, paras. 2, 27, 30, 102.

[230] *LG&E* v. *Argentina*, Liability, paras. 189–95.

[231] *El Paso* v. *Argentina*, Award, paras. 241–5, 269, 278, 299.

[232] *Continental* v. *Argentina*, Award, para. 276.

Although these decisions indicate growing support for the use of proportionality analysis as a method of review or more broadly for employing
the concept of a balance of interests in the determination of liability, brief
references to proportionality or declarations that a measure is proportionate without further explication may conceal impressionistic decision-
making because in such cases, the tribunal's conclusions do not reveal the
methodology undertaken to determine that the measure at issue was a
proportionate exercise of public power.

4.3.4   Other methods of review

Despite the moves towards proportionality-based approaches in the
decided cases, many tribunals have employed other methods of review
that do not involve consideration of alternative measures or proportionality *stricto sensu* testing.

4.3.4.1   Legitimate objective as the test for legality

Several tribunals have assessed the legitimacy of the state's regulatory
objective as a means to determine whether the state had breached fair and
equitable treatment or had undertaken an indirect expropriation. Like
determining breach on the basis of the proportionality *stricto sensu* stage
of proportionality analysis alone, determining breach based solely on an
assessment of the regulatory objective arrogates to tribunals the power
to decide the legality of the measure based on a value judgement. This
approach might also attract criticism from investors on the basis that it
could result in the approval of measures that are ineffective at achieving
their objectives or are overly burdensome in light of alternatives.[233]

The risk of state liability being based solely on a value judgement using
this method of review is highlighted by the *Metalclad* and *Tecmed* cases
in relation to their determination of fair and equitable treatment claims.
Both tribunals appeared to suggest that a legitimate reason for inconsistent
administrative treatment of an investor (here, denial of permit applications for waste disposal facilities) would not breach fair and equitable
treatment, but that the authorities had not acted with a proper purpose
in responding to community concerns about environmental issues.[234]
The *Metalclad* tribunal found that the authorities' reasons for denial of

---

[233] See *UPS* v. *Canada*, Award, Separate Statement of Arbitrator Cass, paras. 131–2.
[234] *Metalclad* v. *Mexico*, Award, paras. 90–8; *Tecmed* v. *Mexico*, Award, 154, 157–8, 164, 166,
172–3.

the permit were 'improper', based on its (contested) interpretation of the relevant considerations that the authorities were obliged to take into account when determining permit applications.[235] Unlike its approach to expropriation, the *Tecmed* tribunal did not refer to proportionality in relation to the fair and equitable treatment claim, instead relying on its prior finding as to the illegitimacy of the regulatory objective as the basis for its finding that fair and equitable treatment had also been breached by the authorities' actions.

In other cases where tribunals adopted this approach, arbitrators briefly remarked that a state would violate fair and equitable treatment if it regulated in the absence of 'justification of an economic, social or other nature',[236] regulated in bad faith[237] or departed from previously made representations without a legitimate objective.[238] While regulating in bad faith would clearly render the measure in breach of fair and equitable treatment, other descriptions of this approach suggest that this method of review permits overly broad adjudicative discretion.

4.3.4.2   Suitability test

Another method of review employed by investment tribunals involves testing the rationality of the connection between the measure and its objective, which approximates to using the suitability stage of proportionality analysis to determine legality. This is the dominant approach taken in discrimination cases to date.[239] Tribunals have also applied this approach in relation to fair and equitable treatment and arbitrary measures claims. For example, the *Electrabel* tribunal determined that Hungary's reintroduction of pricing regulations in the electricity market complied with fair and equitable treatment because it was 'a rational and reasonably appropriate measure' that achieved the government's aim of ensuring affordability and controlling excessive profits while continuing to permit energy generators to procure a reasonable return on their investments.[240]

---

[235] *Metalclad* v. *Mexico*, Award, para. 106. See e.g. Schneiderman, *Constitutionalizing Economic Globalization*, pp. 82–6; Montt, *State Liability in Investment Treaty Arbitration*, pp. 325, 336; Van Harten, *Sovereign Choices and Sovereign Constraints*, p. 74.

[236] *El Paso* v. *Argentina*, Award, para. 372.

[237] *CME* v. *Czech Republic*, Partial Award, paras. 526, 611.

[238] *Lauder* v. *Czech Republic*, Award, paras. 263–4, 297.

[239] For example, *Unglaube* v. *Costa Rica*, Award, para. 262; *GAMI* v. *Mexico*, Final Award, para. 114; *Saluka* v. *Czech Republic*, Partial Award, paras. 344–7, 460; *Consortium RFCC* v. *Morocco*, Award, para. 74 .

[240] *Electrabel S.A.* v. *Republic of Hungary*, Jurisdiction, Applicable Law and Liability, para. 8.34. See also *Roussalis* v. *Romania*, Award (treaty provision prohibiting unjustifiable

Using a suitability test to determine liability may be regarded as problematic by claimants, because it would permit a finding that a measure is lawful in cases where are less restrictive measures reasonably available to the government, even if those alternatives have a substantially less restrictive effect on the investor's interests. This issue is discussed further in Chapter 5.

4.3.4.3 Review for unreasonableness

Finally, a number of investment tribunals have used the concept of reasonableness as the applicable method of review, principally in the context of fair and equitable treatment[241] but also in relation to indirect expropriation claims.[242] Like proportionality, the concept of reasonableness may be understood as a search for equilibrium and appears to require a balancing of divergent interests.[243] In the absence of more detailed decision-making criteria, however, review for reasonableness risks impressionistic decision-making.[244]

To place these tribunals' decisions in a broader context, reasonableness is a concept that is used as a method of review or as a means of limiting governmental discretion in many legal systems.[245] For example, the ECtHR uses reasonableness as a method of review in relation to certain rights such as in relation to whether authorities have discharged their

---

or discriminatory measures) paras. 687–8, 691; *AES* v. *Hungary*, Award (treaty provision prohibiting unreasonable or discriminatory measures) paras. 10.3.1, 10.3.7–10.3.19, 10.3.34–10.3.35.

[241] As well as the cases discussed below, see the brief references to the concept of reasonableness in *Parkerings* v. *Lithuania*, Award, para. 332; *Merrill & Ring* v. *Canada*, Award, para. 213; *Impregilo S.p.A.* v. *Argentina*, Award, para. 291; *L.E.S.I. S.p.A. and ASTALDI S.p.A.* v. *Algeria*, Award, para. 151; *Electrabel* v. *Hungary*, Award, para. 8.22; *El Paso* v. *Argentina*, Award, paras. 364, 371. See also *Continental* v. *Argentina*, Award, para. 254.

[242] *Feldman* v. *Mexico*, Merits, paras. 103–5, 112, 116; *Gemplus S.A., SLP S.A., Gemplus Industrial S.A. de C.V.* v. *Mexico*, Award, paras. 4-117–4-124, 4-175, 4-183, 4-187, 8-27.

[243] See Hickman, 'The Substance and Structure of Proportionality', p. 177; Ortino, 'From 'Non-Discrimination' to 'Reasonableness:' A Paradigm Shift in International Economic Law?' (2005) 1 *New York University School of Law Jean Monnet Working Papers*, pp. 33–4; Bongiovanni et al., 'Introduction', p. xi; Kavanagh, *Constitutional Review*, pp. 246–7; Barak, *Proportionality*, pp. 373–5.

[244] See, in relation to the use of reasonableness as a method of review by investment tribunals, Kingsbury and Schill, 'Investor-State Arbitration as Governance', pp. 49–50; Kingsbury and Schill, 'Public Law Concepts', pp. 96–7; Kläger, *Fair and Equitable Treatment*, pp. 239–40, 245.

[245] See, in relation to reasonableness as a method of review in general international law, Corten, *L'utilisation du "raisonnable" par le juge international: discours juridique, raison et contradictions* (1997) 96–135.

positive obligations to protect the right to life.[246] Many domestic systems of administrative law also rely on the concept of reasonableness to determine the legality of government conduct, though the concept means different things in different legal systems. For example, many Commonwealth countries use *Wednesbury* unreasonableness as the grounds of substantive review in administrative law.[247] Other legal systems including Canada[248] and South Africa[249] use the concept of reasonableness as the grounds of review in certain cases, but the threshold for breach appears to be lower than the *Wednesbury* test. In US administrative law, a review for 'arbitrary and capricious' conduct[250] is a form of reasonableness review, with similarities to the *Wednesbury* approach.[251]

Most investment tribunal decisions in this area briefly refer to reasonableness and conclude whether the measure was reasonable without further explication, which does not shed light on the reasoning processes undertaken by arbitrators. Several tribunals appear to have viewed the concept of reasonableness solely in terms of the significance of changes made to the regulatory environment for the claimant, rather than taking into account both state and investor interests. For example, the *PSEG* tribunal held that Turkey had acted unreasonably by making 'continuous' regulatory changes to the law affecting a contract between the government and the claimant, but did not appear to consider the state's reasons for its actions, even though it acknowledged that the state was acting in good faith.[252] The *Toto* tribunal held that a 'drastic' alteration of the regulatory framework would breach fair and equitable treatment, but that the challenged measures (amendments to taxes and customs duties on cement,

---

[246] See e.g. Hickman, *Public Law after the Human Rights Act* (2010) 213–16.

[247] *Associated Provincial Pictures Houses Ltd* v. *Wednesbury Corporation* per Lord Greene: 'so unreasonable that it might almost be described as being done in bad faith . . . so unreasonable that no reasonable authority could ever have come to it'. See Craig, *Administrative Law*, pp. 646–52 (UK administrative law).

[248] Administrative decisions are reviewed either for correctness or for reasonableness, depending on factors including the relative expertise of the decision-maker with respect to the issue to be determined and the nature of the questions to be answered by the court: see *Dunsmuir* v. *New Brunswick* [2008] 1 SCR 190, paras. 44–64, 53; Jones and de Villars, *Principles of Administrative Law* (2009) 490–1; Lewans, 'Deference and Reasonableness Since *Dunsmuir*' (2012) 38 *Queen's Law Journal* 59, 75, 78.

[249] Bilchitz, *Poverty and Fundamental Rights: The Justification and Enforcement of Socioeconomic Rights* (2008) 139–66.

[250] Section 706, Administrative Procedure Act 5 U.S.C. (2011).

[251] *Ethyl Corp.* v. *Environmental Protection Agency* 426 U.S. 941 (1976) (ruling that the arbitrary and capricious test is an inquiry into whether the agency decision at issue was rational). See e.g. Montt, *State Liability in Investment Treaty Arbitration*, p. 209.

[252] *PSEG* v. *Turkey*, Award, paras. 250–6.

diesel, and construction material) were general in nature and had resulted in a relatively small cost to the claimant, but again did not appear to frame the test in a manner that would also take into account the state's reasons for its actions.[253] There appears to be only one case in which the tribunal explicitly took into account state and investor interests in determining whether a measure was reasonable.[254]

Using the concept of reasonableness as a method of review is problematic, not least because the concept is indeterminate. This method of review has attracted criticism in relation to both domestic and international law on the basis that it lacks a clear analytical structure and that it can conceal the subjective preferences of adjudicators[255] and that judges have decided cases according to their own policy preferences without relying on any particular criteria.[256] The subjectivity inherent in this approach is illuminated by the *BG* case. In *BG*, reviewing Argentina's emergency measures for breach of a treaty provision prohibiting unreasonable measures, the tribunal opined that 'the determination of reasonableness is in its essence a matter for the arbitrator's judgment'.[257] Although stating that it was not the tribunal's role 'to pass judgment on the reasonableness or effectiveness of [Argentina's emergency] measures as a matter of political economy', the tribunal concluded, without further explication, that insofar as Argentina's emergency measures departed from previous commitments made to the claimant by entering into concession agreements and granting licences, the measures were 'by definition unreasonable and a breach of the treaty'.[258]

There is, however, nothing to prevent courts and tribunals from developing the concept of reasonableness with a more structured method of

---

[253] *Toto* v. *Lebanon*, Award, para. 244.

[254] *Mamidoil* v. *Albania*, Award, paras. 791–2, also noting that the measure 'bore a reasonable relationship to some rational policy'.

[255] For example, Schønberg, *Legitimate Expectations in Administrative Law* (2000) 150; Hickman, 'The Reasonableness Principle', p. 166; Bilchitz, *Poverty and Fundamental Rights*, p. 176; Miles and Sunstein, 'The Real World of Arbitrariness Review' (2008) 75 *University of Chicago Law Review* 761, 767–9; Bongiovanni, Sartor and Valentini, 'Introduction' in Bongiovanni, Sartor and Valentini (eds.), *Reasonableness and Law* (2009) xi, xiii, xiv; della Cananea, 'Reasonableness in Administrative Law', in Bongiovanni, Sartor and Valentini (eds.), *Reasonableness and Law* (2009) 295, 305.

[256] Miles and Sunstein, 'The Real World of Arbitrariness Review', pp. 767–9 (in relation to review for arbitrary and capricious conduct under US administrative law). These authors also argue that the political ideology of judges, as discerned by the appointing government, has had a substantial effect on decision-making in such cases.

[257] *BG* v. *Argentina*, Final Award, para. 342, citing *CME* v. *Czech Republic*, Partial Award, para. 158.

[258] *BG* v. *Argentina*, Final Award, paras. 343–4.

review by fleshing out the concept with more detailed criteria.[259] The ICJ has done so on two occasions: in *Dispute Regarding Navigational and Related Rights (Costa Rica v. Nicaragua)*, the Court held that Nicaragua had the right to regulate the exercise by Costa Rica of its freedom of navigation on the San Juan River, but that this right could not be exercised unreasonably, which in the Court's view meant that there should be no other means available to achieve the objective and that the impact of the means chosen 'must not be manifestly excessive when measured against the protection afforded to the purpose invoked'.[260] In *Whaling in the Antarctic (Australia v. Japan)*, the ICJ appeared to imbue the concept of reasonableness with a procedural type of necessity test.[261] The Court held that the determination of whether Japan's whaling programme was undertaken 'for purposes of scientific research' required it to assess whether the design and implementation of the programme were 'reasonable in relation to achieving its stated [scientific] objectives'.[262] In making this determination, the ICJ ascertained whether Japan had considered whether its objective could have been achieved by other methods with a lesser lethal impact on whales or sample sizes causing fewer fatalities, as required by relevant International Whaling Commission resolutions and guidelines. Japan was unable to satisfy the Court that it had done so.[263]

4.3.4.4   Review for arbitrariness

As a related point, a number of other tribunals have held that fair and equitable treatment will only be infringed where the measure is arbitrary in the sense of there being a lack of substantive justification for the measure.[264] Tribunals have found that fair and equitable treatment would be breached where the substance of legislation was arbitrary,[265] regulatory changes were made in bad faith,[266] the authorities could offer no reasons for their actions,[267] there was arbitrary reversal of undertakings made as

---

[259] Barak, *Proportionality*, pp. 375–7.
[260] *Navigational and Related Rights (Costa Rica v. Nicaragua)*, paras. 87, 128.
[261] Chapter 5 discusses investment tribunals' use of a procedural form of necessity test.
[262] *Whaling in the Antarctic (Australia v. Japan)*, para. 88.
[263] *Whaling in the Antarctic (Australia v. Japan)*, paras. 136–7, 141, 156, but see the Dissenting Opinion of Judge Owada, paras. 25, 39, 42, arguing that the Court should have reviewed Japan's actions only for good faith.
[264] Bonnitcha, *Substantive Protection under Investment Treaties*, p. 211.
[265] *Metalpar S.A. and Buen Aire S.A. v. Argentina*, Award, para. 187; *Mobil Investments Canada Inc. and Murphy Oil Corporation v. Canada*, Liability, paras. 152–3.
[266] *Teco Guatemala Holdings LLC v. Guatemala*, Award, paras. 629–30.
[267] *Siemens v. Argentina*, Award, paras. 318–19. See also *Teco v. Guatemala*, Award, para. 587 (suggesting that failure to provide reasons for governmental decisions indicates arbitrary conduct).

to the stability of the legal framework,[268] the authorities had engaged in arbitrary administrative conduct[269] or arbitrarily modified the regulatory framework,[270] arbitrarily differentiated between foreign and domestic investors,[271] or had failed to implement regulations or had implemented them in an arbitrary manner.[272]

However, the law is currently less than clear as to the actual circumstances in which state conduct will be arbitrary. Investment tribunals have frequently referred to the decision of the ICJ in the *ELSI* case to assist in their determination of the level of mistreatment that would establish that the treatment was arbitrary. In *ELSI*, the ICJ interpreted a clause prohibiting arbitrary measures in the US-Italy Friendship, Commerce and Navigation treaty, finding the state liable for arbitrary treatment in the context of the requisition of a factory. The Court stated that arbitrary conduct was conduct 'opposed to the rule of law . . . a wilful disregard of due process of law, an act which shocks, or at least surprises, a sense of juridical propriety'.[273] Investment tribunals have rarely found that a government has acted arbitrarily in breach of fair and equitable treatment, but in *Lemire*, the tribunal found the state to have acted in breach of an arbitrary measures clause by repeatedly awarding radio licences to applicants who were well connected to politicians, even though the claimant established that it better satisfied the licensing criteria.[274] In *Bilcon*, the majority of the tribunal held that the government had acted arbitrarily by assessing the investor's proposed project using what it found were extralegal criteria and by its failure to accord due process in relation to the application of these criteria, although this finding attracted a strongly worded dissent from one arbitrator.[275]

---

[268] *Frontier Petroleum* v. *Czech Republic*, Final Award, para. 285.

[269] *Unglaube* v. *Costa Rica*, Award, paras. 258–9.

[270] *PSEG* v. *Turkey*, Award, paras. 239–40.

[271] *Consortium FRCC* v. *Morocco*, Award, para. 74.

[272] *GAMI* v. *Mexico*, Award, paras. 94, 104–05; *Teco* v. *Guatemala*, Award, paras. 621–2.

[273] *Elettronica Sicula S.p.A. (ELSI) (US* v. *Italy)*, para. 128. See e.g. *LG&E* v. *Argentina*, Liability, para. 157; *Cargill* v. *Mexico*, Award, para. 291; *Rumeli Telekom A.S. and Telsim Mobil Telekomikasyon Hizmetleri A.S.* v. *Kazakhstan*, Award, para. 672; *SAUR* v. *Argentina*, Jurisdiction and Liability, para. 487. See also (treaty provisions prohibiting arbitrary measures) *EDF* v. *Romania*, Award, para. 303 and *Lemire* v. *Ukraine*, Jurisdiction and Liability, para. 262.

[274] *Lemire* v. *Ukraine*, Jurisdiction and Liability, paras. 316, 384–5, 419–20.

[275] *Bilcon* v. *Canada*, para 591; Dissenting Opinion of Professor Donald McRae, para 38: 'The majority makes no attempt, beyond an assertion of arbitrariness, to show how the [authorities'] actions . . . were, in fact, arbitrary. There is no suggestion that the Panel had deliberately or willfully disregarded the law to be applied.'

Arbitrariness is a nebulous concept, particularly where it is used as a method of review. Although the *ELSI* case indicates that there is a high threshold for when the state will be liable in relation to regulatory changes and other administrative conduct affecting investors, the *ELSI* test is difficult to apply to the context of regulatory disputes.[276] The investment tribunals that have employed the concept of arbitrariness as the applicable method of review have not generally elaborated on the circumstances in which the conduct of the state will be arbitrary, which makes it difficult to distil coherent and certain legal tests from these approaches to determining liability.

Two investment tribunals have, however, given more content to the test for arbitrariness. The *Genin* tribunal treated the concept of arbitrariness as being akin to an absence of a rational connection between a measure and its objective. The tribunal found that the government's revocation of the claimant's banking licence did not breach fair and equitable treatment or the prohibition on arbitrary measures because it was a lawful action taken in the course of exercising the government's statutory obligations to regulate the Estonian banking sector. The tribunal held that Estonia's actions amounted to an 'entirely legitimate and fully proper exercise' of public power due to the fact that there were concerns about the management of the bank and its financial soundness.[277] The *Glamis* tribunal appears to be the only investment tribunal that has fleshed out the concept of arbitrariness with a structured approach to determining liability, by relying on the concept of arbitrariness as the grounds of review and then employing proportionality analysis as the method of review.

4.4   Conclusion

The analysis undertaken in this chapter permits two observations: first, that investment tribunals are increasingly adopting methods of review that take into account both state and investor interests in determining state liability, including proportionality-based methodologies, and, second, that arbitrators are in many cases employing an appropriately

---

[276] See Hamrock, 'The *ELSI* Case: Toward an International Definition of "Arbitrary" Conduct' (1992) 27 *Texas International Law Journal* 837, 838, 846, 849–62, arguing that the ICJ was 'overly vague' in its definition of what kind of government conduct would constitute arbitrary measures and proposing a four-part test to give effect to the concept.

[277] *Genin* v. *Estonia*, Award, 352–3, 370.

deferential approach to the standard of review that takes into account arbitrators' institutional limitations in situations of normative or empirical uncertainty. In recent years, many investment tribunals have adopted or referred to proportionality analysis or have employed one or more of its component stages in determining liability in regulatory disputes.

Although proportionality analysis may be criticized for permitting subjectivity and overly broad discretion, these criticisms are also applicable to its alternatives.[278] The concept of reasonableness offers little transparency or certainty as a method of review, as it permits adjudicators to decide cases according to their own subjective preferences because the method does not require that any particular questions are asked of a responding government nor that any particular analytical structure be employed. The concept of arbitrariness – while signalling that a certain level of severity must be made out to establish a breach – also does not entail any degree of transparency in terms of the analytical processes employed by adjudicators. Reasonableness and arbitrariness are better understood as *grounds of review* rather than as appropriate methods of review.

Using a proportionality *stricto sensu* test without the other stages of proportionality analysis also amounts to basing the determination of state liability on a value judgement that is undisciplined by other factual inquiries. Employing neither the legitimate objective nor the suitability stage of proportionality analysis (or their conceptual equivalents) as methods of review do go far enough to inquire into questions such as the capacity of the measure to achieve its objective or whether the objective could reasonably have been achieved in such as way as to affect private interests to a lesser extent. As Chapter 5 will discuss further, the concept of suitability as a method of review may provide insufficient protection to investors and appears to be ill-suited to the discrimination inquiry.

Proportionality analysis is also preferable to the approaches seen in a number of (primarily older) investment tribunal decisions, whereby a tribunal undertakes 'an extensive summary of the facts of the case at hand ... followed by the abrupt determination with little intelligible legal reasoning'[279] as to whether the state has violated an obligation towards an

---

[278] See Barak, *Proportionality*, pp. 521–7.

[279] Kingsbury and Schill, 'Investor-State Arbitration as Governance', p. 50; Kingsbury and Schill, 'Public Law Concepts', p. 103.

investor, or adopts an 'I know it when I see it'[280] or 'smell test'[281] approach. Such approaches to determining state liability not only avoid clarifying the relevant obligation on the basis that the tribunal has concluded that the facts of the case are clearly determinative of whether or not there has been a breach, but also do not reveal the applicable method or standard of review.

Despite its emergence as a method of review, proportionality analysis has thus far been inconsistently applied by investment tribunals, and arbitrators have been less than clear with respect to the methodologies they have employed. Moreover, references to proportionality in the decided cases do not always signal that a particular analytical process will be undertaken.[282] Even when investment tribunals have referred to the approaches of other courts and tribunals in their decision-making, they have not necessarily followed the approaches they have described; in *Tecmed*, the tribunal referred to ECtHR jurisprudence concerning the right to property but went on to construct its own approach to proportionality analysis that went directly from assessing the objective of the measure to the proportionality *stricto sensu* stage and combined this approach with a strict standard of review. Some tribunals, notably *Glamis*, have also employed proportionality-based approaches without referring to proportionality. Other tribunals have used proportionality analysis in relation to some areas of international investment law but not others,[283] or in relation to only some measures while other measures were scrutinized under the same standard of protection using a different method of review.[284]

Although proportionality analysis has been emerging for over a decade as a method of review in investor-state arbitration, its prevalence in the

---

[280] See *Jacobellis* v. *Ohio*, 378 U.S. 184 (1964), concurring opinion of Justice Potter Stewart; Fortier and Drymer, 'Indirect Expropriation', p. 327. See also Heiskanen, 'Arbitrary and Unreasonable Measures', pp. 101–3; Stone Sweet, 'Proportionality's New Frontier', p. 62.

[281] Ranieri, 'Investors' Rights, Legal Concepts and Public Policy in the NAFTA Context' in Trakman and Ranieri (eds.), *Regionalism in International Investment Law* (2013) 400, 442.

[282] See Bomhoff, 'Balancing, the Global and Local', pp. 557–8; Bomhoff, 'Genealogies of Balancing as Discourse', p. 113 (noting, in reference to comparative constitutional law, that the discourse of balancing may mean different things depending on the context).

[283] *Total* v. *Argentina*, Award, paras. 115, 122–3, 162–5, 309, 317–18; *LG&E* v. *Argentina*, Liability, paras. 177, 189–95, 239–42; *Tecmed* v. *Mexico*, Award, paras. 117–19, 121–2, 133–9, 145–8.

[284] *Pope and Talbot* v. *Canada*, Merits, paras. 172–3; *Total* v. *Argentina*, Award, paras. 166–75, 180, 336–8.

decided cases and its degree of acceptance should not be overstated. Investment tribunals have not uniformly embraced least-restrictive means analysis. Most tribunals that have discussed the required connection between a measure and its objective in the context of non-discrimination claims have required only a test of suitability between the challenged measure and a non-discriminatory objective, and none of the decided indirect expropriation cases explicitly refer to the necessity stage of analysis in their decision-making. Outside of the context of the Argentina-US BIT, which mandates the consideration of alternative measures, tribunals appear to have conducted least-restrictive means analysis or referred to the concept of necessity only in response to the parties' pleadings, in circumstances where the relevant treaty or domestic regulatory regime required authorities to consider alternative measures or stipulated such measures, or in cases where there was evidence that the authorities had undertaken this type of analysis on their own motion.[285] Tribunals have been more inclined to rely on the concept of reasonableness as the applicable method of substantive review in relation to fair and equitable treatment claims.[286]

But despite this variance in approaches adopted by tribunals, the decided cases do demonstrate that proportionality analysis can be a workable methodology in regulatory disputes. Chapter 5 picks up on the tentative moves to proportionality analysis in the decided cases, analysing the manner in which investment tribunals have applied the various stages of proportionality analysis in terms of the standard of review, and discussing other factors influencing the way in which the method of review has been applied.

---

[285] I am grateful to Jonathan Bonnitcha for this point. See *Methanex* v. *US*, Final Award; *Pope and Talbot* v. *Canada*, Merits; *UPS* v. *Canada*, Award and *Chemtura* v. *Canada*, Award (pleadings); *SD Myers* v. *Canada*, Partial Award; *AWG* v. *Argentina*, Liability; *InterAgua* v. *Argentina*, Liability and *Glamis* v. *US*, Award (less-restrictive means specified in the treaty or required to be considered by the regulatory framework); *Methanex* v. *US*, Final Award and *AES* v. *Hungary*, Award (less restrictive options considered by primary decision-makers).

[286] Bonnitcha, *Substantive Protection under Investment Treaties*, p. 224.

The development of an institutionally sensitive approach to proportionality analysis in investor-state arbitration

5.1 Introduction

This chapter disaggregates the approaches of investment tribunals to each stage of proportionality analysis in terms of the standard of review and other factors that have influenced the determination of liability. Although the decisions analyzed in this chapter represent a range of approaches to methods of review, this chapter discusses each stage of proportionality analysis separately for heuristic purposes, so as to isolate the considerations that arbitrators have taken into account in undertaking each inquiry. The aim of this exercise is to highlight the foundations upon which an institutionally sensitive approach to proportionality analysis could be built in investor-state arbitration. This chapter also addresses the question of the desirability of investment tribunals employing least-restrictive means analysis and undertaking proportionality *stricto sensu* testing in light of concerns that these analytical processes may have unjustifiably negative effects on the regulatory autonomy of host states.

5.2 Legitimate objective

As noted in Chapter 4, a minority of investment tribunals has held that the objective of the host state is irrelevant to the question of the legality of the measure in the context of indirect expropriation, fair and equitable treatment and discrimination claims. Most tribunals, however, have taken into account, explicitly or implicitly, the objective being pursued by the state in their determination of whether the state had acted lawfully. Assessing the legitimacy of the objective creates the risk that a tribunal will undermine the state's own assessment, both in a general sense and as reflected in the state's chosen level of achievement of the objective (such as the level of health or environmental risk that the state is willing to bear). This risk might also carry through to the necessity stage of inquiry if a tribunal were to adopt a strict approach that did not involve consideration of whether any available alternative measures were as effective at achieving the state's objective as well as to the proportionality *stricto sensu* stage, because the importance that a tribunal ascribes to the objective will strongly influence the outcome of both stages of proportionality analysis.

The other courts and tribunals surveyed in this book are, as discussed in Chapter 3, usually loath to make their own determination of the legitimacy or value of the government's objective, recognizing that the determination what is in the public interest or whether an objective is sufficiently important to limit protected rights or interests is a political decision for which governments should have primary responsibility. Their practice indicates that the purpose of this analysis – whatever the actual method of review adopted – is to identify and exclude measures that have discriminatory or other improper objectives, rather than to second-guess the legitimacy or importance of the measure's objective, including the desired level of protection or achievement of it.[1]

To take the example of indirect expropriation, the concept of police powers potentially encompasses a wide variety of state activities. A decision to intervene in pursuit of a particular objective will naturally be a decision in respect of which opinions may differ. Some states will understand police powers as comprising a range of interventions to promote the public good, whereas the exercise of police powers by other states will be restricted to protecting individuals from harm.[2] One author argues that there should be a 'taxonomy' of permissible regulatory purposes in terms of police powers by reference to common state practice, whereby, for example, measures taken to promote public health or to require businesses to internalize the costs of pollution would be considered to be legitimate, but redistributive economic policies or restrictions on land development would not.[3] Others suggest that certain public purposes but not others would justify what would otherwise be an indirect expropriation.[4] This

---

[1] See Van Harten, *Investment Treaty Arbitration and Public Law*, pp. 144–5; Montt, *State Liability in Investment Treaty Arbitration*, pp. 351–3; Kingsbury and Schill, 'Investor-State Arbitration as Governance', p. 39.

[2] On differing views concerning the role of the state in relation to legitimate interferences with private property in the context of the ECHR, see Çoban, *Protection of Property Rights*, pp. 107–8.

[3] Weiner, 'Indirect Expropriation: The Need for a Taxonomy of "Legitimate" Regulatory Purposes' (2003) 5 *International Law FORUM du droit international* 166, 171–4.

[4] Dalhuisen and Guzman, 'Expropriatory and Non-Expropriatory Takings under International Investment Law' (2013) *Transnational Dispute Management*, pp. 5–7 (referring to government action that promotes public welfare such as the purposes of health, safety and

approach suggests scope for a great deal of value judgement on the part of a tribunal and support for a certain economic ideology that is not shared by all states. As a starting point, the broad discretion enjoyed by states in terms of the right to regulate at international law suggests that a low standard of scrutiny is appropriate in relation to this inquiry and that no particular area of policy should be excluded *ex ante*.[5]

The normative uncertainty inherent in determining whether a particular regulatory objective is legitimate means that its direct evaluation by an investment tribunal would transgress the role of national decision-makers, particularly given arbitrators' lack of embeddedness in the state (or, typically, the region).[6] Tribunal members may hold different opinions to states as to the desirability of enacting regulations or taking other actions in a particular policy area or as to the role of the state in the economy more generally, but engaging in substitutionary review in this respect risks unjustifiable incursions into regulatory autonomy. Taking a deferential approach to this stage of review would not give a host state free rein to adopt any measure and claim it was taken in the public interest so as to defeat a claim. Rather, this assessment seeks to identify measures taken with illegitimate purposes and does not function as a way of preordaining the measure selected.[7]

5.2.1   Strict approaches

The analysis undertaken in Chapter 4 revealed that investment tribunals have, in some cases, held that the state acted with an impermissible objective in circumstances where it was at least arguable that the authorities' objective was to promote public welfare. The *Tecmed* and *Metalclad* decisions illustrate this phenomenon in relation to fair and equitable treatment and expropriation, as do the decisions of the *CMS*, *Enron* and *Sempra* tribunals in relation to whether the Argentine crisis was sufficiently severe to engage the protection of the treaty exception in the

security as a subset of legitimate government action that will constitute a valid exercise of police powers).

5 For example, in relation to the scope of police powers under customary international law, Christie, 'What Constitutes a Taking of Property under International Law?' (1962) 38 *British Yearbook of International Law* 307, 332; UNCTAD, *Expropriation* (2012) 80.

6 See e.g. Maduro, *We the Court*, p. 59; Çoban, *Protection of Property Rights*, p. 199; Burke-White and von Staden, 'Investment Protection in Extraordinary Times', pp. 372–3.

7 Barak, *Proportionality*, p. 464.

Argentina-US BIT.[8] Another example is the *Vivendi* case, where the tribunal found that the authorities had acted improperly in issuing a public warning in relation to an issue of turbidity (cloudiness) in drinking water supplied by the claimant. Whether turbidity was potentially harmful is an issue on which expert opinion is divided, suggesting that a government is entitled to take a precautionary approach.[9] However, the tribunal found that Argentina had acted in bad faith and was motivated by animus towards the claimant due to its status as a foreign investor, summarily concluding that the authorities' actions were 'disproportionate'.[10]

Arbitrators have also generally been less willing to find that the state has acted with a legitimate objective where authorities have acted in response to strongly held public opinion.[11] As discussed in Chapter 4, arbitrators in *Metalclad* and *Tecmed* found that the authorities had acted for impermissible political purposes in responding to community opposition to waste disposal facilities.[12] In *Occidental (No 2)*, the tribunal hinted that public opposition to the claimant undermined the legitimacy of the state's actions in terminating the contract.[13] In *Gemplus*, the tribunal found that the government had acted in bad faith by cancelling the concession for a car registration scheme, noting that the authorities were motivated by public opposition to the increased costs levied on consumers by the new regulatory requirements.[14] However, these tribunals generally did not delve into the reasons why there was public opposition to a particular project or investment.

Decisions such as these demonstrate the crucial connection between the applicable standard of review and state liability. In substituting their views for the legitimacy or importance of the objective of the challenged measures (or the existence of a crisis situation), the approaches of these

---

[8] *Metalclad* v. *Mexico*, Award, paras. 90–8, 106; *Tecmed* v. *Mexico*, Award, paras. 123–49, 154–73; *CMS* v. *Argentina*, Award, paras. 322, 355; *Enron* v. *Argentina*, Award, paras. 306–7; *Sempra* v. *Argentina*, Award, paras. 348–9.

[9] *Vivendi* v. *Argentina*, Award, para. 7.4.18. See van Aaken, 'Defragmentation of Public International Law', pp. 483, 509; Van Harten, *Sovereign Choices and Sovereign Constraints*, p. 5.

[10] *Vivendi* v. *Argentina*, Award, paras. 7.4.18–7.4.19, 7.4.26.

[11] Cf. Cheyne, 'Deference and the Use of the Public Policy Exception' in Gruszczynski and Werner (eds.), *Deference in International Courts and Tribunals: Standard of Review and Margin of Appreciation* (2014) 44, observing that the CJEU 'has been reluctant to accept evidence of strong public opinion on its own' to justify derogations from free movement.

[12] *Metalclad* v. *Mexico*, paras. 86, 92, 109; *Tecmed* v. *Mexico*, paras. 126–7.

[13] *Occidental* v. *Ecuador (No 2)*, Award, paras. 181, 196, 442.

[14] *Gemplus* v. *Mexico*, Award, paras. 4–72–4–92. See also e.g. *Biwater* v. *Tanzania*, Award, para. 500.

tribunals are unsatisfactory from the perspective of the need for international investment law to provide sufficient policy space for host states.

5.2.2   Explicitly deferential approach or endorsement of state policy

Several other tribunals have referred to the right to regulate and have adopted a deferential approach,[15] or have held that a measure's objective would be unlawful only where there was no justification for the measure or where there was clear evidence that authorities had acted improperly.[16] The *Saluka* tribunal, in relation to the challenge to the decision to place the claimant's bank into administration, remarked that the state 'enjoyed a margin of discretion' with respect to its actions and that in the absence of clear and compelling evidence that it had acted improperly, the tribunal would 'accept the justification' offered by the government for its action and not second-guess the decision.[17] In *SD Myers*, the tribunal held that when determining whether a state was in breach of fair and equitable treatment, a tribunal did not have an 'open-ended mandate to second-guess government decision-making' even where, in its view, the government had 'proceeded on the basis of a misguided economic or sociological theory [or] placed too much emphasis on some social values over others'.[18] In his Separate Opinion rendered in this case, Arbitrator Schwartz cautioned that in some circumstances, determining whether the government had made such a mistake depended on subjective judgement rather than objective criteria.[19] Likewise, the *GAMI* tribunal held that, even if the government was 'misguided', that was 'a matter of policy and politics'.[20]

---

[15] As well as the cases discussed in this section, see e.g. *Parkerings* v. *Lithuania*, Award, para. 332; *Total* v. *Argentina*, Award, para. 312; *Teco* v. *Guatemala*, Award, paras. 490–3, 629–38 (but finding breach in relation to the government's actions in disregarding the views of an independent expert commission when determining an electricity tariff rate); *Yuri Bogdanov and Yulia Bogdanova* v. *Moldova*, Final Award, para. 186. See also *Bilcon* v. *Canada*, Award, para. 598: '[Each party] is free under NAFTA to adopt laws that are as demanding as they choose in exercising their sovereign authority.'

[16] For example, *Glamis* v. *US*, Award, paras. 803–5; *Paushok* v. *Mongolia*, Award, para. 299, cf. Van Harten, *Sovereign Choices and Sovereign Constraints*, pp. 15, 49, finding that in no case did a tribunal refer to deference on the basis of 'relative accountability' where the measure was a product of a legislature or was authorized by statute.

[17] *Saluka* v. *Czech Republic*, Award, paras. 272–3 (but see the tribunal's findings of breach in relation to state aid, discussed in Section 5.3).

[18] *SD Myers* v. *Canada*, Partial Award, para. 261. See also *Cargill* v. *Mexico*, para. 292.

[19] *SD Myers* v. *Canada*, Partial Award, Separate Opinion of Arbitrator Schwartz, para. 231.

[20] *GAMI* v. *Mexico*. Award, para. 114.

Other tribunals have referred to the right to regulate in a general sense, including in relation to the idea of proximity. As noted in Chapter 4, the *Continental* tribunal referred to ECtHR jurisprudence in relation to the idea that proximate decision-makers were better placed to determine what was in the state's interest 'because of their direct knowledge of their society and of its needs'.[21] The *Thunderbird* tribunal held that the state should be afforded a high degree of deference in relation to the regulation of 'conduct that it considers illegal', such as gambling, because such regulation reflected 'national views on public morals',[22] and the *Apotex* tribunal held that the *Thunderbird* tribunal's pronouncements 'must be no less true with respect to regulating drug imports to protect the public health of its citizens and residents'.[23] The *Apotex* tribunal also referred to 'the need for international tribunals to exercise caution in cases involving a state regulator's exercise of discretion, particularly in sensitive areas involving protection of public health'.[24] Tribunals have stressed that a deferential approach was appropriate in the context of the Argentine crisis, given the circumstances and the nature of the measures that were adopted.[25]

In a number of other cases, tribunals have, rather than referring to deference, explicitly affirmed the legitimacy of the state's objective. For example, the *Roussalis* tribunal held that food hygiene regulations had 'an important public safety purpose', and the *AES* tribunal held that the introduction of regulated electricity pricing to address excessive profits in the sector had 'a perfectly valid and rational policy objective'.[26] The *Electrabel* tribunal both referred to a margin of appreciation and endorsed the state's policy, holding that 'Hungary would enjoy a reasonable margin of appreciation' in terminating an electricity purchasing agreement with the claimant (which the European Commission had found was an unlawful form of state aid) and in reintroducing regulated electricity pricing, but concluded that 'Hungary requires no such margin in its defence to Electrabel's claim', because regulated electricity pricing 'remains an important measure available to State regulators in liberalized markets for

---

[21] *Continental* v. *Argentina*, Award, para. 181.
[22] *Thunderbird* v. *Mexico*, Award, para. 127. See also *Lemire* v. *Ukraine*, Jurisdiction and Liability, para. 505.
[23] *Apotex* v. *US*, Award, paras. 9.37–9.38.   [24] *Apotex* v. *US*, Award, para. 9.37.
[25] *Total* v. *Argentina*, Award, paras. 163, 165; *Continental* v. *Argentina*, Award, para. 181.
[26] *Roussalis* v. *Romania*, Award, para. 686; *AES* v. *Hungary*, Award, paras. 10.3.31–10.3.34. See also *Genin* v. *Estonia*, Award, paras. 352–3, 370; *EDF* v. *Romania*, Award, paras. 179, 293.

electricity'.[27] While taken at face value, this approach affirms the regulatory autonomy of host states, it might be regarded as potentially problematic insofar as it involves tribunals directly assessing the rationality and importance of the regulatory objectives pursued.

Tribunals have implicitly found a wide range of other objectives to be legitimate including protecting cultural heritage and preserving cultural identity,[28] ensuring access to drinking water and sewerage services,[29] protecting human health and the environment,[30] and maintaining currency stability and promoting the proper functioning of the financial system and financial entities.[31] In the NAFTA context, arbitrators have also given their imprimatur to objectives designed to assist the state's economy, such as removing the threat of countervailing duties and providing for new entrants to an industry,[32] and ensuring the economic strength of local industries.[33] These decisions include cases where the challenged measure was subsequently found to be unlawful due to it being insufficiently connected to the state's putative objective or for failing the least-restrictive means stage of review, indicating that arbitrators conceptually separated the question of the legitimacy of the regulatory objective from the question of the legality of the measure itself.

Despite the tendency of many tribunals to discount the state's reasons for its actions where it responded to community concerns relating to an

---

[27] *Electrabel* v. *Hungary*, Award, para. 8.35. The tribunal also held that Hungary was entitled to a 'modest margin of appreciation' in relation to its decision to challenge the Commission's decision (at para. 6.92). The tribunal found that EU law was applicable law and that the claimant was not protected under the Energy Charter Treaty from Hungary's implementation of the Commission decision (at para. 4.169), but nevertheless reviewed the merits of the claim.

[28] *Parkerings* v. *Lithuania*, Award, paras. 392, 396; *UPS* v. *Canada*, Award, paras. 146–9; *Lemire* v. *Ukraine*, Jurisdiction and Liability, para. 506.

[29] For example, *InterAgua* v. *Argentina*, Liability, para. 215; *AWG* v. *Argentina*, Liability, para. 235.

[30] *Methanex* v. *US*, Final Award, Part IV, Chapter D, para. 15; *Chemtura* v. *Canada*, Award, para. 266.

[31] *Fireman's Fund* v. *Mexico*, Award, para. 47.

[32] *Pope and Talbot* v. *Canada*, Merits, paras. 87, 93.

[33] *SD Myers* v. *Canada*, Partial Award, para. 255 (maintaining provision for domestic disposal of hazardous waste, although this objective was also supported by the Basel Convention); *GAMI* v. *Mexico*, Award, paras. 46, 52–6, 114 and *Archer* v. *Mexico*, Award, paras. 44–7, 55 (sugar industry); *UPS* v. *Canada*, Award, paras. 146, 149 (cultural industries). This approach may be contrasted with the CJEU's approach to mandatory requirements (permissible reasons for interfering with free movement that are not based on the treaty text), which does not permit economic objectives to justify derogating measures, although the approach of the CJEU may be explained by the context of positive integration.

investment,[34] other tribunals have viewed responding to such concerns as an ordinary and legitimate function of governance. For example, in *Electrabel* (discussed above), the tribunal referred to considerations of politics and democratic accountability in determining that the state had acted legitimately in responding to public concerns about excessive profits made by electricity generators.[35] In *AES* (also discussed above), the tribunal held that 'the fact that an issue becomes a political matter . . . does not mean that the existence of a rational policy is erased', and that 'it is normal and common that a public policy matter becomes a political issue'.[36] In *Parkerings*, the tribunal referred to public opposition to the investor's proposed project (construction of a car parking facility in an area that encroached on a site of cultural and historical significance) as an important and legitimate consideration in relation to the authorities' decision to award the tender to a competitor with a differently situated project.[37] These more recent decisions, as well as others where tribunals have not interfered with a government's attempt to take into account the interests of different constituencies, show encouraging signs that tribunals understand that it is not presumptively the case that responding to political pressure is an illegitimate motivation for government action.[38]

5.2.3   The relevance of international harmonization or consensus

Where the objective of a measure is to implement an international treaty or other instrument or reflects common practice, this will provide a strong indication to a tribunal that the measure's objective is non-discriminatory.[39] As discussed in Chapter 3, the CJEU and the ECtHR rely on the existence or otherwise of European consensus as a factor influencing the degree of scrutiny applied to the measure. In the WTO context, the Appellate Body has referred to 'common interests or values' reflected

---

[34] As well as the cases previously discussed (*Metalclad* and *Tecmed*), see the criticism of the majority's decision in *Bilcon v. Canada*, Dissenting Opinion of Professor Donald McRae, paras. 49–51.

[35] *Electrabel* v. *Hungary*, Award, para. 8.23.

[36] *AES* v. *Hungary*, Award, paras. 10.3.23, 10.3.24.

[37] *Parkerings* v. *Lithuania*, Award, paras. 392, 396.

[38] Bonnitcha, *Substantive Protection under Investment Treaties*, p. 45 (but note the Dissenting Opinion in *Bilcon*, discussed above).

[39] Reinisch, 'Expropriation', p. 434; Kingsbury and Schill, 'Investor-State Arbitration as Governance', p. 39; Moloo and Jacinto, 'Environmental and Health Regulation: Assessing Liability under Investment Treaties' (2011) 29 *Berkeley Journal of International Law* 101, 125, 156.

in a measure's objective as a factor influencing the standard of review with respect to necessity testing,[40] and one WTO tribunal has referred to the practice of other WTO members in determining the legitimacy of an objective not specified in the TBT Agreement,[41] but this factor does not appear to have specifically influenced the standard of review that subsequent WTO tribunals have adopted.

Investment tribunals have, on occasion, bolstered their findings that a measure has a legitimate objective by referring to the fact that it sought to implement international treaties or other instruments[42] including EU regulations[43] and NAFTA's side agreements.[44] In other cases, they have remarked that the state's general objective was common in other countries.[45] Investment tribunals do not, however, appear to have based the standard of review on the commonality of the objective pursued

[40] Appellate Body Report, *Korea-Beef*, para. 164.

[41] In *US-Certain Country of Origin Labelling (COOL) Requirements*, the panel remarked that the objective of providing consumers with country of origin information for products for sale 'is in keeping with the requirements of current social norms in a considerable part of the WTO membership' (at paras. 7.645–7.651).

[42] See *SD Myers* v. *Canada*, Partial Award, para. 255 (Basel Convention); *Parkerings* v. *Lithuania*, Award, para. 385 (Convention Concerning the Protection of the World Cultural and Natural Heritage); *UPS* v. *Canada*, Award, para. 118 (Universal Postal Convention and International Convention on the Simplification and Harmonization of Customs Procedures); *Pope and Talbot* v. *Canada*, Merits, para. 18 (Canada-US Softwood Lumber Agreement); *Chemtura* v. *Canada*, Award, para. 135 (Protocol on Persistent Organic Pollutants, Convention on Long-Range Transboundary Air Pollution on Persistent Organic Pollutants); *Glamis* v. *US*, Award, para. 83 (Convention Concerning the Protection of the World Cultural and Natural Heritage and UNESCO Recommendation Concerning the Preservation of Cultural Property Endangered by Public or Private Works). In one case, a tribunal referred to a treaty that neither party to the investment treaty had signed: *Chemtura* v. *Canada*, Award, para. 135 (Convention for the Protection of the Marine Environment of the North-East Atlantic).

[43] *Roussalis* v. *Romania*, Award, paras. 636–9, 688.

[44] *SD Myers* v. *Canada*, Partial Award, paras. 217, 218 and Separate Opinion of Arbitrator Schwartz paras. 109–12, 214 (North American Agreement on Labor Cooperation and North American Agreement on Environmental Cooperation). Article 104(1) NAFTA also states that in the event of any inconsistency between NAFTA and the specific trade obligations set out in the Basel Convention, the Montreal Protocol on Substances that Deplete the Ozone Layer and the Convention on International Trade in Endangered Species of Wild Fauna and Flora, the provisions of the other agreements will prevail.

[45] For example, *Feldman* v. *Mexico*, Merits, para. 115 (dealing with cigarette smuggling); *Roussalis* v. *Romania*, Award, para. 686 (food safety policies). However in *Sempra*, Argentina argued that its actions were justified due to its obligations under the American Convention on Human Rights, but the tribunal held that this was not relevant to whether Argentina's essential security interests were engaged – a point that is, at the very least, arguable: *Sempra* v. *Argentina*, Award, paras. 331–2.

by the measure, apart from using the existence of common practice to confirm the legitimacy of the objective or the *bona fides* of the measure itself. This is appropriate in the context of international investment law: adopting a stricter standard of review on the basis of the absence of international consensus or common practice suggests universality in policy priorities, and may have the effect of constraining governmental discretion to promulgate measures to deal with novel or local issues.[46] Unlike the other treaties discussed in this book that do stipulate legitimate objectives, it may be difficult to discern the values or objectives that are shared by the parties to most investment treaties. Moreover, some policy areas are not amenable to standards or guidance from international instruments.

5.2.4 Discriminatory objectives

Although it is generally appropriate that a tribunal apply a deferential standard of review to determining whether a state is pursuing a legitimate objective, deference is less relevant to determining whether the state is acting with a discriminatory motivation or in pursuit of another objective that may be prohibited by the treaty (or other applicable source of law).[47] Whether the state is acting with a discriminatory motive is generally a question that can be objectively determined on the basis of evidence (whether direct or, more frequently, circumstantial).[48] In *SD Myers*, for example, the record demonstrated that the government was acting with the primary objective of protectionism, meaning that there was no situation of normative uncertainty justifying deference on the basis of the desirability of regulatory autonomy and proximity.

Investment tribunals have, unsurprisingly, found that governmental objectives were illegitimate in cases of intentional discrimination.[49]

---

[46] See Regan, 'The Meaning of "Necessary"' (2007) 6 *World Trade Review* 352–3; McGrady, *Trade and Public Health* (2010) 147 (criticizing reliance by WTO tribunals on the common values of WTO members as relevant to the question of the importance of the measure's objective).

[47] See Mamolea, 'Good Faith Review' in Gruszczynski and Werner (eds.), *Deference in International Courts and Tribunals: Standard of Review and Margin of Appreciation* (2014) 74, 75.

[48] See Von Staden, 'Deference or No Deference, That Is the Question: Legitimacy and Standards of Review in Investor-State Arbitration' (2012) 2 *Investment Treaty News* 3, 4. See also Diebold, *Non-Discrimination in International Trade in Services* (2010) 89–92; Moloo and Jacinto, 'Standards of Review', p. 56.

[49] For example, *Corn Products* v. *Mexico*, Award, para. 137; *Archer* v. *Mexico*, Award, para. 142. In both cases, tribunals found that the government intended to discriminate against the US as retaliations for breaches of NAFTA.

However, it is arguable that at least some tribunals were overly deferential in assessing the legitimacy of the challenged measure's objective, resulting in the approbation of measures with discriminatory objectives. In *GAMI*, the tribunal found that Mexico's nationalization of certain loss-producing sugar mills was 'plausibly connected' to the non-discriminatory objective of ensuring the solvency of the local industry by remedying overproduction, but did not probe the relationship between the measure and its objective any further.[50] Despite the legitimacy of the objective in a general sense, more searching scrutiny may have uncovered protectionist intentions, given that the nationalizations took place in the context of the on-going dispute between the US and Mexico in relation to market access for Mexican sugar and the dumping of US-produced high-fructose corn syrup on the Mexican market.[51]

However, determining the objective of a challenged measure may be more complex in situations where the circumstances suggest that the government acted with more than one motive, or that motives for the challenged measure varied among officials. As the ICJ remarked in the *Whaling* case, a government often seeks to accomplish more than one objective when it pursues a particular policy.[52] According to the Court in that case, the existence of differing motivations among government officials – some of which were impermissible – would not preclude a finding that the measure had a legitimate aim, as long as the permissible objectives alone were sufficient to justify the design and implementation of the measure.[53] The *Methanex* tribunal also suggested that multiple motives were acceptable, remarking that evidence would be crucial to the determination of whether an improper purpose was the 'predominant purpose'.[54] It may be appropriate for a tribunal to afford a measure of deference on the basis of proximity considerations where more than one objective appears to have animated the primary decision-maker, given that it can be difficult to isolate the government's dominant purpose and that a tribunal may be unaware of the way in which the authorities have taken into account the concerns of various stakeholders in designing the measure.[55]

---

[50] *GAMI* v. *Mexico*, Partial Award, paras. 46, 52–6, 114.
[51] Kurtz, 'The Merits and Limits of Comparativism', pp. 275–6.
[52] *Whaling in the Antarctic (Australia* v. *Japan)*, para. 97.
[53] *Whaling in the Antarctic (Australia* v. *Japan)*, para. 97.
[54] *Methanex* v. *US*, Partial Award, para. 158.
[55] Kurtz, 'The Merits and Limits of Comparativism', pp. 274–7; Moloo and Jacinto, 'Environmental and Health Regulation', p. 156.

Investment tribunals have dealt with this issue in different ways. The *Archer* tribunal found that the challenged measure (an excise tax on soft drinks and syrups that used a sweetener other than cane sugar) was, at face value, taken for legitimate 'social and political reasons' relating to the sugar industry, and held that state intervention in the industry was permissible due to the importance of the sector to the Mexican economy.[56] However, the tribunal found, on the basis of statements by government ministers, that protectionism was the government's 'true motive and intent', and concluded that the measure was unlawful.[57] The *SD Myers* tribunal stated that it would accord Canada a 'high measure of deference' in relation to determining the legitimacy of its regulatory objective, even in the face of clear evidence of a discriminatory motivation, but its finding that Canada could have adopted less restrictive measures led it to conclude that protectionism was Canada's dominant purpose.[58] The *Tza Yap Shum* tribunal echoed the statement of the *SD Myers* tribunal, but cautioned that deference was 'not unlimited', noting that even if a measure was adopted with a legitimate objective, it might still be implemented in an arbitrary or discriminatory manner and therefore attract liability.[59]

Another factor that tribunals have taken into account in assessing whether the state's objective is discriminatory is whether the measure at issue is generally applicable legislation, rather than targeted towards a particular investor – the former being a situation that might attract greater deference on the basis of regulatory autonomy and proximity considerations, and the latter a situation that might attract stricter scrutiny as a possible indicator of discrimination.[60] It might also be argued that the case for deference on the basis of regulatory autonomy is weaker in cases involving challenges to specific measures if the nature of the measure means that it does not impact upon other actors, because in the absence

---

[56] *Archer* v. *Mexico*, Award, paras. 44–7, 55.

[57] *Archer* v. *Mexico*, Award, paras. 142, 149–50. Mexico had argued that that tax was levied as a countermeasure against the US, but the tribunal held, *inter alia*, that it had not been levied 'in order to induce compliance' in relation to a previous internationally wrongful act as required by Article 49 of the ILC Articles, but rather as a protective device (at paras. 132, 142).

[58] *SD Myers* v. *Canada*, Partial Award, para. 263. See also Separate Opinion of Arbitrator Schwartz, para. 233.

[59] *Señor Tza Yap Shum* v. *Peru*, Award, paras. 147–8.

[60] See *Total* v. *Argentina*, Award, paras. 163, 197, 312; *EDF* v. *Romania*, Award, para. 180; *Toto* v. *Lebanon*, Award, para. 244; *Continental* v. *Argentina*, Award, para. 232.

of polycentricity, there may be less normative uncertainty – but this will depend on the circumstances.[61]

5.3   Suitability

Courts and tribunals generally treat the suitability stage of proportionality analysis as relatively undemanding, requiring only that a government can demonstrate some connection between the measure and its objective or that the measure has some benefit with respect to its objective. Although most investment tribunals have not addressed the required degree of efficacy of or level of achievement of the challenged measures to satisfy this test, some have suggested that partial fulfilment of the objective would suffice: the *Continental* tribunal found that Argentina's emergency measures were 'sufficient in their design to address the crisis', and the *Glamis* tribunal held that a measure was suitable to achieve its objective, despite it not being 'curative of all of the ills' that it was intended to remedy.[62] More generally, affording deference in relation to the determination of suitability is a practical response to conditions of empirical uncertainty, where the institutional competence and expertise of governments in designing measures and predicting the consequences of interventions may be greater.[63]

5.3.1   Strict approaches

Some tribunals have performed suitability analysis relatively strictly, by second-guessing the connection between the measure and its objective or by assessing the effectiveness of the measure *ex post facto*. The *Saluka* tribunal found that a measure granting state aid to three banks in which the state retained a major shareholding interest (but not to the claimant) appeared to have the legitimate objectives of alleviating the bad debt problem suffered by those banks to ready them for privatization.[64] However, the tribunal held that none of the criteria relied on by the authorities

---

[61] See Van Harten, *Sovereign Choices and Sovereign Constraints*, p. 85. In any event, as Van Harten has observed, tribunals have in some cases characterized what would normally be understood to be general measures as specifically targeting investors in light of their impact of the particular claimant, such as where the former legal framework had been enacted to encourage foreign investment to the sector (at pp. 107–9): e.g. *Enron* v. *Argentina*, Award, para. 26; *LG&E* v. *Argentina*, Liability, para. 175.

[62] *Continental* v. *Argentina*, Award, paras. 196, 232; *Glamis* v. *US*, Award, paras. 625, 803–4.

[63] See e.g. Barak, *Proportionality*, pp. 308–9; Brady, *Proportionality and Deference*, pp. 20–1.

[64] *Saluka* v. *Czech Republic*, Award, para. 337.

to differentiate between the claimant and domestic banks in relation to eligibility for aid (such as their business strategies and liquidity positions) provided a 'rational justification' for the discrepant treatment.[65] The tribunal's approach suggests that measures adopted for apparently non-discriminatory purposes risk being held in breach where the tribunal does not agree with the rationality of the criteria used to differentiate between those in like circumstances, even in the context of empirical uncertainty.[66]

As discussed in Chapter 4, the *Total* tribunal held that a pricing mechanism adopted by Argentina was unsuitable and in breach of fair and equitable treatment, as it had resulted in the undesirable (but unanticipated) side effect of significantly increasing electricity consumption, resulting in supply failures and the need to import electricity while significantly increasing costs to the claimant.[67] Although this is a rather extreme example, the assessment of suitability (and necessity) *ex post facto* may be problematic for governments where a measure was adopted in a crisis situation or other conditions of significant empirical uncertainty. With the benefit of hindsight and expert evidence, a tribunal may readily identify problems with a measure or different courses of action that could have been taken, but this information might not have been available to authorities at the time the measure was adopted. The *Enron* annulment committee suggested that the *Enron* tribunal should have determined Argentina's liability 'on the basis of information reasonably available at the time that the measure was adopted'.[68] This issue was also identified by the *Metalpar* tribunal, which noted the difficulties inherent in determining whether Argentina's emergency measures represented the best solution to the crisis. The tribunal stated that 'to try to abstractly determine whether the actions carried out by Argentina during the crisis were optimal is a difficult or impossible task', especially where this assessment was determinative of liability.[69]

---

[65] *Saluka* v. *Czech Republic*, Award, paras. 344–7, 460.

[66] van Aaken and Kurtz, 'Prudence or Discrimination? Emergency Measures, the Global Financial Crisis and International Economic Law' (2009) 12 *Journal of International Economic Law* 859, 888–9.

[67] *Total* v. *Argentina*, Award, paras. 325–35.

[68] *Enron* v. *Argentina*, Annulment, para. 372, also suggesting that the relevant question for a tribunal was 'whether it was reasonably open to the State . . . to form the opinion that no relevant alternative was open' at the time of adopting the measure. See also *Laboratoires Servier* v. *Poland*, Final Award, where Poland argued that the validity of its regulatory decisions should be assessed in light of the material available to the regulator at the time of its decision (at para. 393).

[69] *Metalpar* v. *Argentina*, Award, paras. 198–9.

These comments are an acknowledgement that states acting in response to emergencies are operating in circumstances of significant empirical uncertainty. These cases suggest that in such situations, a lower standard of review is appropriate in order to give policy-makers the flexibility to respond quickly to the situation without the looming threat of liability. Arguably, arbitrators assessing suitability should take into account the amount of information that was available to primary decision-makers and the level of uncertainty that existed at the time that the measure was adopted, particularly where the situation is subsequently rectified and the breach does not persist.[70] This approach was adopted by several tribunals determining claims against Argentina in relation to the crisis. These tribunals determined that there was no breach of Argentina's obligations until the point in time at which the crisis had abated, at which point there was greater certainty about the extent of the crisis and the effectiveness of interventions.[71]

5.3.2   The desirability of affording a margin for error

More generally, tribunals have suggested that restraint may be appropriate where primary decision-makers turn out to have acted erroneously. The *SD Myers* tribunal observed that governments 'may appear to have made mistakes, to have misjudged the facts [or] . . . adopted solutions that are ultimately ineffective or counterproductive', but that this would not be the basis for a finding of breach of fair and equitable treatment.[72] In this vein, the *Eastern Sugar* tribunal held that a state would not be liable 'each time the law is flawed or not fully and properly implemented'; rather, 'some attempt to balance the interests of the various constituents within a country, some measure of inefficiency, a degree of trial and error, a modicum of human imperfection must be overstepped'.[73] The tribunal concluded that two measures reorganizing the Czech sugar production quota ostensibly to comply with European Union rules but that disadvantaged

---

[70] Which did not appear to be the case in *Total*.

[71] *National Grid* v. *Argentina*, Award, paras. 179–80; *LG&E* v. *Argentina*, Liability, para. 195; *EDF* v. *Argentina*, Award, paras. 1002, 1005. See also *SAUR* v. *Argentina*, Jurisdiction and Liability, paras. 504–5; Separate Opinions of Arbitrator Nikken in *InterAgua* v. *Argentina*, Liability, para. 39 and *AWG* v. *Argentina*, Liability, para. 39.

[72] *SD Myers* v. *Canada*, Partial Award, para. 261.

[73] *Eastern Sugar B.V.* v. *Czech Republic*, Partial Award, para. 272. Arbitrator Volterra criticized this approach in a Partial Dissenting Opinion, opining that it was imprecise and implied an overly 'low threshold' with respect to liability: *Eastern Sugar* v. *Czech Republic*, Partial Award, Partial Dissenting Opinion of Robert Volterra, paras. 9–11.

the claimant did not breach fair and equitable treatment even though the measures were 'rashly introduced on an insufficient legislative basis', 'ineffectively implemented' and contained 'illogical' elements.[74] However, the tribunal found that a third reorganization of the quota was in breach because the state could offer no justification for the fact that the claimant was heavily burdened by the measure when compared to other producers.[75] In *GAMI*, the tribunal held that although the government 'may have been clumsy in its analysis of the relevant criteria for the cut-off line between candidates and non-candidates for expropriation' and '[its] understanding of corporate finance may have been deficient', this ineffectiveness would not on its own be sufficient to establish liability.[76] The *Paushok* tribunal went so far as to hold that the fact that a measure that was 'a poor instrument to achieve [its] objectives', 'ill-conceived' or 'counter-productive' would not necessarily entail a breach of the state's obligations, noting that parliaments frequently amend legislation so as to bring statutory provisions into line with current circumstances or to correct errors made when the legislation was originally enacted.[77]

This approach is difficult to fit neatly within either the category of deference on the basis of the desirability of regulatory autonomy and proximity or relative institutional competence and expertise, but may encompass elements of both.[78] The decided cases in this area do not shed any clear light on how adjudicators conceptualized their role in relation to primary decision-makers when affording deference on this basis, but there are some suggestions that they afforded deference on the

---

[74] *Eastern Sugar* v. *Czech Republic*, Partial Award, paras. 265, 274, 284–5.

[75] *Eastern Sugar* v. *Czech Republic*, Partial Award, para. 333–7.

[76] *GAMI* v. *Mexico*, Award, para. 114 (but note criticisms of this decision, discussed below).

[77] *Paushok* v. *Mongolia*, Award, paras. 299, 316. See also *Bilcon* v. *Canada*, Award, para. 572: 'As lessons of experience are learned, as new policy ideas are advanced, as governments change in response to democratic choice, state authorities with the power to change law or policy must have reasonable freedom to proceed without being tasked with having breached the minimum standard under international law.'

[78] For example, Leonhardsen, 'Treaty Change, Arbitral Practice and the Search for a Balance: Standards of Review and the Margin of Appreciation in International Investment Law' in Gruszczynski and Werner (eds.), *Deference in International Courts and Tribunals: Standard of Review and Margin of Appreciation* (2014) 135, 147–8; Cohen-Eliya and Porat, *Proportionality and Constitutional Culture*, p. 114, noting that in US administrative law 'even in cases of clear mistakes, a court will respect the autonomy of the authorized institution and bow to its special expertise when it identifies areas that are within the scope of the institution's exclusive authority'. See also Van Harten, *Sovereign Choices and Sovereign Constraints*, p. 78, suggesting that decision-making in times of crisis should attract deference on the basis of democratic or political accountability.

basis of the greater institutional competence of governments vis-à-vis adjudicators.[79] Where a tribunal permits a margin within which it would tolerate errors made by authorities without making a finding of breach along with recognition of governments' generally greater institutional capacity, it arguably represents a sound reason for exhibiting deference. However, the *Paushok* tribunal's view that a measure would be permissible, even if 'counter-productive' might test the limits of this approach.

5.3.3 Reliance on the state's expertise

Other investment tribunals have afforded a measure of deference to the host state by explicitly relying on the authorities' own assessments as to the suitability of the measure, including in cases where the primary decision-maker's decision was based on specialist expertise.[80] When reviewing measures in this area, tribunals must determine two issues: first, whether the expert evidence appears to be from a properly qualified source and, second, whether there is a rational relationship between the evidence and the measure at issue. This distinction is illustrated by WTO case law in relation to the SPS Agreement. In *US-Continued Suspension*, the Appellate Body held that rather than substituting their own views as to the correctness of the risk assessment undertaken by a government, panels must verify that the scientific evidence on which the measure was based was from a respected and qualified source, that the evidence itself had 'the necessary scientific and methodological rigour to be considered reputable science' and that it was rationally related to the measure itself in the sense that the result of the risk assessment must 'sufficiently warrant' the measure.[81]

In *Methanex*, the tribunal did not itself attempt to review the scientific evidence relied on by the authorities in banning MTBE, having found that the expert report relied on by the authorities was credible and had

---

[79] See Andenas and Zleptnig, 'The Rule of Law and Proportionality in WTO Law' in Shan, Simons and Singh (eds.), *Redefining Sovereignty in International Economic Law* (2008) 171, 175 (arguing that in domestic legal systems, legislators are permitted a 'right to err' with respect to the suitability of a measure); Kulick, *Global Public Interest*, p. 187 (suggesting that a 'good faith misjudgement' of suitability should not result in liability on this basis).

[80] Cf. Van Harten, *Sovereign Choices and Sovereign Constraints*, p. 90, criticizing tribunals for not mentioning terms that might signal restraint in their review of specialized decision-making or decision-making involving science.

[81] See Appellate Body Report, *US-Continued Suspension*, paras. 590–1. See also Appellate Body Report, *EC-Hormones*, para. 193.

been peer-reviewed and subject to public consultation.[82] The tribunal held that claimant had not established that the scientific evidence relied on by the primary decision-maker was 'so faulty that the Tribunal may reasonably infer that the science merely provided a convenient excuse for the hidden regulation of methanol producers'.[83] The tribunal also stressed that the fact that some of the methodologies, analyses and conclusions in the scientific studies relied on by the authorities were the subject of disagreement among scientists and researchers did not undermine the rationality of the measure, which suggests that a government is entitled to take a precautionary approach in the face of uncertainty as to the degree of risk.[84] In *Chemtura*, the tribunal held that it would not be appropriate for it 'to judge the correctness or adequacy of the scientific results' or 'second-guess the correctness of the science-based decision-making of highly specialized national regulatory agencies'.[85] The tribunal did not make any explicit findings as to the rationality of the connection between the measures and the objective of protecting health and the environment, instead appearing to accept the suitability of the measure through its findings in relation to the expertise of the authorities, the existence of relevant international instruments and the practice of other states.[86]

Tribunals have also acknowledged their relative lack of expertise in other areas.[87] The *Glamis* tribunal, noting the superior qualifications of the primary decision-makers, cautioned that it was not its role to 'become archaeologists or ethnographers' in determining the appropriateness of administrative decisions.[88] The *Electrabel* tribunal acknowledged that regulating electricity tariffs was 'a difficult discretionary exercise involving many complex factors' and, as discussed above, held that regulators were

---

[82] *Methanex* v. *US*, Final Award, Part III, Chapter A, paras. 101–2.

[83] *Methanex* v. *US*, Final Award, Part IV, Chapter E, para. 19.

[84] *Methanex* v. *US*, Final Award, Part III, Chapter A, para. 101. This reasoning reflects the approaches of WTO tribunals under the SPS Agreement, which permits members to adopt measures based on 'divergent or minority' opinions as long as they are from qualified and respected sources: see Appellate Body Reports, *EC-Hormones*, para. 194; *Australia-Apples*, para. 364; *US-Continued Suspension*, para. 591.

[85] *Chemtura* v. *Canada*, Award, paras. 134, 153.

[86] *Chemtura* v. *Canada*, Award, paras. 135–6. Similarly, the *Laboratoires Servier* tribunal held that it 'must accord due deference to the decisions of specialized Polish administrators' (but ultimately concluded that the government's actions were discriminatory): *Laboratoires Servier* v. *Poland*, Final Award, para. 568.

[87] Cf. Van Harten, *Sovereign Choices and Sovereign Constraints*, p. 90, finding that arbitrators did not refer to their potential fallibility as a basis for restraint.

[88] *Glamis* v. *US*, Award, para. 779.

entitled to a margin of appreciation.[89] The *Apotex* tribunal remarked that it lacked the expertise, 'by inclination, qualification and training' to 'step into the shoes' of the regulator.[90] The tribunal noted that the regulation of cross-border trade in pharmaceutical products was 'inherently a complex and specialised process involving professional judgments as to public health'.[91] The tribunal also observed that other investment tribunals had emphasized 'the need for international tribunals to recognize the special roles and responsibilities of regulatory bodies charged with protecting public health and other important public interests'.[92]

The approaches of these tribunals – which recognized the expertise of scientists and primary decision-makers, evaluated the propriety of decision-making processes and relied on these issues in the determination of the suitability of the measures – reflect the relative strengths of authorities and give weight to their assessment of relevant matters. This approach limits the potential for the decision-making of investment tribunals to impede legitimate regulation and administrative decision-making through overly strict scrutiny.

5.3.4   *The relevance of common state practice*

Like their approach to whether a state's regulatory objective was legitimate, tribunals have relied on the fact that a particular type of measure was common among states as a means of confirming the legitimacy of the means by which a state had pursued its objective. For example, the *Noble Ventures* tribunal held that judicial reorganization proceedings for insolvency were 'provided for in all legal systems', the *ADF* tribunal held that domestic content and performance requirements in government procurement programmes were common practice in many states, and the *Link-Trading* tribunal held that the challenged tax measures 'were not dissimilar to the policies of many countries in the world'.[93]

---

[89] *Electrabel* v. *Hungary*, Award, para. 8.35.

[90] *Apotex* v. *US*, Award, para. 9.39 (in the context of determining whether the customary international law minimum standard of treatment required that the claimant be afforded certain procedural rights before an administrative decision was taken).

[91] *Apotex* v. *US*, Award, para. 9.48.   [92] *Apotex* v. *US*, Award, para. 9.37.

[93] *Noble Ventures* v. *Romania*, Award, paras. 178, 182; *ADF Group* v. *US*, Final Award, para. 188; *Link-Trading Joint Stock Company* v. *Moldova*, Final Award, para. 72. See also *Chemtura* v. *Canada*, Award, para. 135; (ban on pesticide); *Plama Consortium* v. *Bulgaria*, Award, 27 August 2008, para. 269 (tax policies); *Total* v. *Argentina*, Award, para. 214 (maintaining

It is arguable that the greater the degree of international harmonization or consensus with respect to the subject matter of the measure, the lesser the degree of normative or empirical uncertainty in relation to the appropriateness of the measure itself. Therefore, the argument for deference would be weaker where a state's actions in pursuit of a particular regulatory objective were greatly at odds with the actions of other states, as this might suggest that the government's stated objective is pretextual. However, divergence from the practice of other states in the area being regulated should not be decisive of whether the measure is rationally connected to the objective; there may be good reasons why the local context requires a different approach. In this vein, the *Genin* tribunal emphasized that although the actions of the authorities were 'contrary to generally accepted banking and regulatory practice', this was not enough to amount to a breach,[94] and the *Paushok* tribunal remarked that the fact that a windfall profit tax on gold 'went beyond the taxation levels in application at the time in most countries of the world' was not enough to establish a breach of fair and equitable treatment.[95]

5.3.5 Using the suitability stage to identify pretextual objectives

The suitability stage of proportionality analysis can also be used to determine whether a measure has an impermissible objective in light of the connection between the stated objective and the measure as designed and applied. In several investment cases, the insufficiency of the connection between the measure and the objective suggested that the state's ostensible objective was pretextual. In *Feldman*, although the authorities' stated objectives were adjudged to be legitimate (protecting intellectual property and discouraging smoking, smuggling and grey market sales of cigarettes), the tribunal found Mexico in breach of national treatment for not demonstrating a 'reasonable nexus' between those objectives and the authorities' actions in conducting an audit of the claimant's business and in refusing to register the claimant's company and rebate excise taxes.[96] In *ADC*, the tribunal held that Hungary had failed to substantiate its claim that the challenged measure (a governmental take-over of the operations

---

low energy prices to bolster other sectors of the economy); *Lemire* v. *Ukraine*, Jurisdiction and Liability, para. 506 (local content requirements for radio stations); *Mamidoil* v. *Albania*, Award, para. 787 (method of calculating taxes).

[94] *Genin* v. *Estonia*, Award, para. 364.   [95] *Paushok* v. *Mongolia*, Award, para. 303.

[96] *Feldman* v. *Mexico*, Merits, paras. 73, 78, 170, 182–7.

of Budapest airport, for which the claimant held a contract) was taken with the purpose of harmonizing domestic regulations with EU law, concluding that the measure was discriminatory and amounted to an unlawful expropriation.[97] The *Bilcon* tribunal held that Canada had breached national treatment by not establishing a rational nexus between the less favourable treatment provided to the claimant compared to like Canadian investors with respect to regulatory approval for proposed projects with environmental impacts.[98] Arguably, the *GAMI* tribunal (discussed above) could have used suitability testing in this way, as it appeared that the government's objective was legitimate in a general sense, but the surrounding circumstances strongly suggested that the challenged measure was not properly connected to this objective. The challenge for tribunals in this context is to approach the standard of review in such a way as to be able to identify measures with discriminatory or other impermissible objectives, but not to apply overly rigorous scrutiny so as to require a host state to prove a high degree of effectiveness or achievement of the objective in circumstances where this might not be possible.

5.4   Necessity

Necessity testing, as Chapters 2 and 3 have discussed, is a potentially intrusive method because it permits adjudicators to substitute their view with respect to the choice of measure. The necessity test can be applied strictly, such as by requiring that an alternative measure be adopted even where it does not achieve the objective as effectively, or by not considering the feasibility and likely effectiveness of potential alternative measures. Such an approach risks significant incursions into regulatory autonomy.

There are, however, several ways in which adjudicators can soften the necessity test in a way that acknowledges the empirical uncertainties inherent in policy-making. Such an approach has several advantages over a strict necessity test. Only measures that are practically available and do not unduly burden a government will be considered to be viable alternatives. The requirement that measures be equally as effective at achieving the objective precludes a court or tribunal from substituting its view with respect to the appropriate level of benefit that a measure should achieve

---

[97] *ADC Affiliate Limited and ADC & ADMC Management Limited* v. *Hungary*, Award, paras. 429–33, 443.
[98] *Bilcon* v *Canada*, Award, para. 274.

in relation to its objective. Permitting a state to rely on its institutional competence and any relevant expertise lessens the risk that a tribunal will hold that a measure is an available alternative in circumstances where the measure is infeasible, would be overly burdensome to the state, or would unjustifiably impact on the rights and interests of others.

5.4.1 Strict approaches

Strict approaches to necessity testing now appear to be less prevalent than the more flexible approaches employed by investment tribunals that are discussed below. However, as discussed in detail in Chapter 4, earlier tribunals took strict approaches to necessity testing in relation to the exception clause in the Argentina-US BIT. The *CMS*, *Enron* and *Sempra* tribunals, conflating the nexus requirement of Article XI of the Argentina-US BIT with the substance of the customary plea of necessity, proposed alternative measures on their own motion or accepted the submissions of the claimants, but did not analyze whether those alternatives would have been effective in dealing with the crisis and feasible in the circumstances.[99] The *AWG* and *InterAgua* tribunals also adopted a strict approach in their review of Argentine provincial measures.[100] These decisions are open to the criticism that arbitrators did not give due consideration to whether, in the circumstances of the crisis, the authorities possessed the capacity to devise and implement alternative measures. These arbitrators did not recognize their own institutional weaknesses in evaluating regulatory policy.

5.4.2 Reliance on the state's institutional competence or expertise

Other tribunals have explicitly referred to the desirability of a deferential approach to least-restrictive means analysis, particularly in the context of the Argentine crisis. As discussed in Chapter 4, the *Continental* tribunal referred to the undesirability of substituting its judgment in relation to the necessity of the emergency measures due to the significant empirical uncertainty existing at the time the measures were enacted and the urgency of the measures in view of the potentially grave consequences of not

---

[99] *CMS* v. *Argentina*, Award, para. 323; *Sempra* v. *Argentina*, Award, paras. 339, 351; *Enron* v. *Argentina*, Award, paras. 300, 309.

[100] *InterAgua* v. *Argentina*, Liability, para. 215; *AWG* v. *Argentina*, Liability, para. 235.

intervening in the economy.[101] The *LG&E* tribunal also appeared to take these matters into account in relation to its determination of the necessity of the emergency measures.[102]

Tribunals and tribunal members have, in some cases, implied that the necessity test functions as a margin within which a government may select a reasonable alternative. The *LG&E* tribunal stated that although there were potentially 'several responses' at Argentina's disposal to deal with the crisis, the measures adopted were 'legitimate' and 'reasonable' in the circumstances.[103] This approach is also apparent in other cases unrelated to the Argentine crisis. The *Pope and Talbot* tribunal held that it would not substitute its judgment as to the necessity of one of the challenged measures unless the impact of the measure was especially severe or appeared to be unreasonable in light of potential alternatives.[104] The Separate Opinions rendered by Arbitrator Nikken in the *AWG* and *InterAgua* cases stressed that tribunals should adopt a deferential approach, provided that the measures fell 'within the range of decisions that any reasonable government could have adopted under the same circumstances'.[105] In *Saluka*, the tribunal remarked that the obligation of fair and equitable treatment 'does not set out totally subjective standards which would allow the Tribunal to substitute . . . its judgment on the choice of solutions for the Czech Republic's', which might indicate a preference for a deferential approach to necessity testing – although this point was not further developed in the decision and, as noted above, the tribunal adopted a strict approach to suitability in relation to measures it reviewed for fair and equitable treatment.[106] These approaches might, however, like ECtHR case law in this area, be criticized for not articulating a principled basis for when a measure will or will not be lawful, permitting a tribunal to set the boundaries of legality according to its own preferences.

Moreover, while deference is appropriate in circumstances of empirical uncertainty, an overly deferential approach can mean that instances of protectionism are not uncovered. In this respect, the *UPS* award is

---

[101] *Continental* v. *Argentina*, Award, para. 199. See also *Enron* v. *Argentina*, Annulment, para. 372 (in relation to the customary plea).

[102] *LG&E* v. *Argentina*, Liability, paras. 241–2.

[103] *LG&E* v. *Argentina*, Liability, para. 239. See Sloane, 'On the Use and Abuse of Necessity', p. 501; Kurtz, 'Adjudging the Exceptional', pp. 355–6.

[104] *Pope and Talbot* v. *Canada*, Merits, para. 155.

[105] *InterAgua* v. *Argentina*, Liability, Separate Opinion of Arbitrator Nikken, paras. 37, 42; *AWG* v. *Argentina*, Liability, Separate Opinion of Arbitrator Nikken, paras. 37, 42.

[106] *Saluka* v. *Czech Republic*, Award, para. 284.

amenable to the criticism that the tribunal accepted the state's justification for its chosen measure, granting Canada Post the exclusive right to receive subsidies for delivering Canadian periodicals, was 'the most efficient' means of achieving its objective, without proper scrutiny of the alternative measure proposed by the claimant.[107]

5.4.3 Procedural approach to necessity

As noted in Chapter 3, courts and tribunals can manifest deference when undertaking proportionality analysis by permitting a government to demonstrate that it had considered alternative measures in decision-making. The basis for such in approach is that well-functioning governmental processes are less likely to lead to decisions being made that disproportionately affect protected rights and interests. Under this approach, adjudicators will not engage in substantive review unless this procedural burden has not been discharged or the choice of measures appears to be arbitrary or irrational in light of available alternatives, but will engage in more robust scrutiny of the decision-making processes undertaken by primary decision-makers.[108]

There are several hints of this approach in the decided investment cases. The *Glamis* tribunal took into account that pursuant to domestic legislation, the authorities had considered alternatives to the impugned regulations and alternative courses of action in administrative decision-making.[109] In *Methanex* and *Chemtura*, tribunals briefly referred to alternative measures considered by the primary decision-makers, but it is not clear whether these tribunals regarded the consideration of alternatives as mandatory for compliance with fair and equitable treatment and in any event in *Chemtura*, international practice strongly supported the ban that the authorities had placed on the substance.[110]

---

[107] See *UPS* v. *Canada*, Award, paras. 165, 173–81 and Separate Statement of Arbitrator Cass, paras. 115, 119. See also the criticism levelled at the majority decision in Kurtz, 'The Merits and Limits of Comparativism', p. 276.

[108] Schueler, 'Proportionality Principle in Environmental Law' (2008) 35 *Legal Issues of Economic Integration* 237–8; Gerards, 'How to Improve the Necessity Test', pp. 487–8.

[109] See *Glamis* v. *US*, Award, paras. 63–4, 70, 99–101, 109–10, 133–51, 181.

[110] *Methanex* v. *US*, Final Award, Part III, Chapter A, paras. 13, 15; *Chemtura* v. *Canada*, Award, paras. 181–2, 192. See also *Bilcon* v. *Canada*, Award, para. 452: the tribunal held that the authorities' failure to consider potential environmental mitigation measures for the investors' project (in a sense, alternative measures) amounted to a breach of fair and equitable treatment.

It is arguable that the adoption by a tribunal of a procedural approach to necessity testing (or proportionality *stricto sensu* analysis) should not oblige a government to perform a judicial form of proportionality analysis as part of the design of a measure or prior to its implementation. In other words, proportionality analysis – as a method of review used by adjudicators to structure decision-making in the determination of liability – should not, as a consequence, function as a procedural precondition to the legality of government action.[111] The relevant issue for determination by a tribunal is whether the state has violated its obligations towards the claimant through an impermissible motive or disproportionately targeted measure, rather than whether the challenged measure was the product of a particular decision-making process. Focusing only on decision-making processes at the expense of substantive outcomes could lead to problematic results, such as finding a measure is in breach where it was based on sound evidence and turned out to be the least-restrictive measure available, but where the primary decision-maker had not considered alternatives before making the relevant decision.[112] Arguably, therefore, failure to consider alternatives in the decision-making process should not result in a finding of breach, provided that the measure itself is the least-restrictive measure reasonably available, except perhaps in specific cases where the prior analysis of the availability of alternative measures could be regarded as a mandatory relevant consideration under the domestic law in question. However, it seems reasonable that a tribunal might adopt a more deferential approach if the decision-maker had considered alternatives in arriving at the decision to pursue a particular measure or otherwise conscientiously had paid attention to investors' interests in its decision-making.[113]

---

[111] See, in relation to this issue in UK public law, *R (Begum)* v. *Governors of Denbigh High School* (House of Lords), paras. 31, 68, c.f. *R (SB)* v. *Governors of Denbigh High School* (Court of Appeal), para. 75. See also Poole, 'Of Headscarves and Heresies: The *Denbigh High School* Case and Public Authority Decision-Making Under the Human Rights Act' (2005) *Public Law* 685, 689–91; Taggart, 'Proportionality, Deference, *Wednesbury*', p. 460.

[112] But see Hickman, *Public Law after the Human Rights Act* (2010) 240, arguing that this approach could lead to uncertainty because where a government can justify its conduct *ex post facto*, it will be difficult for claimants to predict their chances of success; Mead, 'Outcomes Aren't All: Defending Process-Based Review of Public Authority Decisions under the Human Rights Act' (2012) *Public Law* 61, 81, arguing that this approach is undesirable as it does not provide any incentive for governments to improve their decision-making processes in such cases.

[113] See Hickman, *Public Law after the Human Rights Act*, p. 149; Gerards, 'How to Improve the Necessity Test', p. 487; *Belfast City Council v. Miss Behavin' Ltd*, paras. 37, 91. See also

5.4.4   The burden of proof

In international law, the burden of proof is understood to rest with the party invoking the provision.[114] However, international courts and tribunals rarely refer expressly to the burden of proof or the applicable standard of proof.[115] In relation to least-restrictive means analysis, several themes emerge from comparative case law. Courts and tribunals typically do not require governments to prove that there were no less restrictive alternative measures available to achieve their objective; this would involve proof of a negative, which is notoriously difficult.[116] Rather, a responding state is required to rebut the claimant's assertions as to the availability of alternatives.[117]

For example, under the WTO agreements' general exceptions, the responding government is required to establish that the challenged measure complies with the requirements of the exception, including the necessity of the measure.[118] A complaining government need only point to a potential alternative measure, at which point the burden shifts to the responding government to establish that the alternative measure was

---

Hunt, 'Sovereignty's Blight', p. 354; Kavanagh, 'Reasoning about Proportionality under the Human Rights Act 1998: Outcomes, Substance and Process' (2014) 130 *Law Quarterly Review* 235, 239–40, 242; Kavanagh, 'Proportionality and Parliamentary Debates', pp. 444–5, 470. See also the ECtHR case of *Animal Defenders International* v. *UK*, paras. 114–17, in which the ECtHR attached significant weight to the government's consideration of the proportionality of the measure.

[114] See e.g. *Military and Paramilitary Activities in and Against Nicaragua (Nicaragua* v. *US)*, Jurisdiction and Admissibility, para. 101; *Pulp Mills on the River Uruguay (Argentina* v. *Uruguay)*, para. 162; Foster, 'Burden of Proof in International Courts and Tribunals' (2010) 29 *Australian Yearbook of International Law* 27, 31, 40. Neither the ICSID Convention nor the ICSID Rules of Procedure for Arbitration Proceedings (2006) contain provisions with respect to the burden of proof. However, Rule 27.1 UNCITRAL Arbitration Rules (2010) and Article 24.1 Permanent Court of Arbitration Rules (2012) provide that each party has the burden of proving the facts relied on to support its claim or defence.

[115] Foster, 'Burden of Proof', pp. 27–8.

[116] See Regan, 'The Meaning of "Necessary"', p. 364; Barak, *Proportionality*, p. 449; Rivers, 'The Presumption of Proportionality' (2014) 77 *Modern Law Review* 409, 425; Jans, 'Proportionality Revisited', pp. 259–60; but see Foster, 'Burden of Proof', p. 49, noting that in matters before international courts and tribunals, '[the] burden of proof is often allocated regardless of the question of which party may have to prove a negative proposition'.

[117] See e.g. Cases C-131/93 *Commission* v. *Germany (Crayfish)*, paras. 24–6; C-62/90; *Commission* v. *Germany (Medicines)*, paras. 24–5; C-110/05, *Commission* v. *Italy (Trailers)*, paras. 65–7; Appellate Body Report, *US-Gambling*, para. 109.

[118] Appellate Body Report, *Korea-Beef*, para. 157.

not reasonably available.[119] Similarly, in the context of derogations and mandatory requirements, the CJEU appears to require that the applicant point to an alternative measure or measures that it considers the member state could have adopted, at which point the member state must prove that the alternative measures were ineffective or otherwise unavailable.[120]

The burden of proof operates differently where the necessity test forms part of a positive obligation rather than an exception. Under the SPS and TBT agreements, a complainant must make a *prima facie* case that the measure is more trade-restrictive than necessary in light of alternative measures before the burden shifts to the respondent.[121] This is a higher burden than that placed on the complaining government under the general exceptions. The ICJ adopted a similar approach in *Navigational and Related Rights*, where Costa Rica was required to establish that Nicaragua's regulations constituted an unreasonable restriction on its freedom of navigation. Costa Rica argued that Nicaragua could have pursued alternative measures rather than restricting night-time navigation on the San Juan river such as 'requiring boats travelling at night to have lights and to have dangerous places marked by lights'.[122] However, the Court held that Costa Rica had not discharged its burden of establishing the practicality of the alternative measures, including their cost and likely effectiveness.[123] The ICJ also took this approach in the *Pulp Mills* case. In that case, the Court held that Uruguay was obliged to conduct an environmental impact assessment prior to the construction of pulp mills on the River Uruguay, which was to include, as a minimum, a description of practical alternatives to the proposed project.[124] The Court found that Uruguay had considered four other possible sites and found that they were unsuitable,

---

[119] Appellate Body Reports, *US-Gambling*, paras. 308–10; *China-Publications*, paras. 319, 328.

[120] See Jans, 'Proportionality Revisited', pp. 259–60; Ortino, *Basic Legal Instruments*, p. 410; Sauter, 'Proportionality in EU Law: A Balancing Act?' (2013) 15 *Cambridge Yearbook of European Legal Studies* 439, 460.

[121] Appellate Body Reports, *EC-Hormones*, paras. 97–109; *Japan-Measures Affecting the Importation of Apples*, paras. 152–3; *US-Tuna II*, paras. 321–3. See Mitchell and Henckels, 'Variations on a Theme', pp. 140–2. A *prima facie* case is 'one which, in the absence of effective refutation by the defending party, requires a panel, as a matter of law, to rule in favour of the complaining party presenting the *prima facie* case': Appellate Body Report, *EC-Hormones*, para. 104. See, discussing the concept further, Grando, *Evidence, Proof and Fact-finding in WTO Dispute Settlement* (2010) 105–49.

[122] *Navigational and Related Rights (Nicaragua v. Costa Rica)*, para. 128.

[123] *Navigational and Related Rights (Nicaragua v. Costa Rica)*, para. 128.

[124] *Pulp Mills on the River Uruguay (Argentina v. Uruguay)*, paras. 204, 205, 210.

and concluded overall that Argentina had failed to establish that Uruguay had not acted with the requisite degree of due diligence in conducting the assessment.[125]

Investment tribunals have not developed a consistent approach to the burden of proof with respect to necessity testing.[126] In several of the Argentine cases, tribunals referred to alternative measures proposed by the claimants' expert witnesses in the context of both fair and equitable treatment and the exception clause, but did not discuss the relevance for the burden of proof of whether the determination of necessity was being made in terms of a positive obligation or treaty exception.[127] The *Continental* annulment committee, however, appeared to suggest that once the claimant had identified alternative measures that 'could have been adopted', the burden would shift to Argentina to demonstrate that those measures were not available, suggesting an approach similar to that taken by WTO tribunals under the general exceptions.[128] More recently, the *Laboratoires Servier* tribunal held that if the claimant could produce sufficient evidence to establish that the measures were inconsistent with a legitimate exercise of police powers, the burden would shift to Poland to rebut it.[129] If Poland could point to evidence that it had acted with a legitimate objective, it would, according to the tribunal, be 'unreasonable to demand that Poland "prove the negative" in the sense of demonstrating... the lack of disproportionateness of the measures taken'.[130]

In the context of positive obligations such as fair and equitable treatment and the prohibition on uncompensated expropriations, an approach to the burden of proof such as that taken by the *Laboratoires Servier* tribunal and by WTO tribunals in SPS and TBT cases would require a claimant to establish a *prima facie* case that another measure was

---

[125] *Pulp Mills on the River Uruguay (Argentina v. Uruguay)*, paras. 210, 265. However, Judge *ad hoc* Vinuesa questioned this analysis, arguing that the evaluation of alternative sites was overly brief and had been completed after Argentina first raised its objections: Dissenting Opinion of Judge *ad hoc* Vinuesa, paras. 54–6.

[126] Mitchell and Henckels, 'Variations on a Theme', pp. 156–7.

[127] *Sempra v. Argentina*, Award, paras. 339, 350; *Enron v. Argentina*, Award, paras. 300, 308; *InterAgua v. Argentina*, Liability, para. 215; *AWG v. Argentina*, Liability, para. 235. See Mitchell and Henckels, 'Variations on a Theme', p. 157.

[128] *Continental v. Argentina*, Annulment, para. 139. See also *Total v. Argentina*, Award, para. 223: in relation to the customary plea, the tribunal stated that Argentina had the burden of persuading the tribunal that there were no reasonable alternatives measures available to it, which required Argentina to establish that its measures were *prima facie* necessary and rebut the investor's argument that there were alternative measures available.

[129] *Laboratoires Servier v. Poland*, Final Award, para. 584.

[130] *Laboratoires Servier v. Poland*, Final Award, para. 583.

available before the burden shifted to the host state, rather than simply pointing to alternatives.[131] Arguably, there is no reason why most investors should not be able to marshal expert evidence to assist them to discharge this burden; several of the Argentine decisions refer extensively to the evidence of economic experts retained by the claimants in the determination of the necessity of the emergency measures.[132] An argument can be made, however, that this approach might disadvantage certain smaller investors vis-à-vis states, who may have certain evidence available that is not available to the claimant.[133] This is a point of difference compared to the context of inter-state dispute settlement, where states can rely on their experience in regulatory policy-making in proposing alternative measures.

5.4.5   The desirability of least-restrictive means analysis in investor-state arbitration

5.4.5.1   Deleterious effects on regulatory autonomy can be mitigated through the standard of review

A necessity test imposes greater restrictions on regulatory autonomy than a suitability test, because it narrows the pool of potential measures available to a state to achieve its objective. Some investment arbitrators have opined that necessity testing is undesirable in the context of investor-state arbitration – but, in doing so, appear to have viewed necessity testing in its strict sense, rather than the more flexible approach developed by other courts and tribunals. In *UPS*, Arbitrator Cass opined that necessity testing would place undue power in investment tribunals to 'evaluate the legitimacy of government objectives and efficacy of governmentally chosen means', appearing to hold the view that least-restrictive means analysis would permit a tribunal to hold that there was an alternative measure available even where it did not achieve the regulatory objective to the same degree.[134] In *AWG* and *InterAgua*, Arbitrator Nikken rejected

---

[131] Mitchell and Henckels, 'Variations on a Theme', pp. 157–8.

[132] Mitchell and Henckels, 'Variations on a Theme', pp. 157–8.

[133] But see Kurtz, 'Use and Abuse of WTO Law', p. 758, arguing that consideration of the allocation of the burden of proof should bear in mind that in many cases, relevant parts of the factual record will be held solely by the state. More broadly, commentators have argued that the allocation of the burden of proof should depend in part on which party has greater resources to prove the existence of certain facts, e.g. Grando, *Evidence, Proof and Fact-Finding*, pp. 196, 330–1, 361–2.

[134] *UPS* v. *Canada*, Award, Separate Statement of Arbitrator Cass paras. 113, 117, 119–25.

a least-restrictive means approach on the basis that it would entail a tribunal inappropriately engaging in substitutionary review – again, perhaps not appreciating the way in which adjudicators can soften the application of the necessity test.[135]

Commentators have also argued against investment tribunals using a necessity test in the determination of state liability. Montt argues that least-restrictive means analysis blurs the distinction between policy-making and adjudication, and that tribunals should instead determine whether the measure's objective was *bona fide*, the measure was evidence-based, and the authorities had followed proper decision-making processes.[136] This approach – which might be described as a form of suitability testing with particular regard paid to the government's decision-making processes – has merit, but as argued above, arbitrators should focus on substance rather than procedure, and as will be argued below, testing only for suitability may not offer sufficient protection to investors. Bonnitcha argues that investment tribunals should use a suitability test (which he terms a 'margin of appreciation') to determine liability in indirect expropriation and fair and equitable treatment claims. He contends that the constraints placed by least-restrictive means testing on the range of measures lawfully available to achieve a particular regulatory objective would have a chilling effect on socially desirable regulation.[137] However, Bonnitcha acknowledges that arbitrators' application of an institutionally sensitive approach to the standard of review could moderate any such effects.[138]

5.4.5.2 The suitability test may provide insufficient protection to investors and is ill-suited to the discrimination inquiry

It is arguable that using a suitability test to determine liability may not grant sufficient protection to investors in all circumstances. Leonhardsen,

---

[135] *InterAgua* v. *Argentina*, Liability, Separate Opinion of Arbitrator Nikken, paras. 37, 42; *AWG* v. *Argentina*, Liability, Separate Opinion of Arbitrator Nikken, paras. 37, 42.

[136] Montt, *State Liability in Investment Treaty Arbitration*, p. 354. Somewhat confusingly, Montt also appears to advocate that arbitrators employ a proportionality *stricto sensu* test in determining liability in regulatory disputes, but does not acknowledge the concerns that this technique creates (at pp. 355–8).

[137] Bonnitcha, *Substantive Protection under Investment Treaties*, pp. 304–5, 307–8, also arguing that a requirement of proportionality 'confers protections on foreign investors that go beyond their entitlements under the domestic law of many host states'. This is an issue worthy of further comparative research.

[138] Bonnitcha, *Substantive Protection under Investment Treaties*, pp. 307–8.

for example, argues that fairness (in the context of fair and equitable treatment) requires that a government adopt a measure that impacts on the investor as little as reasonably possible in light of available alternatives.[139] Moreover, a suitability test may not encourage efficient regulation where other measures are available that would achieve the state's objective yet impact to a lesser degree on the investor's interests. It has been argued that the necessity test expresses the idea of Pareto optimality: no other distribution of costs and benefits could make at least one person better off without making anyone else worse off, meaning that a measure is Pareto optimal (and the least restrictive alternative) when no further Pareto improvements can be made.[140] But, as has been emphasized throughout this book, it is important that necessity testing be applied in a way that does not undermine a state's ability to determine the appropriate level of protection or achievement of the regulatory objective. Tribunals can also afford a measure of deference in situations of empirical uncertainty on the basis of governments' greater institutional competence and expertise in relation to designing and evaluating policy options, where this competence or expertise is relevant to the measure at issue.

Another potential problem with the suitability test relates to the extent to which it can delineate discriminatory from non-discriminatory measures. This issue arises in part due to the contested purpose of the non-discrimination obligations in international investment law. Whether the purpose of these obligations is to prohibit only deliberately discriminatory measures or whether their purpose is also to prohibit measures that inadvertently cause detriment to foreign investors through the drawing of distinctions between them is, as noted in Chapter 4, an issue that remains unresolved in the decided cases and academic commentary.[141]

There is substantial incoherence in the decided national treatment cases. Some tribunals have held that the purpose of the obligation is to

---

[139] See Leonhardsen, 'Looking for Legitimacy: Exploring Proportionality Analysis in Investment Treaty Arbitration' (2011) *Journal of International Dispute Settlement* 1, 40. See also e.g. Sykes, *Product Standards for Internationally Integrated Goods Markets* (1995) 118: '[I]f a given objective can be expressed in a variety of ways, the trading community benefits in the aggregate when the least-cost way is selected.'

[140] Alexy, *A Theory of Constitutional Rights*, pp. 398–9; Rivers, 'Proportionality and Variable Intensity of Review', p. 198; Alexy, 'Balancing, Constitutional Review, and Representation' (2005) 3 *International Journal of Constitutional Law* 572, 573. Brems and Lavrysen. '"A Sledgehammer to Crack a Nut"', p. 142.

[141] A measure can be intentionally discriminatory whether it is an instance of *de jure* or *de facto* discrimination.

proscribe only deliberately discriminatory treatment of foreign investors and that intent must be proven.[142] Others have emphasized that, although the purpose of the obligation is to prohibit intentional discrimination, discriminatory intent need not be proven for practical reasons.[143] Still others have taken the view that a discriminatory intention is not essential and that the obligation extends to cover measures that inadvertently discriminate.[144] In relation to the non-discrimination element of fair and equitable treatment, the decided cases generally suggest that the objective is to prohibit treatment based on animus towards the investor based on their foreignness or other characteristics such as race, ethnicity or religion.[145] The situation in relation to clauses prohibiting discriminatory measures is less clear, with approximately equal numbers of tribunals holding that a discriminatory intention is and is not required.[146]

An argument can be made that if an obligation of non-discrimination (such as national treatment) prohibits only deliberate discrimination, it should suffice for a state to demonstrate that the challenged measure is

---

[142] *SD Myers* v. *Canada*, Partial Award, para. 254; *Methanex* v. *US*, Final Award, Part IV, Chapter B, para. 12 (but see Part IV, Chapter B, para. 1, where the tribunal appeared to suggest that 'malign intent' was not a precondition of breach); *UPS* v. *Canada*, Award, para. 177; *The Loewen Group and Raymond L. Loewen* v. *US*, Award, para. 139; *Total* v. *Argentina*, Award, para. 213.

[143] *Feldman* v. *Mexico*, Merits, paras. 181–3; *Pope and Talbot* v. *Canada*, Merits, paras. 78–9; *Thunderbird* v. *Mexico*, Award, para. 177; *ADF* v. *US*, Final Award, para. 157; *Bayindir* v. *Pakistan*, Award, para. 390; *Bilcon* v. *Canada*, para. 719.

[144] *Corn Products* v. *Mexico*, Award, para. 138; *Occidental* v. *Ecuador (No 1)*, Award, para. 177; *Consortium RFCC* v. *Morocco*, Award, para. 74. See also *Cargill* v. *Mexico*, Award, paras. 219–20 (measure intended to discriminate, but the tribunal suggested that this was not a necessary prerequisite for a finding of less favourable treatment).

[145] *Waste Management* v. *Mexico*, Award, para. 115; *Glamis* v. *US*, Award, paras. 542, 828; *Lemire* v. *Ukraine*, Jurisdiction and Liability, paras. 261, 283; *Loewen* v. *US*, Award, paras. 135–6; *Methanex* v. *US*, Final Award, Part IV, Chapter C, para. 26; but see *Consortium RFCC* v. *Morocco*, Award, para. 74 (discriminatory intention not a prerequisite for breach); *Saluka* v. *Czech Republic*, Award, paras. 307–9 (appearing to hold that discriminatory intention was not a prerequisite for breach).

[146] See *Lauder* v. *Czech Republic*, Award, paras. 213, 270; *Noble Ventures* v. *Romania*, Award, para. 180; *Eastern Sugar* v. *Czech Republic*, Partial Award, para. 338; *Genin* v. *Estonia*, Award, para. 369; *Biwater Gauff* v. *Tanzania*, Award, paras. 676, 710; *Sempra* v. *Argentina*, Award, para. 319; *Enron* v. *Argentina*, Award, para. 282 (obligation prohibits only intentional discrimination); cf. *Siemens* v. *Argentina*, Award, para. 321; *LG&E* v. *Argentina*, Liability, para. 146; *El Paso* v. *Argentina*, Award, para. 305; *Unglaube* v. *Costa Rica*, Award, paras. 262–3; *Plama* v. *Bulgaria*, Award, para. 184; *Ulysseas* v. *Ecuador*, Final Award, para. 293 (obligation also prohibits inadvertently discriminatory measures).

suitable to achieve a legitimate objective to defeat a claim, which would embody an appropriate balance between the objectives of preventing deliberate discrimination and the retention of an appropriate degree of regulatory flexibility for host states.[147] However, this approach encounters criticisms. First, it is not altogether clear that the objective of the obligations of non-discrimination in international investment law is to outlaw only deliberate discrimination.[148] If a breach can be established in cases of inadvertent discrimination, a suitability test does not provide any further criteria by which to determine the legality of the measure, suggesting that such a test would not capture all instances of discrimination. A necessity test, on the other hand, would allow a state to demonstrate that despite the unintentionally greater adverse impact on foreign investors, the measure was the least-restrictive means available to achieve the objective.[149] Second, even if only intentional discrimination was proscribed, a suitability test might be under-inclusive in the sense that it might not capture all instances of hidden discrimination where the state was able to point to another legitimate objective that appeared to be rationally connected to the measure. In SD Myers, for example, the presence of less restrictive alternative measures revealed that the government's dominant motive was to protect domestic industries, rather than to comply with its international environmental obligations.

One approach that has been proposed is to require necessity testing in the context of de jure discrimination, but apply a less stringent test in cases of de facto discrimination.[150] Arguably, a stricter standard of review is appropriate in cases of de jure discrimination on the basis that measures that discriminate de jure should be regarded with particular suspicion and that it is less likely that there will be a situation of normative uncertainty

---

[147] See Kurtz, 'The Merits and Limits of Comparativism', pp. 255, 275 (in relation to national treatment).

[148] See DiMascio and Pauwelyn, 'Nondiscrimination in Trade and Investment Treaties' (2008) 102 American Journal of International Law 41, 79; Newcombe and Paradell, Law and Practice of Investment Treaties (2009) 174–5; Dolzer and Schreuer, Principles of International Investment Law (2012) 201 (arguing that national treatment does not require deliberate discrimination as a precondition of breach and extends to cover inadvertent discrimination).

[149] See also Diebold, 'Standards of Non-Discrimination' (2011) 60 International and Comparative Law Quarterly 860 (arguing that discrimination claims should be determined using a necessity or proportionality stricto sensu test, but not clearly setting out what is envisaged).

[150] DiMascio and Pauwelyn, 'Nondiscrimination in Trade and Investment Treaties', p. 88; UPS v. Canada, Award, Separate Statement of Arbitrator Cass, paras. 118, 125.

would justify a deferential approach. However, taking a variegated approach to the *method* of review could also be under-inclusive, for the reasons stated above. To use the *SD Myers* example again, the measure at issue was an instance of *de facto* discrimination in that the ban on the export of toxic waste, while facially neutral, had the effect of disadvantaging foreign investors in toxic waste remediation with disposal facilities located outside the jurisdiction rather than their domestic counterparts, who would be more likely to conduct their activities in Canada. A suitability test might not have revealed the government's dominant motive.

Another argument that has been made is that the required connection between a measure and its objective (and thus the applicable method of review) should vary according to the importance of the interests or values that the measure seeks to further.[151] Depending on the degree of importance that the tribunal ascribes to the regulatory objective, the measure would be required to 'relate to', 'substantially relate to' or be 'necessary to' achieve its objective.[152] DiMascio and Pauwelyn argue that this approach reflects WTO case law in relation to the general exceptions.[153] However, this approach is not apparent from the decided WTO cases, and would in any case be at odds with the text of the provisions. In *Korea-Beef*, the Appellate Body suggested that it would vary the applicable *standard* of review – rather than the method of review – under the necessity-based general exceptions, depending on the level of importance it ascribed to the government's objective.[154] But there are no clear indications that WTO tribunals have done so in subsequent cases, beyond the observation that the case law suggests that measures with objectives that the Appellate Body has viewed as particularly important tend to be upheld, or substantially upheld, more frequently.[155]

---

[151] See DiMascio and Pauwelyn, 'Nondiscrimination in Trade and Investment Treaties', p. 87.

[152] See DiMascio and Pauwelyn, 'Nondiscrimination in Trade and Investment Treaties', p. 87; Diebold, 'Standards of Non-discrimination', pp. 861–2. See also Pauwelyn, 'Comment: The Unbearable Lightness of Likeness' in Panizzon, Pohl and Sauvé (eds.), *GATS and the Regulation of International Trade in Services* (2008) 358, 368–9 (also advocating this approach in the context of national treatment under GATT and GATS).

[153] DiMascio and Pauwelyn, 'Nondiscrimination in Trade and Investment Treaties', p. 87, citing Appellate Body Reports, *Korea–Beef*, para. 162; *US-Gambling*, para. 306; *EC-Asbestos*, para. 172.

[154] See Appellate Body Report, *Korea-Beef*, para. 162.

[155] Mitchell and Henckels, 'Variations on a Theme', p. 150. See e.g. Appellate Body Reports, *EC-Asbestos* and *Brazil-Tyres*; cf. *Korea-Beef*, *US-Gambling* and *China-Publications*.

A method of review that varies according to the tribunal's perception of the importance of the objective is inherently uncertain. It creates the risk that a tribunal's value judgement will be determinative of or be highly influential upon the ultimate outcome of the case, particularly if this value judgement carries over to its application of the standard of review more broadly (for example, affecting the strictness of any necessity test employed). Moreover, it is difficult to determine what is envisaged in terms of the criteria that tribunals should take into account in determining the importance of the objective. Investment treaties generally do not articulate a shared set of values in terms of regulatory objectives, including ranking them in the same way as the WTO Agreements' general exceptions through the varied nexus requirements. In the absence of such provisions, although investment tribunals may be able to rely on more general statements of the parties' shared objectives in treaty preambles, they will not be able to draw on any objectively ascertainable and specific manifestation of the consensus of the treaty parties with respect to the normative value of any particular objective. Given the problems identified in Chapter 1 concerning the inconsistent and uncertain approaches to state liability adopted by investment tribunals, an open-ended test can only perpetuate these difficulties. It would not, therefore, seem appropriate that tribunals vary the method of review according to the perceived importance of the value of the regulatory objective.

5.5   Proportionality *stricto sensu*

The proportionality *stricto sensu* stage of proportionality analysis gives rise to the greatest concerns about the discretion of investment tribunals negatively impacting on regulatory freedom, because it involves the explicit weighing and balancing of the importance of avoiding the harm caused by the measure against the importance of achieving the measure's objective. The *Tecmed* and *Occidental (No 2)* decisions are visible reminders of the potential for the outcome of a proportionality *stricto sensu* test to weigh in favour of the foreign investor at the expense of the host state in circumstances where the state appeared to be acting to promote public welfare. But apart from these two cases, investment tribunals that have undertaken this stage of proportionality analysis have found that the balance of interests weighed in favour of the host state, which might allay concerns that tribunals will inevitably approach this stage of proportionality analysis with a pro-investor orientation.

5.5.1   Restatement of the threshold of (dis)proportionality

Some tribunals have articulated a high threshold for lack of proportionality by altering the threshold at which a measure would be found to be in breach. In *EDF (Romania)*, the tribunal referred to the balance of interests being upset only where the claimant bore an 'individual and excessive burden'.[156] Although neither tribunal actually undertook the proportionality *stricto sensu* stage, the *Saluka* tribunal suggested that the outcome of a proportionality *stricto sensu* test would have to 'manifestly violate' the principle of stability or be 'manifestly unreasonable' in order to breach fair and equitable treatment,[157] and the *LG&E* tribunal remarked that a measure with a social or general welfare purpose would not be regarded as expropriatory 'except in cases where the State's action is obviously disproportionate to the need being addressed'.[158] By the use of terms such as 'manifestly', 'obviously' and 'excessively', these tribunals indicated that they would permit the government a margin of appreciation within which to conduct the proportionality *stricto sensu* test and would not substitute their own views in this respect unless the impact on the claimant was particularly harsh. This approach reflects that of the ECtHR in property cases, whereby a measure will comply with the proportionality *stricto sensu* test unless the outcome of the balancing exercise is 'manifestly disproportionate', and echoes the ICJ's approach in *Navigational and Related Rights*, where the Court held that the 'negative impact on the exercise of the right in question must not be manifestly excessive when measured against the protection afforded to the purpose invoked'.[159]

5.5.2   Procedural approach to proportionality stricto sensu

As discussed above in relation to necessity testing, a procedural approach to proportionality analysis permits greater discretion for governments because it generally precludes substantive review. However, a procedural approach is likely to place greater obligations on host states to demonstrate that the decision-making procedure involved balancing the public

---

[156] *EDF* v. *Romania*, Award, para. 293 ('individual and excessive burden'). See also, more generally, *Glamis* v. *US*, Award, para. 22 and *Thunderbird* v. *Mexico*, Award, para. 194 ('manifest arbitrariness'); *AES* v. *Hungary*, Award, para. 9.3.40 ('manifestly unfair or unreasonable'); *Paushok* v. *Mongolia*, Award, para. 299 (suggesting that even 'excessively burdensome' legislation would not inevitably result in a finding of breach).

[157] *Saluka* v. *Czech Republic*, Award, paras. 305–9, 337.

[158] *LG&E* v. *Argentina*, Liability, para. 195.

[159] *Navigational and Related Rights (Nicaragua* v. *Costa Rica)*, para. 87.

and private interests at issue. Two investment tribunals have hinted at a procedural approach in this regard, although neither tribunal articulated the circumstances in which this obligation would be fulfilled. The *Glamis* tribunal noted that the challenged legislation appeared to reflect 'a compromise between the conflicting desires and needs of the various affected parties' and indicated that it would respect the legislature's approach unless it resulted in an outcome that was 'manifestly arbitrary'.[160] The *LG&E* tribunal might also be regarded as taking this approach in relation to a treaty provision prohibiting arbitrary measures, stating that the purpose of the obligation was to prevent states from implementing measures affecting foreign investors without 'consideration of the effect of [the] measure on foreign investments and a balance of the interests of the State with any burden imposed on such investments'.[161] The tribunal noted that the government had negotiated with foreign investors before adopting the measures and held that '[even] though the measures adopted by Argentina may not have been the best, they were not taken lightly, without due consideration'.[162]

5.5.3   The extent of interference with the investment

There are two different ways in which the extent of interference with a protected right or interest might affect the manner in which a court or tribunal conducts proportionality analysis.

The first approach is one whereby the greater the interference with the right or interest, the stricter the standard of review with respect to all stages of proportionality analysis. A greater interference will place a higher burden on the authorities in terms of establishing the importance of the objective, the reliability of the prognosis of the efficacy of the measure, the unavailability of alternative measures and, potentially, the question of proportionality *stricto sensu*.[163] The CJEU, the ECtHR and WTO tribunals all take this approach. The CJEU reviews more significant interferences with free movement (such as import bans) with greater intensity than lesser interferences.[164] The ECtHR is less deferential in cases involving interferences with the 'core' or 'essence' of a right (in property cases, the

---

[160] *Glamis* v. *US*, Award, paras. 625, 803–5.   [161] *LG&E* v. *Argentina*, Liability, para. 158.

[162] *LG&E* v. *Argentina*, Liability, para. 162.

[163] See Alexy, 'On Balancing and Subsumption' (2003) 16 *Ratio Juris* 446; Rivers, 'Variable Intensity of Review', pp. 205–6; Rivers, 'Second Law of Balancing', p. 187.

[164] See Jans, 'Proportionality Revisited', p. 264; Tridimas, *The General Principles of EU Law* (2006) 223.

extinguishment of the rights of ownership) than other interferences.[165] In WTO cases, the Appellate Body has indicated that the greater the degree of interference with trade created by a measure, the more closely any justification advanced under the general exceptions should be scrutinized.[166] There are, however, no clear examples of investment tribunals taking this approach.

The second approach is one whereby the greater the interference with the protected right or interest, the more urgent or compelling the regulatory objective must be for the measure to be adjudged proportionate.[167] This approach is taken in many domestic constitutional contexts, where it might be considered more legitimate for adjudicators to engage in the proportionality *stricto sensu* stage of review. This approach gives greater discretion to adjudicators, because it more clearly directs them to evaluate the relative weight of competing interests rather than vary the applicable degree of scrutiny in a general sense. Unlike the first approach, which is applicable to all stages of proportionality analysis, the second approach is reliant on a tribunal undertaking the proportionality *stricto sensu* stage of review.

Investment tribunals that have referred to the degree of interference with an investment in conducting proportionality analysis have favoured this approach. In *Tecmed*, the tribunal's finding as to the severity of the interference with the investment was a substantial influence on the proportionality *stricto sensu* test it employed.[168] In *EDF (Romania)*, the relatively small degree of interference with the investment caused by the revocation of the claimant's operating licence in light of the perceived importance of the objective led the tribunal to find that the measure was proportionate. In *Total*, the tribunal found that although the pesification and related emergency measures had a severely deleterious impact on the claimant, this impact was outweighed by the compelling

---

[165] For example, *Družstevnízáložna Pria and Others* v. *Czech Republic*, para. 93; *Dickson* v. *UK*, para. 78; *Evans* v. *UK*, para. 77; *Sporrong* v. *Sweden*, para. 73. See Arai-Takarashi, *Margin of Appreciation and Proportionality*, pp. 155, 159; Rivers, 'Variable Intensity of Review', p. 206; Gerards, 'Pluralism, Deference and the Margin of Appreciation Doctrine' (2011) 17 *European Law Journal* 112. See also Christoffersen, *Fair Balance*, pp. 184, 187.

[166] Whether actual trade flows (Appellate Body Report, *Korea-Beef*, para. 163) or restrictions on the 'right to trade' (Appellate Body Report, *China-Publications*, para. 307): see Mitchell and Henckels, 'Variations on a Theme', p. 132.

[167] See Alexy, *A Theory of Constitutional Rights*, p. 418; Alexy, 'Thirteen Replies' in Pavlakos (ed.), *Law, Rights and Discourse: The Legal Philosophy of Robert Alexy* (2007) 333, 345–6.

[168] *Tecmed* v. *Mexico*, Award, para. 115.

importance of arresting Argentina's economic crisis.[169] Although this assessment has not always impacted negatively on states, given the problems inherent in investment arbitrators directly assessing the relative weights of state and investor interests (discussed further below), the first approach is preferable.

5.5.4   The desirability of proportionality stricto sensu in investor-state arbitration

It is questionable whether investment tribunals can – or should – assess the importance of achieving a state's objective vis-à-vis the importance of avoiding the negative impact on an investment. Not only is the problem of incommensurability always present in relation to proportionality *stricto sensu* review, but arguably it will never be appropriate for investment tribunals to engage in this form of analysis due to arbitrators' lack of embeddedness in the state or region, the *ad hoc* nature of investment arbitration and the absence of an appellate facility.[170] Some of these arguments reflect those marshalled against proportionality *stricto sensu* testing in the WTO context, but have even greater resonance in relation to investor-state arbitration, given the absence of a mechanism for appellate review.

By comparison, the CJEU and ECtHR are embedded within particular regional institutional settings that suggest it is more legitimate to undertake this stage of review. The EU's institutional imperative of economic integration gives the CJEU the authority to take an activist approach to measures interfering with free movement, which is reflected in its approach to both the applicable method and standard of review.[171] The

---

[169] *EDF* v. *Romania*, Award, paras. 179, 293–4; *Total* v. *Argentina*, Award, paras. 163–5, 309, 429.

[170] Been and Beauvais, 'The Global Fifth Amendment? NAFTA's Investment Protections and the Misguided Quest for an International "Regulatory Takings" Doctrine' (2003) 78 *New York University Law Review* 30, 108; Kurtz, 'Adjudging the Exceptional', pp. 366–8; Kleinlein, 'Judicial Lawmaking by Judicial Restraint? The Potential of Balancing in International Economic Law' (2011) 12 *German Law Journal* 1141, 1154; Kurtz, 'The Shifting Landscape', p. 693; Calamita, 'International Human Rights and the Interpretation of International Investment Treaties: Constitutional Considerations' in Baetens (ed.), *Investment Law within International Law: Integrationist Perspectives* (2013) 164, 180–1; Foster, 'Diminished Ambitions? Public International Legal Authority in the Transnational Economic Era' (2014) 17 *Journal of International Economic Law* 355, 395; Bonnitcha, *Substantive Protection under Investment Treaties*, pp. 307–8.

[171] For example, Kurtz, 'Adjudging the Exceptional', pp. 367–8.

CJEU, however, is sensitive to the legitimacy implications of undertaking this stage of proportionality analysis, and almost invariably structures its judgments so as to avoid explicit balancing (but on occasion does so in the guise of necessity testing). As discussed in Chapter 3, WTO tribunals have very rarely, if at all, undertaken the proportionality *stricto sensu* stage of proportionality analysis.

The proportionality *stricto sensu* stage might also be regarded as generally less problematic in the context of the ECHR. Despite its diverse membership and the fact that it is a regime of negative integration, there is an increasing degree of consensus among state parties as to the normative quality of human rights and the desirability of strictly scrutinizing interferences with them. This increasing consensus legitimizes the ECtHR's broad discretion in terms of its approach to the method and standard of review, including engaging in the proportionality *stricto sensu* stage – although the ECtHR takes a more deferential approach to scrutiny of interferences with property than in relation to other ECHR rights. The margin of appreciation has been subject to more intense criticism than proportionality *stricto sensu* analysis in the ECHR context, on the basis that it might encourage cultural relativism and a weakening in the human rights protections guaranteed by the ECHR.[172]

However, most proponents of proportionality analysis in investor-state arbitration do not acknowledge concerns that arise in relation to the proportionality *stricto sensu* stage, either in a general sense or in relation to the particular context of investor-state arbitration.[173] While Kulick

---

[172] See e.g. Benvenisti, 'Margin of Appreciation, Consensus, and Universal Standards' (1999) 31 *International Law and Politics* 843; Brauch, 'The Margin of Appreciation and the Jurisprudence of the European Court of Human Rights: Threat to the Rule of Law' (2005) 11 *Columbia Journal of European Law* 113; del Moral, 'The Increasingly Marginal Appreciation of the Margin-of-Appreciation Doctrine' (2006) 7 *German Law Journal* 611.

[173] Freeman, 'Regulatory Expropriation Under NAFTA Chapter 11', pp. 212–13; Stone Sweet and Grisel, 'Transnational Investment Arbitration', pp. 118, 130–1; Brower and Schill, 'Is Arbitration a Threat on a Boon to the Legitimacy of International Investment Law?' (2009) 9 *Chicago Journal of International Law* 471, 484–6; Montt, *State Liability in Investment Treaty Arbitration*, pp. 355–8; Krommendijk and Morijn, '"Proportional" by What Measure(s)? Balancing Investor Interests and Human Rights by Way of Applying the Proportionality Principle in Investor-State Arbitration' in Dupuy, Petersmann and Francioni (eds.), *Human Rights in International Investment Law and Arbitration* (2009) 422; UNCTAD, *The Protection of National Security in IIAs* (2009) 127–9; Stone Sweet, 'Proportionality's New Frontier', pp. 63–4; Leonhardsen, 'Looking for Legitimacy', p. 19 (but acknowledging that the application of this stage 'can be regarded as the difference between hard and soft proportionality analysis'); Diebold, 'Standards of Non-discrimination', p. 860,

acknowledges that undertaking the proportionality *stricto sensu* stage risks subjectivity in adjudication, suggesting that a tribunal might conclude at the outset that one of the competing interests should take priority and then undertake this analysis in an instrumental fashion, he does not suggest any adjustment to the way in which investment tribunals might carry out this stage so as to mitigate these concerns.[174]

Other commentators, while advocating proportionality *stricto sensu* testing, have acknowledged the risks inherent in undertaking this stage of review but suggest that these concerns could be attenuated by way of the standard of review. Kingsbury and Schill argue that investment tribunals should employ the proportionality *stricto sensu* stage as part of proportionality analysis because not doing so 'would allow restricting a right severely in order to protect a negligible public interest'.[175] They acknowledge the criticism that proportionality analysis 'confers power on judges to take policy-driven decisions' and that this stage might be used to 'justify particular judicial preferences'.[176] To address these concerns, they suggest that arbitrators determine whether the government had taken into account all relevant interests in decision-making and tried to minimize the interference with the investment.[177] This would be done by ascertaining whether the authorities had 'stayed in a basically proportionate manner within an outer framework that is spanned by the recognition of property and investment protection on the one hand and the legitimate public interest on the other'.[178] Here, these authors appear to suggest either that the proportionality *stricto sensu* stage of proportionality analysis could be discharged procedurally or that arbitrators should apply a margin of appreciation in performing proportionality *stricto sensu* review, although this is not altogether clear.[179] More generally, Schill argues that

Radi, 'Human Rights in Investment Treaty Arbitration' pp. 1151, 1166–81 (although it is not entirely clear whether he supports an approach involving proportionality *stricto sensu*, see pp. 1170–1); Wagner, 'Regulatory Space in International Investment Law and International Trade Law' (2015) 36 *University of Pennsylvania Journal of International Law* 1, 50–1.

[174] Kulick, *Global Public Interest*, pp. 171–3.

[175] Kingsbury and Schill, 'Investor-State Arbitration as Governance', p. 39; Kingsbury and Schill, 'Public Law Concepts', p. 87.

[176] Kingsbury and Schill, 'Investor-State Arbitration as Governance', pp. 30, 49–50; Kingsbury and Schill, 'Public Law Concepts', pp. 87–8, 102–3.

[177] Kingsbury and Schill, 'Investor-State Arbitration as Governance', p. 30; Kingsbury and Schill, 'Public Law Concepts', pp. 87–8.

[178] Kingsbury and Schill, 'Investor-State Arbitration as Governance', p. 39; Kingsbury and Schill, 'Public Law Concepts', pp. 78, 87–8.

[179] See Kingsbury and Schill, 'Investor-State Arbitration as Governance', p. 31; Kingsbury and Schill, 'Public Law Concepts', p. 103.

investment tribunals should refrain from employing an intrusive standard of review when undertaking proportionality analysis so as to permit sufficient policy space for host states.[180] Burke-White and von Staden also argue that, due to arbitrators' lack of embeddedness in the host state, national governments should have primary responsibility for undertaking proportionality analysis, including the proportionality *stricto sensu* stage – but that it may be appropriate for tribunals to undertake this stage of review moderated by the application of a margin of appreciation.[181]

Pirker, however, is more specific in cautioning that investment tribunals should be circumspect in undertaking this stage of proportionality analysis due to arbitrators' lack of embeddedness within the host state polity. He contends that investment tribunals should not generally undertake the proportionality *stricto sensu* stage but that they should retain a residual capacity to do so in 'rare' or 'exceptional' circumstances, such as cases where 'the interest of investment seems to be severely underrepresented in the domestic political process' or (in the case of treaty exceptions) where 'elements of an abuse of the provision are apparent'.[182] It is not clear what is meant by underrepresentation in the political process and how a tribunal would establish this fact as the basis for performing the proportionality *stricto sensu* stage. Moreover, the structure of proportionality analysis means that abuses of governmental power would likely be filtered out by the stages of legitimate objective (whether the measure is discriminatory or pursues another impermissible objective), suitability (whether the measure is in fact directed at and capable of achieving its asserted objective) and necessity (whether there are alternative measures available to authorities).[183] This being the case, it is not clear why it would be necessary or desirable for an investment tribunal to deploy proportionality *stricto sensu* testing in these circumstances.

It might be argued that the approach of the ECtHR in property cases demonstrates the potential for a relatively deferential approach to

---

[180] Schill, 'Fair and Equitable Treatment', p. 170. See also Diehl, *The Core Standard in International Investment Protection: Fair and Equitable Treatment* (2012) 337.

[181] Burke-White and von Staden, 'Private Litigation', pp. 337–8; Burke-White and von Staden, 'Public Law Standards', pp. 717–19. However, their work appears to characterize the margin of appreciation as a separate method of review rather than a doctrine of deference: see Stone Sweet, 'Arbitration and Judicialization' (2011) 1 *Oñati Socio-Legal Series* 16 (criticizing Burke-White and von Staden's characterization of the margin of appreciation).

[182] Pirker, *Proportionality Analysis and Judicial Review*, pp. 335, 342, 348, 361, 376, 378.

[183] See Matthews and Stone Sweet, 'All Things in Proportion?', p. 109.

proportionality *stricto sensu* testing to attenuate some of the concerns raised about this approach in the context of investor-state arbitration.[184] As noted above, the *Glamis, Saluka, LG&E* and *EDF (Romania)* tribunals adopted an approach whereby a measure would only be held to lack proportionality where it was manifestly disproportionate. This approach is preferable to an unconstrained balancing test, because it reduces the ambit of tribunals' discretion to undermine the legitimate policy choices of host states. However, whether the effect of a measure on an investment or investor is 'manifestly' disproportionate nevertheless places a high degree of discretion in arbitrators and hardly provides greater certainty for governments or for investors.[185] Even where the proportionality *stricto sensu* stage is moderated by the application of a margin of appreciation, it is difficult to determine the circumstances in which an investment tribunal should find that a measure – that is, the least-restrictive means reasonably available to achieve a legitimate objective – is outweighed by the importance of avoiding harm to the claimant's interests. The proportionality *stricto sensu* stage by its very nature can only operate to reduce the regulatory autonomy of states compared to the application of a necessity test, as it can result in a tribunal ruling unlawful the only way that the government has available to achieve its aim. It is strongly arguable, therefore, that least-restrictive means analysis should be the limit of review in investor-state arbitration.

5.6   Conclusion

Analysis of the decided cases reveals a range of approaches to the various stages of proportionality analysis by investment tribunals, including a number of instances where arbitrators did not pay regard to the concept of deference in circumstances of normative or empirical uncertainty. However, a number of recent decisions where tribunals employed proportionality analysis or one or more of its component stages demonstrate that the review of regulatory and administrative measures can be

---

[184] This argument was made in Henckels, 'Indirect Expropriation and the Right to Regulate: Revisiting Proportionality Analysis and the Standard of Review in Investor-State Arbitration' (2012) 15 *Journal of International Economic Law* 223.

[185] See Ranjan, 'Using the Public Law Concept of Proportionality to Balance Investment Protection with Regulation in International Investment Law: A Critical Reappraisal' (2014) 3 *Cambridge Journal of International and Comparative Law* 853, 878–80 (noting that determining whether a measure is 'obviously disproportionate' risks unprincipled decision-making).

undertaken in a manner that pays due regard to the need for restraint in such situations. These decisions clearly show that proportionality analysis can permit variable intensity of review, depending on the issues raised in the dispute.

Tribunals have infrequently ruled that a measure was not pursuing a legitimate objective in regulatory disputes, or that the objective of a measure was irrelevant to the question of its legality. Several tribunals have referred to the need for deference or specifically affirmed the legitimacy and/or importance of the objective. In undertaking this assessment, many tribunals have referred to the fact that an objective aligned with common state practice or implemented the government's international obligations, although this factor was not determinative of whether a state was pursuing a legitimate objective.

In relation to the requirement of suitability, some tribunals have adopted strict approaches by substituting their view for the rationality of the measure or by assessing suitability *ex post facto*. These strict approaches diverge from the way in which other international and supranational courts and tribunals conduct this assessment. However, other tribunals expressly relied on the host state's assessment of suitability, whether in general or by referring to the primary decision-maker's expertise. In some cases, tribunals referred to the desirability of allowing states a margin for error in policy-making without liability, such as where the measure proved to be less than effective at achieving its objective, or adopted a deferential approach to this analysis in the light of Argentina's economic crisis and the urgency of the measures' adoption.

In the context of necessity testing, the trend in tribunals' decision-making is somewhat skewed by the first tranche of decisions by tribunals assessing Argentina's emergency measures under the exception clause in the Argentina-US BIT, an approach which did not permit consideration of the feasibility and effectiveness of alternative measures. Most other tribunals, however, have adopted an approach that requires that an alternative measure be equally effective at achieving the desired objective and/or that takes into account the actual likelihood that the government could adopt it in the circumstances. Still other tribunals have permitted states more discretion by allowing the necessity stage to be discharged procedurally. These approaches considerably lessen the effect that least-restrictive means analysis can have on regulatory autonomy.

Aside from two notable exceptions, investment tribunals have conducted proportionality *stricto sensu* testing with a high threshold for breach, have ascribed greater weight to the state's interests or have permitted this stage of analysis to be discharged procedurally. These approaches may assuage concerns that arbitrators will invariably approach the proportionality *stricto sensu* stage with a predisposition towards the protection of investment over other legitimate objectives. However, this stage of proportionality analysis nevertheless places an undesirably high degree of discretion in arbitrators, which can only reduce the regulatory autonomy of host states and appears to be inappropriate to the institutional context of investor-state arbitration. Future tribunals considering whether to engage in the proportionality *stricto sensu* stage should, at the very least, be mindful of the significant concerns arising from this stage of review; the analysis undertaken in this book suggests they should avoid this stage altogether.

It could be argued that tentative moves by investment tribunals towards proportionality analysis alongside the absence of a coherent approach to deference risks sending a signal to future tribunals that scrutiny of measures should be heightened.[186] Cases such as *Tecmed* and *Occidental (No 2)* – in which tribunals explicitly adopted proportionality-based reasoning alongside a strict approach to the applicable standard of review – have raised anxieties in this respect. To be sure, there are several other examples of tribunals referring to proportionality to suggest an approach to the relevant standard of investment protection that would seem to presumptively afford greater weight to the investor's interests.[187] However, as investment tribunals develop a better understanding of the structure of

---

[186] See, in relation to the anxieties caused by the introduction of proportionality analysis as a method of review in UK public law following the enactment of the Human Rights Act 1998, Craig, 'Unreasonableness and Proportionality in UK Law' in Ellis (ed.), *The Principle of Proportionality in the Laws of Europe* (1999) 85, 100–3; Elliott, 'Substantive Review', p. 107; Taggart, 'Proportionality, Deference, Wednesbury', p. 438; King, 'Proportionality – A Halfway House' (2010) *New Zealand Law Review* 332, 337.

[187] *Sempra* v. *Argentina*, Award, para. 299 (referring to the need for a balancing of interests in determining breach of fair and equitable treatment, but then finding that there was an obligation to ensure stability in the regulatory environment that could not be displaced by the circumstances of the crisis); *Fireman's Fund* v. *Mexico*, Award, para. 176 (referring to a balancing test for indirect expropriation claims, but noting that the effect on the investment would be 'dispositive'); *Corn Products* v. *Mexico*, Award, paras. 87–8 (citing *Fireman's Fund*); *MTD* v. *Chile*, Award, para. 109 (stating that fair and equitable treatment encompassed an obligation of proportionality, but then taking a strict approach to the circumstances when a government could change a course of administrative conduct that did not permit consideration of the government's reasons for acting); *AWG* v. *Argentina*, Award, para. 236 (referring to legitimate expectations as a balance of interests, but taking a strict approach to the permissibility of certain actions by provincial authorities in the context of the crisis). See also (citing *Tecmed* with approval) *Azurix* v. *Argentina*, Award, para. 311.

proportionality analysis and rationales for deference it may be less likely that they will make decisions on the basis of reasoning that contradicts the institutional premises underlying an institutionally sensitive approach to this method of review.[188] The decided cases demonstrate that investment tribunals are capable of employing the various stages of proportionality analysis in such a way as to lay the foundations upon which a more structured, coherent and appropriately deferential approach to proportionality analysis could develop.

Such an approach would draw inspiration from the other courts and tribunals that are examined in this book. Briefly stated, tribunals would afford a measure of deference on the basis of regulatory autonomy and proximity concerns when evaluating the legitimacy of a measure's objective, and would use this stage of proportionality analysis only to identify cases whether states were acting with discriminatory or other impermissible objectives. They would apply the suitability test in a way that takes account of any empirical uncertainty, and would permit states to adduce evidence to demonstrate that a measure would be expected to achieve its objective in future. They might afford a measure of deference even where states have, acting in good faith, made mistakes. Tribunals would also permit states to rely upon any relevant institutional competence and expertise in demonstrating the necessity of the challenged measure in light of possible alternatives, and would approach the burden of proof in a way that accords with the character of the relevant treaty provision (a positive obligation or an exception). Tribunals might also afford deference on the basis that states have thoroughly investigated alternative options before promulgating the measure in question or carefully balanced the interests at stake. Finally, investment tribunals would refrain from employing the proportionality *stricto sensu* stage of proportionality analysis in light of the significant legitimacy implications that this form of analysis causes for both certainty and regulatory autonomy.

---

[188] See Brady, *Proportionality and Deference*, p. 263 (in relation to UK public law).

6

Other issues affecting the method and standard of review in investor-state arbitration

6.1 Introduction

This chapter addresses several further issues. First, it clarifies the circumstances in which proportionality analysis will – and will not – be an appropriate method of review in regulatory disputes. Next, it discusses the proper place for the use of proportionality analysis in the context of treaties with an exception clause, and deals with a potential argument relating to the impact of available remedies in international investment law on the preferable method of review. Turning to the issue of the standard of review, the chapter discusses the relevance of the institutional context, considers other factors that have animated arbitrators' approaches with particular reference to NAFTA cases and notes the problem of conflating the grounds of review with the standard of review. Finally, the chapter addresses potential criticisms of and limitations to a deferential approach to adjudicating regulatory disputes in international investment law.

6.2 The appropriateness of proportionality analysis as a method of review

Although its limitations must be acknowledged, proportionality analysis is a rational method of review that has been tried and tested by a number of other international and supranational courts and tribunals in a variety of contexts. Its analytical structure provides a degree of transparency and certainty to adjudication – attributes that are lacking in many of the decided investment cases. The consistent adoption of this method of review by investment tribunals could also deal with the problem of inconsistencies in the manner in which tribunals determine liability in regulatory disputes. As this book has argued, the problems inherent in proportionality analysis can, arguably, be attenuated through an institutionally sensitive approach to the standard of review and by avoiding the value-laden proportionality *stricto sensu* stage.

6.2.1 The limits of proportionality analysis in investor-state arbitration

Chapters 4 and 5 analyzed investment tribunals' approaches to determining state liability in four areas that are the primary sites of tension between the exercise of public power by host states and the interests of foreign investors: fair and equitable treatment and arbitrary measures clauses, indirect expropriation, non-discrimination and treaty exceptions. Apart from treaty exceptions, where the applicable method of review will be guided by the text of the provision, these are also areas where the treaty text typically sheds no light on the manner in which tribunals should take into account the state's reasons for its actions in determining liability and as such, where methods of treaty interpretation are of little assistance. As Chapter 1 has argued, a proportionality-based approach to review of government action need not be explicitly mandated by the text of the treaty and is permitted where the relevant treaty provision does not detail the relationship between the state's obligations towards foreign investors and its continued regulatory powers. Such an approach accords with the purpose of the international investment law regime, which cannot be described as solely to protect foreign investment at the expense of other legitimate interests of host states.

Proportionality analysis will not, however, be an appropriate method of review in all circumstances. Its use will be precluded where a treaty provision or rule of customary international law establishes clear rules of priority between public and private interests or stipulates a different nexus requirement between a measure and a permissible objective. For example, the customary international law of expropriation provides that whether a direct expropriation has been effected for a public purpose is only relevant insofar as it affects the issue of whether an expropriation is lawful or unlawful, and not the issue of whether an expropriation has taken place.[1] Additionally, provisions on indirect expropriation in some

---

[1] Whether an expropriation is lawful or unlawful affects the amount of compensation payable. In the case of an unlawful expropriation, the dominant view is that the state must compensate the investor for lost profits (consequential losses) as well as direct losses, see Crawford, *Brownlie's Principles of Public International Law*, p. 625. Indirect expropriations are by definition unlawful expropriations: Marboe, *Calculation of Compensation and Damages in International Investment Law* (2009) 59–62.

investment treaties stipulate a less stringent nexus requirement between the measure and its objective, such as by providing that regulatory measures that are 'designed and applied' to protect certain policy objectives do not constitute indirect expropriations.[2] As discussed in Chapter 3, exception clauses stipulate a range of nexus requirements, many of which will preclude proportionality analysis. Proportionality analysis would also be precluded in circumstances where an investor-state contract contains an express term authorizing the state to terminate the conduct or take other action against the investor in certain circumstances, to which the investor has explicitly agreed in entering the contract – an issue that caused controversy in *Occidental (No 2)*. Tribunals will need to show fidelity to the treaty text, any applicable customary international law, and the terms of any contract between the state and the claimant.[3]

Moreover, proportionality analysis does not appear to be an appropriate method of review in relation to certain obligations owed by states under international investment law that are largely fact-driven inquiries – even though determining whether the state has complied with these obligations might by understood as involving a balance between public and private interests. One example is the requirement that a government be impartial in its dealings with investors (a requirement of due process, which is regarded as an element of fair and equitable treatment).[4] It is difficult to see how the requirement of impartiality (in terms of a decision-maker not being tainted by actual or apprehended bias) could be subject to proportionality analysis. Rather, this is an inquiry into whether the facts establish that the decision-makers closed their mind to the decision or

---

[2] See e.g. Annex 11-B [4] US-Australia FTA; Annex 3(1)(e) India-Singapore FTA.

[3] See also *Abaclat and others* v. *Argentina*, Jurisdiction and Admissibility, para. 582; Dissenting Opinion of Arbitrator Abi-Saab, paras. 31, 250–1. Arbitrator Abi-Saab strongly criticized the majority decision for undertaking a balancing exercise in order to determine whether the claimant was required to negotiate with the host state and resort to domestic courts for a period of 18 months before bringing an investment arbitration claim. In his view, this approach overrode the clear text of the treaty and 'rebalanced' the interests of the state and the investor in a subjective manner; it was beyond the power of the tribunal to 'arrogate to itself the legislative jurisdiction or power of re-examining the rules in order to revise or refashion them . . . according to its will or whim'.

[4] For example, *Waste Management* v. *Mexico*, Award, para. 98; *Methanex* v. *US*, Final Award, Part IV Chapter C, para. 12; *Rumeli* v. *Kazakhstan*, Award, para. 609; *Saluka* v. *Czech Republic*, Award, para. 308 (finding an obligation of due process as part of fair and equitable treatment). See Kläger, *Fair and Equitable Treatment*, p. 213; Dolzer and Schreuer, *Principles of International Investment Law*, p. 154 (discussing the elements of due process); Montt, *State Liability in Investment Treaty Arbitration*, p. 349; Kläger, *Fair and Equitable Treatment*, pp. 213–14 (discussing the requirement of impartiality).

whether an apprehension of bias may reasonably be raised. Other examples include the prohibitions on coercion and harassment, which are also elements of fair and equitable treatment. Whether the state has engaged in this conduct is a matter for factual determination by the tribunal and is not a question of the proportionality of the state's actions.

6.2.2   The proper place for proportionality analysis in determining liability

It is arguable that tribunals adjudicating disputes under treaties containing an exception clause should consider the proportionality of the measure (where relevant) in the context of determining whether a breach has occurred in the first place, rather than quarantining consideration of regulatory purpose to the determination of whether the state's conduct is justified in terms of the exception clause. The presence of the exception clause in the Argentina-US BIT appears to have directed the attention of both the *LG&E* and *Continental* tribunals to consider the necessity of Argentina's actions to arrest its economic crisis only in the context of the exceptions, rather than in the context of fair and equitable treatment. It is difficult to see why a tribunal should find conduct to breach a state's obligations in the circumstances, but then take those same circumstances into account in finding that the state could invoke the exception.[5] By comparison, the *Total* tribunal found that the same measures did not breach fair and equitable treatment in the context of the France-Argentina BIT, which contains no exception clause.[6]

However, there is a risk that tribunals that are less sensitive to the need to adopt a balanced interpretation of the obligations of host states will view the proper place for taking into account the state's regulatory objective as only in the context of exception clauses, where they exist in the relevant treaty, or even view the absence of an exception clause as signalling that the purpose of the measure is not relevant to the determination of breach of the state's substantive obligations.[7] Moreover, exception clauses frame government action to promote public welfare as something that should only take place in exceptional or highly defined circumstances, which creates the risk that tribunals might interpret such clauses in a very

---

[5] See Desierto, 'Necessity and "Supplementary Means of Interpretation"', p. 893.
[6] *Total* v. *Argentina*, Award, paras. 122–3, 162–3, 309, 429.
[7] Alvarez and Brink, 'Revisiting the Necessity Defense' in Sauvant (ed.), *Yearbook on International Investment Law and Policy 2010–2011* (2011) 358.

narrow way, employ a stricter standard of review than would otherwise be employed in the context of the primary norm, or permit states to rely only on policy objectives stipulated in the exception clause to justify measures interfering with an investment when examining those measures in the context of the state's substantive obligations.[8] For these reasons, commentators have questioned the desirability of the approach taken by WTO tribunals under GATT and GATS,[9] which examines the justification for measures in breach of national treatment and most-favoured nation treatment only in the context of the general exceptions.[10]

This is not to suggest that treaty exceptions should play no role, as this would render such clauses redundant – rather, the exceptions would only come into play where the obligation at issue does not permit a tribunal to take into account the host state's reasons for its actions in the context of determining whether there has been a breach of that obligation. Consideration would, however, need to be given to the interplay of methods of review where the exception stipulates a less stringent test than necessity.[11] To require a necessity test in the context of the substantive obligations (such as non-discrimination or fair and equitable treatment)

---

[8] See Ortino, 'The Social Dimension of International Investment Agreements: Drafting a New BIT/MIT Model?' (2005) 7 *International Law FORUM du Droit International* 243, 245; Spears, 'The Quest for Policy Space' p. 13 *Journal of International Economic Law* 1063; Alvarez and Brink, 'Revisiting the Necessity Defense', p. 357.

[9] See Hudec, 'GATT/WTO Constraints on National Regulation: Requiem for an "Aim and Effects"' Test' (1998) 31 *International Lawyer* 619, 622, 626, 628, 633, 638; Regan, 'Further Thoughts on the Role of Regulatory Purpose Under Article III of the General Agreement on Tariffs and Trade: A Tribute to Bob Hudec' (2003) 37 *Journal of World Trade* 737, 745, 749, 752–3; Roessler, 'Beyond the Ostensible – A Tribute to Professor Robert Hudec's Insights Under the National Treatment Provisions of the General Agreement on Tariffs and Trade' (2003) 37 *Journal of World Trade* 771, 777–80; Porges and Trachtman, 'Robert Hudec and Domestic Regulation: The Resurrection of Aim and Effects' (2003) 37 *Journal of World Trade* 783, 786–97; Zhou, '*US–Clove Cigarettes* and *US–Tuna II* (*Mexico*): Implications for the Role of Regulatory Purpose Under Article III:4 of the GATT' (2012) 15 *Journal of International Economic Law* 1075, 1111–14; Flett, 'WTO Space for National Regulation: Requiem for a Diagonal Vector Test' (2013) 16 *Journal of International Economic Law* 37, 88–90.

[10] This rule/exception structure was recently confirmed by the Appellate Body in *EC-Seal Products* at para. 5.125, where it held that these obligations were 'balanced by a Member's right to regulate in a manner consistent with the requirements of the separate general exception clause of Article XX and its chapeau'. However, regulatory purpose may still play a role in relation to the second sentence of Article III:2 GATT in terms of whether the measure was adopted 'so as to afford protection to domestic production': Appellate Body Report, *Chile-Tax Measures on Alcoholic Beverages*, para. 62.

[11] For example, Article 1(1) Chapter 24 New Zealand-Taiwan FTA (which incorporates GATT Article XX by reference).

could be problematic if the applicable treaty exception had a nexus requirement that was less stringent than a necessity test, such as 'relating to', because the rule would be stricter than the exception.[12] In such cases, the treaty read as a whole would appear to preclude proportionality analysis as the appropriate method of review applicable to the substantive obligations.

6.2.3   The issue of remedies

A potential objection to the use of proportionality analysis by investment tribunals is the issue of remedies in international investment law.[13] In many legal systems where courts and tribunals use proportionality analysis in the determination of liability including domestic law, WTO[14] and ECHR[15] law, the principal remedies available are primary remedies such as quashing orders, declarations and injunctions.[16] In these fields, remedies are directed at the illegality of the measure as such and are preventive or restorative, aiming to induce the authorities to reconsider the measure or decision and take it again in light of the finding of unlawfulness.[17]

---

[12] See, in relation to this issue in relation to national treatment under GATT and GATS, Pauwelyn, 'The Unbearable Lightness of Likeness', p. 368.

[13] Many BITs are silent as to whether the tribunal can award remedies other than pecuniary remedies, but not, for example, Article 1134.1 NAFTA, which provides that a tribunal 'may award only: (a) monetary damages, and any applicable interest; or (b) restitution of property, in which case the award shall provide that the disputing Party may pay monetary damages, and any applicable interest, in lieu of restitution'.

[14] Where a report of the panel or the Appellate Body concludes that a measure is inconsistent and the report has been adopted by the Dispute Settlement Body, it is generally up to the WTO member to determine how it will bring the measure into compliance. WTO remedies operate prospectively, requiring withdrawal or modification of an impugned measure within a reasonable period of time. See Articles 19–22 DSU.

[15] The ECHR principally has a system of declaratory remedies: the state must afford reparation (such as by amending a law or revoking a decision) or, failing that, provide 'just satisfaction' (including compensation) to the claimant: Article 41 ECHR. Compensation is the principal remedy in cases of deprivation of property, but not other types of interference with property: Article 1, 1st Protocol ECHR. However, the ECtHR typically affords a wide margin of appreciation in relation to a state's method of calculating compensation and, as discussed in Chapter 3, is generally reluctant to find that a deprivation has taken place.

[16] van Aaken, 'Primary and Secondary Remedies in International Investment Law and National State Liability: A Functional and Comparative View' in Schill (ed.), *International Investment Law and Comparative Public Law* (2010) 721, 732–3, 745 (referring to public law remedies in domestic legal systems and remedies in WTO law and ECHR law). The situation in EU law is more complex: see Craig, *EU Administrative Law*, pp. 703–38.

[17] van Aaken, 'Primary and Secondary Remedies', p. 724.

In a typical situation arising in investor-state arbitration, however, the investment has been terminated and the investor is seeking compensation rather than a change in government policy; in any case, non-monetary remedies are likely to be less attractive to claimants because they are difficult to enforce compared to orders for monetary compensation.[18] However, the claimants in the pending cases of *Philip Morris* v. *Australia* and *Philip Morris* v. *Uruguay* have requested the suspension, and respectively the 'discontinuance' and 'cessation' of tobacco packaging measures.[19] Whether this is the beginning of a trend in remedies sought by claimants in respect of generally applicable regulatory measures remains to be seen.

The argument against the use of proportionality analysis on the basis of remedies is that if an investment tribunal finds the host state in breach of its obligations through applying proportionality analysis, the state will be obliged to pay compensation but will not be obliged to rescind the measure or take the decision again in light of the tribunal ruling; therefore, it should not be the role of an investment tribunal to assess matters such as the necessity of a challenged measure, because this decision will have no practical effect on the measure itself as a matter of law.[20] Yet, it is also arguable that a well-reasoned decision made by a court or tribunal using proportionality analysis (or, indeed, other methods of review that reveal the adjudicators' reasons for the decision) may induce the host state to

---

[18] van Aaken, 'Primary and Secondary Remedies', p. 734. An award may be enforced by way of seizure of the state's assets in any state that is a party to the ICSID Convention (for ICSID disputes) or the Convention on the Recognition and Enforcement of Foreign Arbitral Awards (for non-ICSID disputes). Article 54(1) ICSID Convention provides that only pecuniary remedies are enforceable in domestic courts through seizure and sale of state assets. The only known cases in which an investment tribunal awarded a non-pecuniary remedy are *Antoine Goetz* v. *Burundi*, Award, para. 133, where the tribunal offered the host state a choice between paying compensation to the investor and revoking the measure and the state chose the latter, and *ATA Construction and Trading Company* v. *Jordan*, Award, paras. 127–32, where the tribunal ordered (at the urging of the host state) that legislation be revoked so as to reinstate the claimant's right to arbitrate disputes under a contract. See Bonnitcha, *Substantive Protection under Investment Treaties*, pp. 60–1.

[19] See Notification of Claim, *Philip Morris* v. *Australia*, para. 11; Request for Arbitration, *Philip Morris Brands Sàrl, Philip Morris Products S.A. and Abal Hermanos S.A.* v. *Oriental Republic of Uruguay*, para. 88.

[20] See Pirker, *Proportionality Analysis and Judicial Review*, pp. 336, 346–7, arguing that the issue of remedies generally militates against investment tribunals undertaking proportionality *stricto sensu* analysis, because the arbitrators' role is not to '[reassess] the balancing of interests undertaken by a legislator or administrator in order to suggest a "better" balance'. This argument could, however, be broadened to object to proportionality analysis more generally, including the necessity stage.

amend or repeal the impugned measure, or may influence future administrative decision-making by the state so as to avoid future liability in relation to investors in similar circumstances. Such decisions may also have broader systemic effects, inducing other states to amend similar measures or act differently in future in order to avoid liability.[21] It is therefore not clear why the question of remedies should preclude the use of proportionality analysis as a method of review.

However, the extent to which the adoption of proportionality analysis by adjudicators would have such salutary effects may depend on the context and the particular legal system at issue. Bonnitcha, for example, argues that there is no evidence that adopting proportionality analysis as a method of review in the context of investor-state arbitration would have such an effect on governmental decision-making, in part because 'investment treaty protections are unlikely to be deeply internalised by primary decision-makers at the time when original regulatory decisions are made'.[22] Whether this is currently the case and will remain so in relation to the impact of investment tribunal decisions on domestic regulators is an issue worthy of further research. To be sure, studies concerning the impact of judicial review on administrative decision-making and legislative development in domestic legal systems give mixed results.[23] Yet, it is certainly clear that the outcome of the challenges to Australia's and Uruguay's tobacco packaging measures may influence the design of other states' measures in this area.[24]

---

[21] Kulick, 'Review: Stephan W. Schill (ed.). *International Investment Law and Comparative Public Law*' (2011) 22 *European Journal of International Law* 917, 919. See also Pauwelyn, 'At the Edge of Chaos? Foreign Investment Law as a Complex Adaptive System, How It Emerged and How It Can Be Reformed' (2014) 29 *ICSID Review* 372, 410 (noting the chilling effect of the threat of monetary compensation combined with the vagueness of investment treaty obligations).

[22] Bonnitcha, *Substantive Protection under Investment Treaties*, p. 307.

[23] See e.g. the contributions in Campbell, Ewing and Tomkins (eds.), *Sceptical Essays on Human Rights* (2001); Hertogh and Halliday (eds.), *Judicial Review and Bureaucratic Impact: International and Interdisciplinary Perspectives* (2004). See also Stone Sweet, *The Judicial Construction of Europe* (2004) 119: in the context of EU law, 'if governments are rational actors, they will learn to pursue their pertinent "national interests" in doctrinally defensible ways'; Feldman, 'The Impact of Human Rights on the UK Legislative Process' (2004) 25 *Statute Law Review* 91, concluding that the introduction of the Human Rights Act 1998 (which incorporates the ECHR into domestic law) has resulted in government departments being more sensitive to human rights considerations standards in drafting legislation.

[24] For example, New Zealand Government, 'Government Moves Forward with Plain Packaging of Tobacco Products' (2013).

6.3   The standard of review: other influencing factors and the desirability of a deferential approach

As indicated in Chapter 2, as well as deference based on the characteristics of primary decision-makers, courts and tribunals may be influenced by additional factors in the determination of the applicable standard of review more broadly. In the context of investor-state arbitration, the grounds of review in terms of the threshold for liability for breach of fair and equitable treatment (the required seriousness of the conduct vis-à-vis the claimant in light of the circumstances) also appear to have influenced tribunals' approach to the applicable standard of review, particularly in NAFTA cases. Moreover, strategic considerations – in particular, a view that arbitrators have a role to play in sustaining the system of investor-state arbitration under the relevant treaty – have animated arbitrators' approach to the standard of review, again in the context of NAFTA. However, a number of tribunals have adopted less-than-clear approaches to the standard of review, or appear to have misunderstood the concepts of deference and the margin of appreciation.

The clearest examples of a conscious approach to the standard of review (both in relation to proportionality analysis and more generally) have occurred in the NAFTA context. NAFTA tribunals and tribunal members issuing separate opinions have referred on several occasions to the desirability of deference, policy space, regulatory autonomy and the expertise of primary decision-makers, and have stated that their role was not to second-guess the policy decisions of governments.[25] NAFTA tribunals have rarely adopted an excessively strict approach to the standard of review in relation to regulatory or administrative acts of states.[26]

---

[25] See e.g. *SD Myers* v. *Canada*, Partial Award, para. 263 and Separate Opinion of Arbitrator Schwartz, para. 233; *Thunderbird* v. *Mexico*, Award, para. 127; *Glamis* v. *US*, Award, paras. 625, 779, 803–5.

[26] Notable exceptions being *Metalclad* v. *Mexico* and *Gemplus* v. *Mexico*, in which tribunals held that states acted illegitimately in responding to community opposition to the claimants' operations. The majority decision in *Bilcon* v. *Canada* was also criticised on this basis by the dissenting arbitrator. It might also be argued that the *Merrill & Ring* v. *Canada* tribunal adopted an overly expansive approach to the grounds of review in holding that Article 1105 NAFTA 'provides for the fair and equitable treatment of alien investors within the confines of reasonableness', suggesting a lower threshold than the customary international law standard would breach fair and equitable treatment (Award, para. 213): see Ortino, 'The Investment Treaty System as Judicial Review', pp. 259–60. However, the question of the threshold for liability, as part of the grounds of review, is conceptually a separate question to the standard of review.

6.3.1 Conflating the grounds of review with the standard of review in fair and equitable treatment cases

NAFTA's fair and equitable treatment clause provides that states must 'accord to investments of investors of another Party treatment in accordance with international law, including fair and equitable treatment'.[27] Early NAFTA cases such as *Metalclad*, where tribunals took an expansive approach to the obligation of fair and equitable treatment,[28] influenced the NAFTA parties to take steps to clarify the extent of the obligation by issuing a binding Note of Interpretation stating that fair and equitable treatment in the context of NAFTA 'prescribes' and does not require 'treatment in addition to or beyond' the customary international law standard of treatment of aliens.[29] The customary international law standard was traditionally understood to prohibit only egregious or outrageous treatment.[30] This interpretation gives governments far greater scope to act in the ordinary course of governance without risking liability than under other types of fair and equitable treatment clause,[31] in relation to which the dominant view is that breach can arise through conduct that

---

[27] Article 1105 NAFTA. [28] *Metalclad* v. *Mexico*, Award, paras. 75–6.

[29] NAFTA Free Trade Commission, *Note of Interpretation of Certain Chapter 11 Provisions* (2001). See Van Harten, *Investment Treaty Arbitration and Public Law*, pp. 88, 145–6; Kläger, *Fair and Equitable Treatment*, pp. 62–70.

[30] It has frequently been argued that the customary international law minimum standard is set out in the (non-investment) case of *LFH Neer and Pauline E Neer (US* v. *Mexico)*, pp. 61–2: '[The] treatment of an alien, in order to constitute an international delinquency, should amount to an outrage, to bad faith, to wilful neglect of duty, or to an insufficiency of governmental action so far short of international standards that every reasonable and impartial man would readily recognise its insufficiency.' However, the content of the customary international law standard itself is open to debate and tribunals have adopted varying interpretations of it, some taking a more liberal approach to when a breach may be established and holding that the required level of misconduct to breach the standard has lessened over time as international law holds states to more exacting standards of treatment (but not setting out systematically exactly how customary international law has evolved). For example, *Waste Management* v. *Mexico*, Award, paras. 91–3; *Thunderbird* v. *Mexico*, Award, para. 19; *Merrill & Ring* v. *Canada*, Award, para. 213. See Kläger, *Fair and Equitable Treatment*, pp. 48–61, 71–2, 75–6, 87–8.

[31] Such as clauses stating that governments must accord treatment in accordance with international law, e.g. Article 3(2) Croatia-Oman BIT; Article 10(1) Energy Charter Treaty; Article II 3(a) US-Ecuador BIT or providing that states must accord fair and equitable treatment without any further elaboration, e.g. Article 4(1) United Arab Emirates-Switzerland BIT; Article 3 Belgium-Luxembourg Economic Union-Tajikistan BIT. Another formulation contains text expanding upon the obligations, e.g. Article 2(2) Hong Kong-Australia BIT (which also requires parties to refrain from unreasonable or discriminatory measures and requires parties to observe any obligations they have entered into with regard to investments of investors of the other party).

does not reach the level of mistreatment that the customary international law standard seeks to proscribe.[32]

The NAFTA parties' clarification concerns the normative content of fair and equitable treatment (and thus the grounds of review) rather than deference based on the characteristics of primary decision-makers.[33] This clarification nevertheless appears to have animated a discourse of deference among NAFTA tribunals, although at times tribunals have conflated these two concepts. For example, the *Glamis* tribunal stated that the customary international law threshold for breach of fair and equitable treatment meant that the concept of deference was inherent in determining whether fair and equitable treatment had been breached, rather than 'being additive to that standard'.[34] As Van Harten has observed, rationales for restraint in adjudication based on the characteristics of primary decision-makers are the same regardless of the grounds of review.[35]

Both the *Glamis* and *Chemtura* tribunals also purported to reject the concept of deference while simultaneously adopting a deferential approach. The *Glamis* tribunal stated that it 'disagrees that domestic deference in national court systems is necessarily applicable to international tribunals', but went on to refer to the desirability of democratically legitimate and expert decision-makers having primary decision-making responsibility.[36] Although rationales for deference relevantly differ between the domestic and international contexts (the concept of democratic accountability may uneasily transfer to the international sphere and separation of powers considerations may affect the degree of deference that a domestic court affords to the primary decision-makers), the *Glamis* tribunal could have acknowledged the way that deference also operates in international adjudication. The *Chemtura* tribunal, for its part, stated that the determination of whether fair and equitable treatment had been violated was 'not an abstract assessment circumscribed by a legal doctrine about the margin of appreciation of specialized regulatory agencies'.[37] However, the tribunal went on to state that it would 'take into account all the circumstances, including the

---

[32] See Kläger, *Fair and Equitable Treatment*, pp. 48–55, 85; UNCTAD, *Fair and Equitable Treatment* (2012) 22, 28; but see Paparinskis, *The International Minimum Standard* p. 162.

[33] Cf. *Waste Management* v. *Mexico*, Award, para. 98, referring to the normative content of Article 1105 NAFTA: 'The search here is for the Article 1105 standard of review.'

[34] *Glamis* v. *US*, Award, para. 617.

[35] Van Harten, *Sovereign Choices and Sovereign Constraints*, pp. 96–100.

[36] *Glamis* v. *US*, Award, para. 617.   [37] *Glamis* v. *US*, Award, para. 617.

fact that certain agencies manage highly specialized domains involving scientific and public policy determinations'.[38] In this respect, the tribunal afforded a significant measure of deference to the expertise of the authorities – one of the bases upon which a court or tribunal may afford a margin of appreciation.[39]

These decisions both highlight arbitrators' lack of understanding of the theoretical underpinnings of deference in the context of regulatory adjudication, while at the same time revealing that they have an implicit understanding of their institutional limitations. As was argued in Chapter 2, whether it is appropriate to afford a measure of deference and the broader issues surrounding the appropriate standard of review are conceptually separate matters to the grounds of review and interpretations of treaty provisions that permit greater or lesser autonomy for host states.

6.3.2 Misunderstanding deference and the margin of appreciation

It should also be noted that some (non-NAFTA) tribunals have expressly rejected a deferential approach.[40] The *Siemens* tribunal rejected the applicability of the margin of appreciation to its decision-making on the basis that the doctrine was neither part of customary international law nor referred to in the treaty in question.[41] The tribunal did not appear to appreciate that the ECtHR developed the margin of appreciation in the absence of a textual basis in the ECHR[42] or how the margin actually operates in case law. In *Quasar de Valores*, the tribunal remarked that unlike human rights treaties, investment treaties 'contain undertakings which are explicitly designed to induce foreigners to make investments in reliance upon them' that 'should not be diluted' through the application of a margin of appreciation.[43] In *EDF (Argentina)*, the tribunal rejected the respondent's submissions (relying on *Glamis*) that it should afford a margin of appreciation on the basis that the NAFTA Commission's Note of Interpretation recalibrated the applicable standard of review for

---

[38] *Glamis* v. *US*, Award, para. 617. [39] *Glamis* v. *US*, Award, para. 617.
[40] *Siemens* v. *Argentina*, Award, para. 354. [41] *Siemens* v. *Argentina*, Award, para. 354.
[42] However, Article 1 of the recently concluded 15th Protocol to the ECHR provides that the parties 'enjoy a margin of appreciation, subject to the supervisory jurisdiction of the European Court of Human Rights established by this Convention'. The Protocol will enter into force as soon as all the parties to the Convention have signed and ratified it.
[43] *Renta 4 S.V.S.A, Ahorro Corporación Emergentes F.I., Ahorro Corporación Eurofondo F.I., Rovime Inversiones SICAV S.A., Quasar de Valores SICAV S.A., Orgor de Valores SICAV S.A., GBI 9000 SICAV S.A.* v. *Russia*, Award, para. 22.

NAFTA cases.[44] Again, these approaches misunderstand the nature of a margin of appreciation and the circumstances in which deference may be due. Still other tribunals mentioned the state's plea for deference but failed to address this question in their reasoning, perhaps indicating a lack of understanding of how to apply the concept in practice.[45] Finally, as discussed in Chapter 4, other tribunals (*Tecmed* and *Gemplus*) referred to the concept of deference while employing a strict standard of review. The *Tecmed* tribunal purported to align its decision with the jurisprudence of the ECtHR,[46] and in early cases against Argentina in relation to its economic crisis, tribunals stated they would take into account the crisis situation in the determination of whether Argentina had complied with fair and equitable treatment, but then failed to do so.[47]

6.3.3   Strategic considerations affecting the standard of review

As Guzman has observed, international courts and tribunals may act strategically by 'tailoring their judgments to the political realities of the situation before them' in order to 'avoid too severe a deviation from the preferences of states'.[48] The Appellate Body, for example, acted strategically in its early years of operation following the move from diplomacy-oriented to legalized dispute settlement by employing a strict textual approach to interpretation.[49] In relation to the standard of review, the ECtHR took a strategic approach in the first few years following its inception through the development and application of the margin of appreciation, mindful of its fragile status and reliance on the continuing support of the state parties.[50] Arguably, the CJEU acts strategically in cases where it disguises the proportionality *stricto sensu* stage of proportionality analysis

---

[44] *EDF* v. *Argentina*, Award, paras. 1003, 1106.

[45] See *Biwater Gauff* v. *Tanzania*, Award, paras. 434–6; *National Grid* v. *Argentina*, Award, para. 247; *EDF International S.A., SAUR International S.A. and León Participaciones Argentinas S.A.* v. *Argentine Republic*, Award, para. 489.

[46] *Tecmed* v. *Mexico*, Award, para. 122; *Gemplus* v. *Mexico*, Award, paras. 4-72–4-92, 6-26.

[47] *CMS* v. *Argentina*, Award, paras. 277–81; *Enron* v. *Argentina*, Award, paras. 260–8; *Sempra* v. *Argentina*, Award, paras. 300–4.

[48] Guzman, 'International Tribunals: A Rational Choice Analysis' (2008) 157 *University of Pennsylvania Law Review* 171, 184. See also (in the domestic context) Kavanagh, 'Deference or Defiance?', pp. 188–9.

[49] Wagner, 'Law Talk v. Science Talk', p. 163.

[50] Macdonald, 'The Margin of Appreciation' in Macdonald, Matscher and Petzold (eds.), *The European System for the Protection of Human Rights* (1993) 83, 123; Marks, 'Civil Liberties at the Margin: The UK Derogation and the European Court of Human Rights' (1995) 15 *Oxford Journal of Legal Studies* 69, 93; Jones, 'The Devaluation of Human Rights

within least-restrictive means analysis because in doing so, it attempts to avoid the perception of overreach into national regulatory autonomy.[51] Whether this approach is desirable is another question. Giving strategic concerns primacy over substantive legal issues may be problematic for both normative reasons and from the perspective of the need for clarity in tribunals' reasoning – particularly where a tribunal seeks to underplay these considerations and frame the decision in such a way as to present its decision as being solely based on the tribunal's assessment of the substantive legal issues.[52]

NAFTA tribunals also appear to have been motivated by strategic concerns in terms of maintaining the institution of NAFTA as an instrument of economic integration. In *Glamis*, the tribunal stressed that maintaining the integrity of NAFTA's investment chapter required it to decide the case with an awareness of the systemic implications of its decision, noting the NAFTA parties' 'indefinite commitment to the deepening of their economic relations' and remarking that 'the long-term maintenance of this commitment requires both governmental and public faith in the integrity of the process of arbitration'.[53] There is also evidence that strategic considerations influenced arbitrators' approaches to deference in cases in which tribunals ruled that it was permissible for governments to pursue policy initiatives designed to assist the host state's economy, such as preferential treatment of domestic industries.

It remains to be seen whether investment tribunals adjudicating disputes under other treaties will, like NAFTA tribunals, adopt a strategic approach to the standard of review. While it might be argued that the imperative of maintaining continued support for an institution such as NAFTA is not generally present in international investment law, given the

Under the European Convention' (1995) *Public Law* 430, 437; Kavanagh, 'Deference or Defiance?', pp. 203–4.

[51] See Chapter 3. Federalist tensions may also explain the CJEU's approach to national measures, in the sense that those measures fall within member state competence: Bermann, 'Proportionality and Subsidiarity' in Barnard and Scott (eds.), *The Law of the Single European Market: Unpacking the Premises* (2002) 76–7.

[52] Kavanagh, 'Deference or Defiance?', pp. 204–5; Kurtz, 'Access to Justice, Denial and Justice and International Investment Law: A Reply to Francesco Francioni' (2009) 20 *European Journal of International Law* 1077, 1081.

[53] *Glamis* v. *US*, Award, para. 8. Although not an issue concerning the standard of review *per se*, in the earlier case of *Loewen*, the tribunal referred to the continuing viability of NAFTA in declining to exercise jurisdiction over a claim involving a challenge to the decision of a US trial court: *Loewen* v. *US*, Award, para. 242. See Van Harten, *Investment Treaty Arbitration and Public Law*, pp. 146–7; Kurtz, 'Access to Justice', p. 1081.

dominance of bilateral treaties between capital-importing and capital-exporting states, recent negotiations for mega-regional trade and investment treaties suggest that this intensity-influencing factor may become more relevant over time. In any event, it can be argued that strategic concerns may become a relevant consideration in a broader sense. Although investment tribunals do not depend on the support of states for the purpose of exercising jurisdiction (governments having given general consent to the arbitration of disputes on entering into investment treaties), individual arbitrators are dependent on both foreign investors and states for the continued use of their services and are thus subject to their own constraints in terms of not alienating potential appointing parties. It is arguable that investment arbitrators might increasingly respond to concerns expressed by states in relation to regulatory autonomy – particularly the threat of exit – by adopting a less strict approach to the standard of review.[54]

6.3.4   The desirability of deference in determining state liability

The central argument made in this book is that investment tribunals should calibrate the appropriate standard of review to the circumstances and afford a measure of deference to governments in situations of normative or empirical uncertainty. Where the treaty at issue does not stipulate or provide guidance as to the applicable standard of review – which is the case in relation to the vast majority of investment treaties – the determination of the appropriate standard of review is, as noted in Chapter 1, an inherent power of the tribunal.

In performing proportionality analysis, the regulatory autonomy and proximity rationale for deference will, provided that the objective is not discriminatory or otherwise impermissible, be relevant to the assessment of the legitimacy of the objective of a challenged measure. This reason for deference will equally be applicable to any proportionality *stricto sensu* review undertaken by a tribunal, because this stage of proportionality analysis is, in essence, a value judgement. Moreover, in many cases, it will be appropriate for arbitrators to take into account the institutional competence and/or expertise of primary decision-makers in determining the suitability and necessity of a challenged measure. These rationales for

---

[54] See Roberts, 'Clash of Paradigms', p. 89. See also Leonhardsen, 'Treaty Change, Arbitral Practice and the Search for a Balance', p. 135.

deference are, in any case, relevant regardless of the method of review that a tribunal employs.

Yet, it is not argued that tribunals should apply a universally deferential approach in all cases. The appropriateness of deference and the applicable degree of deference will depend on the circumstances. Deference will not be indicated where the issues for determination are clear-cut and there is no uncertainty as to normative or empirical matters because in such cases, there will be no need to rely on the assessments of primary decision-makers.

6.3.4.1 Deference versus non-justiciability

Reliance on the standard of review as a means of allocating authority between host states and investment tribunals is not without its critics. Foster, for example, argues that recourse to the concept of the standard of review would result in international adjudicators' role 'falling short of full adjudication, involving a decreased depth of enquiry into compliance with international law', which would result in a court or tribunal avoiding the determination of 'what ought to be the ultimate factual and legal issues in a dispute'.[55]

This criticism is in one sense reminiscent of a debate that has taken place in the context of UK public law, principally between Allan and Kavanagh.[56] Allan famously described deference as 'non-justiciability

---

[55] Foster, 'Adjudication, Arbitration and the Turn to Public Law "Standards of Review": Putting the Precautionary Principle in the Crucible' (2012) 3 *Journal of International Dispute Settlement* 525, 526; Foster, 'Diminished Ambitions? Public International Legal Authority in the Transnational Economic Era' (2014) 17 *Journal of International Economic Law* 374–5. See also Alvarez, 'Beware: Boundary Crossings', pp. 36–7. However, Foster has also expressed support for the concept of a margin of appreciation, at least with respect to expertise in relation to risk regulation undertaken by domestic authorities, acknowledging that 'a tribunal's 'depth of review' must always depend on what is required by the relevant international obligation', and that very seldom is a court or tribunal called upon to 'assess the absolute correctness of the science supporting a State's regulatory measure'; rather, there is 'a margin of regulatory appreciation' applicable to the state's determination: Foster, 'Adjudication, Arbitration', pp. 535–6.

[56] See Allan, 'Human Rights and Judicial Review: A Critique of Due Deference' (2006) 65 *Cambridge Law Journal* 671; Kavanagh, 'Deference or Defiance?'; Kavanagh, 'Defending Deference', Allan, 'Deference, Defiance and Doctrine: Defining the Limits of Judicial Review' (2010) 60 *University of Toronto Law Journal* 41; Kavanagh, 'Judicial Restraint in the Pursuit of Justice' (2010) 60 *University of Toronto Law Journal* 23; Allan, 'Judicial Deference and Judicial Review: Legal Doctrine and Legal Theory' (2011) 127 *Law Quarterly Review* 96; Allan, *The Sovereignty of Law: Freedom, Constitution and Common Law* (2013).

dressed in pastel colours', arguing that courts should only rely on the greater expertise, institutional competence and democratic legitimacy of governments where this resulted in superior arguments that would have persuaded the court in any event.[57] The basis for this criticism is Allan's apprehension that proponents of deference advocate that courts apply a 'doctrine' of deference for its own sake at the outset of the inquiry, accepting the justifications given by primary decision-makers and avoiding full scrutiny of rights-limiting measures. As a result, in Allan's view, the concept of deference collapses into a doctrine of non-justiciability in the sense of abdication of judicial responsibility – a court declining to exercise jurisdiction in cases where it ought to be exercised.[58] But deference differs from non-justiciability, which is a substantive bar on adjudication that is self-imposed by a court or tribunal on the basis that the matter is not suitable for judicial resolution.[59] This critique also arguably neither considers the variety of ways and degrees in which deference can be afforded (i.e. it is not an all-or-nothing approach), nor appears to acknowledge that adjudicators labour under conditions of uncertainty.[60] Nor does deference, as Foster suggests, entail reviewing only governmental decision-making processes and refraining from examining the merits of the decision.[61] Courts and tribunals undertaking both substantive and procedural forms of adjudication must confront the applicable standard of review as an inherent part of the adjudicatory process.

6.3.4.2   Deference does not require particular treaty language

Another argument is that investment tribunals should only adopt a deferential approach where the treaty text so indicates. Burke-White and von Staden argue that deference should be restricted to situations where the text of the treaty indicates that states intend to preserve regulatory

---

[57] Allan, 'Human Rights and Judicial Review: A Critique of Due Deference' (2006) 65 *Cambridge Law Journal* 688–9; Allan, *The Sovereignty of Law*, pp. 249, 269, 275–6, 278.

[58] Allan, 'Human Rights and Judicial Review', pp. 675, 688; Allan, *The Sovereignty of Law*, pp. 274–5. See King, *Judging Social Rights* (2012) 148–50.

[59] Kavanagh, *Constitutional Review*, p. 173; Legg, *The Margin of Appreciation in International Human Rights Law: Deference and Proportionality* (2012) 36.

[60] King, 'The Pervasiveness of Polycentricity' (2008) *Public Law* 101, 143; Kavanagh, 'Judicial Restraint' 23, 28. Brady, *Proportionality and Deference*, p. 28.

[61] Cf. Foster, 'Adjudication, Arbitration', p. 526; Foster, 'Diminished Ambitions?', p. 374.

autonomy, such as treaty exceptions or the requirement that an expropriation be carried out for a 'public purpose'.[62] The applicable degree of deference would be further discerned from the treaty language, with arbitrators granting more deference in relation to more open-textured treaty terms (such as whether a measure was adopted to protect public morals) than those amenable to objective determination (such as whether a measure was adopted to protect public health).[63]

To be sure, the degree of specificity of treaty language may affect the standard of review more broadly. More specific norms are likely to attract a stricter standard of review than more generally expressed norms on the basis that whether the state has complied with a more vaguely expressed norm may be open to a greater range of interpretations.[64] However, Burke-White and von Staden adopt an overly restrictive approach to when deference may be appropriate. Although the applicable standard of review may be guided by and should never be inconsistent with the treaty text, restricting deference to situations where the relevant treaty text indicates an intention to preserve regulatory autonomy would not permit tribunals to take a deferential approach under the vast majority of investment treaties that do not detail or even suggest the existence of the state's continued regulatory powers. The method of review and standard of review, while not usually as visible in treaties as the grounds of review, will always be components of an adjudicator's role.

Burke-White and von Staden justify their restrictive approach on the basis that it is necessary 'to prevent states from seeking more deferential review where it is not appropriate'.[65] But this perspective does not take account of the reasons why deference might be indicated: where a situation of normative or empirical uncertainty means that a tribunal's assessment is more likely to be correct (or viewed as legitimate) where the tribunal relies upon the assessment of the primary decision-maker, due to the greater reliability of the assessment made by that decision-maker. Presumably, it is a natural inclination for a government to argue that a

---

[62] Burke-White and von Staden, 'Investment Protection in Extraordinary Times', pp. 370–6; Burke-White and von Staden, 'Private Litigation', pp. 293–6; Burke-White and von Staden, 'Public Law Standards', p. 695.

[63] Burke-White and von Staden, 'Investment Protection in Extraordinary Times', pp. 372, 375; Burke-White and von Staden, 'Private Litigation', p. 295; Burke-White and von Staden, 'Public Law Standards', p. 695.

[64] See Shany, Margin of Appreciation p. 914.

[65] Burke-White and von Staden, 'Private Litigation', p. 296.

high degree of deference should be granted, regardless of the circumstances. It is the role of the tribunal to determine whether deference is warranted according to the circumstances of the case, rather than applying a restrictive approach *ex ante*. There will be situations in which the public interest asserted by the host state is pretextual or is peripheral to other impermissible objectives. But approaching the concept of deference with the understanding that it is only due in circumstances of *uncertainty* should address these concerns. Additionally, the structure of proportionality analysis provides for appropriate scrutiny of these issues through the examination of the regulatory objective and the suitability and necessity of the means to achieve it, identifying situations where the state has not acted in good faith or has adopted measures that are ineffective or overly burdensome, compared to available alternatives.

6.4   Conclusion

Proportionality analysis is a method of review that has stood the test of time in many other legal systems as a means of determining liability in regulatory disputes engaging competing public and private interests. In international investment law, the normative vagueness of many of the substantive obligations owed by host states to foreign investors strongly suggests that tribunals should take into account the state's reasons for its actions in the determination of liability. It could hardly be argued that state parties to investment treaties intended otherwise.

In the absence of textual guidance concerning how to take state and investor interests into account in determining liability – or where the treaty provision so permits, such as certain exception clauses – it will be legitimate for tribunals to look to how other courts and tribunals undertaking similar functions have approached this task. But this is not to say that proportionality analysis is an appropriate method of review in all circumstances: where customary international law, the treaty text or an investor-state contract stipulate a different method of review, do not envisage taking into account state and investor interests or otherwise preclude proportionality analysis, adopting this method of review would be beyond the power of investment arbitrators. This chapter has also argued that the proper place for consideration of the state's reasons for its actions, including proportionality analysis where relevant, is in the context of the primary norm rather than any exception clause. Moreover, arguments against the use of proportionality analysis by investment tribunals based on the primary remedy of compensation are unconvincing.

As well as deference based on the characteristics of primary decision-makers, other considerations have also affected the standard of review in NAFTA cases: the clarification of the normative content of fair and equitable treatment by the NAFTA parties in response to expansive interpretations of the concept by early tribunals suggests that NAFTA tribunals' approaches to the standard of review have been underpinned by broader considerations of the desirability of restraint in interpreting states' obligations. A parallel discourse of restraint as a means of maintaining the institution of NAFTA as an instrument of regional economic integration is also evident. However, NAFTA tribunals in particular have been less than clear about their approaches to deference, conflating the appropriate degree of deference with the normative content of fair and equitable treatment (and thus the grounds of review), or rejecting the idea of deference while adopting a deferential approach (and vice versa). Other tribunals appear to have rejected a deferential approach based on a misunderstanding of the concept. This suggests that arbitrators should be more explicit in their determination of the appropriate standard of review, including setting out why they have (or have not) been deferential in the circumstances.[66] Greater predictability and transparency in this respect will send signals to states, investors and future tribunals about the circumstances in which a deferential approach to review will – and will not – be appropriate. This in turn could improve the decision-making processes of states to the extent that governments may be influenced to make their decisions in a defensible manner, for example, by relying on available expertise.[67]

This chapter also has responded to criticisms about deferential approaches to determining state liability in the context of investor-state arbitration. Deference cannot be equated with non-justiciability, or be restricted to situations where the treaty text leaves room for different interpretations of key terms. The determination of the applicable standard of review – including the appropriate degree of deference – neither amounts to an abdication of the adjudicatory function of tribunals nor

---

[66] Kläger, *Fair and Equitable Treatment*, p. 248; von Staden, 'Deference or No Deference, That is the Question: Legitimacy and Standards of Review in Investor-State Arbitration' (2012) 2 *Investment Treaty News* 4.
[67] See Gerards, 'Margin of Appreciation', p. 89.

will invariably result in a high level of deference, preclude state liability[68] or politicize the role of investment tribunals.[69] In reviewing measures adopted in the exercise of public power by host states, investment tribunals function as part of the system of governance of the state. Taking into account the relative characteristics and strengths of different actors in decision-making in situations of uncertainty is an essential aspect of governance, including adjudication.[70]

---

[68] Roberts, 'The Next Battleground', p. 177; Chen, 'The Standard of Review', p. 28; Van Harten, *Sovereign Choices and Sovereign Constraints*, p. 18.

[69] Cf. Moloo and Jacinto, 'Standards of Review', p. 566.

[70] See Van Harten, *Investment Treaty Arbitration and Public Law*, p. 144.

CONCLUSION

This book has analyzed the manner in which investment tribunals have balanced the protection of foreign investment with the right of host states to regulate and take other actions in the public interest. In doing so, this study has focused on the *method of review* and the *standard of review* employed by investment tribunals. Both the method of review and the standard of review are critical – not only in terms of the extent to which the system of international investment law can provide sufficient space for regulatory autonomy, but also in the development of a more certain and consistent methodology for deciding regulatory disputes. It is also crucial to view these two aspects of tribunals' decision-making together in terms of an integrated approach to the method and standard of review, which tribunals have not yet done on a consistent basis. These two concepts exist in a symbiotic relationship and must be addressed together.

This book has two main arguments at its heart. First, it argues that proportionality analysis represents a tried and tested method of review for regulatory disputes involving competing public and private interests, and that is is a rational and coherent means of determining state liability. In particular, the technique is preferable to other methods employed by investment tribunals such as review for reasonableness or other approaches that give arbitrators overly broad discretion. These other methods of review also fall short of proportionality analysis in terms of their coherency and transparency. This book contends that investment tribunals should undertake least-restrictive means analysis in fairness to investors, provided that an institutionally sensitive approach is employed. However, investment tribunals are not institutionally well placed to engage in the proportionality *stricto sensu* stage of analysis and should not do so in order to reduce the scope for subjectivity and value judgements in their decision-making – and the negative impact that this approach can have on both legal certainty and regulatory autonomy.

The second main argument made in this book is that as international adjudicators of regulatory disputes, investment tribunals should grant states an appropriate measure of deference where indicated by the circumstances of the case. Deference may be due in situations of normative or empirical uncertainty for two different reasons: the normative desirability of regulatory autonomy and decision-making by embedded or proximate decision-makers, and the practical advantages that inhere in reliance by adjudicators upon the institutional competence and expertise of governments. The decided cases evidence an increasing number of occasions where arbitrators have afforded states a measure of deference in their decision-making, including in combination with proportionality-based approaches to a review of government action.

Adopting proportionality analysis as a method of review together with an appropriate measure of deference in the circumstances of the case would have two significant benefits for investor-state arbitration and for international investment law as a whole. The first benefit is that the consistent use of this method of review could provide greater structure and transparency in tribunals' decision-making, leading to greater consistency in the decided cases and, therefore, greater predictability for states and investors. The other benefit of this approach is that it pays due regard to the circumstances in which the characteristics of host state decision-makers render them better placed to have primary responsibility for deciding the matter in question. It can accommodate varying levels of intensity depending on the circumstances of the case, and thus attenuate the negative effects of tribunals' decision-making on the regulatory autonomy of host states. The proposal made in this book is a means of dealing with the above concerns within the current system of investor-state arbitration, building on approaches taken by arbitrators in the decided investment cases to date and inspired by the approaches of other courts and tribunals undertaking functionally similar tasks.

However, it is arguable that institutional constraints may militate against the adoption of the approach proposed in this book. The absence of a standing court or tribunal or other appellate structure was highlighted in Chapter 1 as a factor affecting the potential for international investment law to develop a coherent approach to the determination of liability in regulatory disputes, including consensus as to the normative content of standards of investment protection and the appropriate approach to the applicable method of review and standard of review. This being the case, the question that arises is whether it is realistic to expect tribunals to consistently adopt proportionality analysis and an appropriately deferential approach to the standard of review at this time.[1] The approaches of other courts and tribunals surveyed in this book demonstrate that even standing courts or legal systems that provide for appellate review do not necessarily approach these issues in a consistent and coherent manner. However, although it may be more difficult to develop the proposed approach to these issues in the context of the current system, it is also arguable that as international investment law continues to evolve, the decision-making of tribunals will begin to coalesce around certain approaches to the method and standard of review. There is no reason why consensus in relation to these issues cannot emerge just as consensus is building around certain other procedural and substantive issues in investor-state arbitration[2] – although tribunals will be reliant on suitable claims being brought in order to employ the proposed approach.

However, commentators have argued that it might be preferable for investment treaties to define the applicable rules with respect to the applicable method and standard of review, either as a means of exerting greater control over the discretion of arbitrators in a manner supportive of regulatory autonomy[3] or on the basis that it is legitimate for investment tribunals to adopt new approaches to the method and standard of review only where the treaty text expressly so permits.[4] Although this book argues that a tribunal's approach to these matters need not be mandated by treaty text, stipulation of these matters would, at a practical level, have the advantage of providing clearer guidance to arbitrators in their decision-making, with the aim of reducing inconsistencies among tribunal decisions and promoting decision-making that takes both state and investor interests into account.

---

[1] See Van Harten, *Sovereign Choices and Sovereign Constraints*, p. 159; Wagner, 'Regulatory Space', p. 85.

[2] Roberts, 'The Next Battleground', p. 178. See also Burke-White and von Staden, 'Public Law Standards', p. 720, arguing that although a new approach to the standard of review could be relatively easily implemented, it would rely on tribunals engaging in dialogue with one another through their awards.

[3] See van Aaken, 'Control Mechanisms in International Investment Law' in Douglas, Pauwelyn and Viñuales (eds.), *The Foundations of International Investment Law: Bringing Theory into Practice* (2014) 409, 423–4.

[4] See Katselas, 'Do Investment Treaties Prescribe a Deferential Standard of Review?' (2012) 34 *Michigan Journal of International Law* 87, 148; Calamita, 'Constitutional Considerations', p. 184; Alvarez, 'Beware: Boundary Crossings', pp. 58–9; Ranjan, 'Using the Public Law Concept of Proportionality', p. 857.

A number of states have concluded or are negotiating new investment treaties that provide for greater regulatory space in the context of substantive obligations owed to foreign investors, including stipulation or guidance as to the applicable method of review. For example, several recent treaties define indirect expropriation with reference to the principle of proportionality, so that non-discriminatory measures directed at legitimate objectives will not be considered to be expropriatory unless the effect of the measure on the investor is adjudged to be disproportionate in light of the importance of the regulatory objective pursued.[5] Other treaty provisions more categorically state that, generally speaking, non-discriminatory regulations directed at the protection of public welfare objectives do not constitute indirect expropriations,[6] or have made exception clauses self-judging.[7] Given this gradual but piecemeal approach to specifying these matters in investment treaties, the proposals made in this book are in one sense an intermediate solution – although there is no reason why the principles underpinning the approaches to the method and standard of review proposed in this book cannot be used to inform future treaty negotiations.

To conclude, the protections granted to foreign investors through investment treaties should be viewed as protections from misuse of public power, whether intended by host states or inadvertently arising through measures that are ineffective at achieving their objectives or that have an undue impact on foreign investment in the light of available alternatives. Seen in this light, proportionality analysis is a useful analytical tool for tribunals to employ in order to identify and control such instances of misuse of power. Using proportionality analysis in combination with an appropriately deferential approach to the standard of review can also provide the basis for a more coherent means of determining liability in these areas of investment law. By approaching the method and standard of review in such a way as to permit host states sufficient freedom to design and implement policies to promote public welfare, investment tribunals can protect the legitimate interests of states while still exercising proper oversight of governments' compliance with their treaty obligations. As

---

[5] See e.g. Annex 11-B [3(b)] US-South Korea FTA; Chapter 8, Section D, Annex 811(2)(b) Colombia-Canada FTA; Annex 13 China-New Zealand FTA; Annex 2 Article 3(c) ASEAN Comprehensive Investment Agreement; Article VIII(2)(c) UK-Colombia BIT.

[6] See e.g. Annex 11-B [4] US-Australia FTA; Annex 11-B US-South Korea FTA; Article 20(8) COMESA Investment Agreement.

[7] See e.g. Article XI US-Ecuador BIT, Article XIV US-Albania BIT.

such, this approach has the potential to assuage concerns about both the fragmented and inconsistent nature of investment tribunals' decision-making in determining state liability in regulatory disputes, and the negative impact of their decision-making on regulatory autonomy. Adopting such an approach may, therefore, go some way towards addressing concerns expressed by states and commentators about the need for a fairer balance between the interests of host states and investors in international investment law.

BIBLIOGRAPHY

Alexy R, *A Theory of Constitutional Rights* (Oxford University Press, J Rivers trans., 2002)

'On Balancing and Subsumption: A Structural Comparison' (2003) 16 *Ratio Juris* 433

'Balancing, Constitutional Review, and Representation' (2005) 3 *International Journal of Constitutional Law* 572

'Thirteen Replies' in G Pavlakos (ed.), *Law, Rights and Discourse: The Legal Philosophy of Robert Alexy* (Oxford: Hart, 2007) 333

Allan T R S, 'Human Rights and Judicial Review: A Critique of Due Deference' (2006) 65 *Cambridge Law Journal* 671

'Deference, Defiance and Doctrine: Defining the Limits of Judicial Review' (2010) 60 *University of Toronto Law Journal* 41

'Judicial Deference and Judicial Review: Legal Doctrine and Legal Theory' (2011) 127 *Law Quarterly Review* 96

The Sovereignty of Law: Freedom, Constitution and Common Law (Oxford University Press, 2013)

Alvarez J E, 'Review: *Investment Treaty Arbitration and Public Law* by Gus Van Harten' (2008) 102 *American Journal of International Law* 909

'The Return of the State' (2011) 20 *Minnesota Journal of International Law* 223

'Beware: Boundary Crossings' (2014) in T Kahana and A Schnicov (eds.), *Boundaries of Rights, Boundaries of State* (forthcoming) http://papers.ssrn.com/sol3/papers.cfm?abstract_id=2498182

Alvarez J E and Brink T, 'Revisiting the Necessity Defense: *Continental Casualty v. Argentina*' in K P Sauvant (ed.), *Yearbook on International Investment Law and Policy 2010–2011* (Oxford University Press, 2011) 319

Alvarez J E and Khamsi K, 'The Argentine Crisis and Foreign Investors: A Glimpse into the Heart of the Investment Regime' in K P Sauvant (ed.), *Yearbook on International Investment Law and Policy 2008–2009* (Oxford University Press, 2009) 379

American Law Institute, *Restatement of the Law Third, Foreign Relations of the United States*, Volume 1 (Philadelphia, PA: American Law Institute, 1987)

Andenas M and Zleptnig S, 'Proportionality: WTO Law in Comparative Perspective' (2007) 42 *Texas International Law Journal* 371

'The Rule of Law and Proportionality in WTO Law' in W Shan, P Simons and D Singh (eds.), *Redefining Sovereignty in International Economic Law* (Oxford: Hart, 2008) 171

Arai-Takahashi Y, *The Margin of Appreciation Doctrine and the Principle of Proportionality in the Jurisprudence of the ECHR* (Antwerp: Intersentia, 2002)

Arato J, 'The Margin of Appreciation in International Investment Law' (2014) 54 *Virginia Journal of International Law* 545

Aust A, *Modern Treaty Law and Practice* (Cambridge University Press, 2007)

Barak A, *Proportionality: Constitutional Rights and Their Limitations* (Cambridge University Press, 2012)

'Proportionality (2)' in M Rosenfeld and A Sajo (eds.), *The Oxford Handbook of Comparative Constitutional Law* (Oxford University Press, 2012) 739

Bartels L, 'The Chapeau of the General Exceptions in the WTO GATT and GATS Agreements: A Reconstruction' (2015) 109 *American Journal of International Law* 95

Baudenbacher C and Clifton M, 'Courts of Regional Economic and Political Integration Agreements' in C Romano, K Alter and Y Shany (eds.), *The Oxford Handbook of International Adjudication* (Oxford University Press, 2014) 250

Been V and Beauvais J C, 'The Global Fifth Amendment? NAFTA's Investment Protections and the Misguided Quest for an International "Regulatory Takings" Doctrine' (2003) 78 *New York University Law Review* 30

Behrens P, 'Towards the Constitutionalization of International Investment Protection' (2007) 45 *Archiv des Völkerrechts* 153

Beloff M, 'The Concept of Deference in Public Law' (2006) 11 *Judicial Review* 213

Benvenisti E, 'Margin of Appreciation, Consensus, and Universal Standards' (1999) 31 *International Law and Politics* 843

Bermann G A, 'Proportionality and Subsidiarity' in C Barnard and J Scott (eds.), *The Law of the Single European Market: Unpacking the Premises* (Oxford: Hart, 2002) 75

Bilchitz D, *Poverty and Fundamental Rights: The Justification and Enforcement of Socio-Economic Rights* (Oxford University Press, 2008)

Binder C and Reinisch A, 'Economic Emergency Powers: A Comparative Law Perspective' in S W Schill (ed.), *International Investment Law and Comparative Public Law* (Oxford University Press, 2010) 503

Bjorklund A K, 'Investment Treaty Arbitral Decisions as Jurisprudence Constante' in C Picker, I Bunn and D Arner (eds.), *International Economic Law: The State and Future of the Discipline* (Oxford: Hart, 2008) 265

'The National Treatment Obligation' in K Yannaca-Small (ed.), *Arbitration Under International Investment Agreements: A Guide to the Key Issues* (Oxford University Press, 2010) 411

Bohanes J and Lockhart N, 'Standard of Review in WTO Law' in D Bethlehem, D McRae, R Neufeld and I Van Damme (eds.), *The Oxford Handbook of International Trade Law* (Oxford University Press, 2009) 378

Bomhoff J, 'Balancing, the Global and Local: Judicial Balancing as a Problematic Topic in Comparative (Constitutional) Law' (2008) 31 *Hastings International and Comparative Law Review* 555

'Genealogies of Balancing as Discourse' (2010) 4 *Law and Ethics of Human Rights* 108

Balancing Constitutional Rights: The Origins and Meanings of Postwar Legal Discourse (Cambridge University Press, 2013)

Bongiovanni G, Sartor G and Valentini C, 'Introduction' in G Bongiovanni, G Sartor and C Valentini (eds.), *Reasonableness and Law* (Dordrecht: Springer, 2009) xi

Bonnitcha J, *Substantive Protection under Investment Treaties* (Cambridge University Press, 2014)

Bown C P and Trachtman J P, '*Brazil – Measures Affecting Imports of Retreaded Tyres*: A Balancing Act' (2009) 8 *World Trade Review* 85

Brady A D P, *Proportionality and Deference under the UK Human Rights Act: An Institutionally Sensitive Approach* (Cambridge University Press, 2012)

Brauch J A, 'The Margin of Appreciation and the Jurisprudence of the European Court of Human Rights: Threat to the Rule of Law' (2005) 11 *Columbia Journal of European Law* 113

Brems E and Lavrysen L, '"Don't Use a Sledgehammer to Crack a Nut": Less Restrictive Means in the Case Law of the European Court of Human Rights' (2015) 15 *Human Rights Law Review* 139

Brower C H, 'Structure, Legitimacy, and NAFTA's Investment Chapter' (2003) 36 *Vanderbilt Journal of Transnational Law* 37

'Obstacles and Pathways to Consideration of the Public Interest in Investment Treaty Disputes' in K P Sauvant (ed.), *Yearbook on International Investment Law & Policy 2008–2009* (Oxford University Press, 2009) 274

Brower C N and Schill S W, 'Is Arbitration a Threat on a Boon to the Legitimacy of International Investment Law?' (2009) 9 *Chicago Journal of International Law* 471

Brown C, 'The Inherent Powers of Courts and Tribunals' (2005) 76 *British Yearbook of International and Comparative Law* 195

Burke-White W W and von Staden A, 'Investment Protection in Extraordinary Times: The Interpretation and Application of Non-Precluded Measures Provisions in Bilateral Investment Treaties' (2008) 48 *Virginia Journal of International Law* 307

'Private Litigation in a Public Law Sphere: The Standard of Review in Investor-State Arbitrations' (2010) 35 *Yale Journal of International Law* 283

'The Need for Public Law Standards of Review in Investor-State Arbitrations' in S W Schill (ed.), *International Investment Law and Comparative Public Law* (Oxford University Press, 2010) 689

Button C, *The Power to Protect: Trade, Health and Uncertainty in the WTO* (Oxford: Hart, 2004)

Calamita N J, 'International Human Rights and the Interpretation of International Investment Treaties: Constitutional Considerations' in F Baetens (ed.), *Investment Law within International Law: Integrationist Perspectives* (Cambridge University Press, 2013) 164

Çali B, 'Balancing Human Rights? Methodological Problems with Weights, Scales and Proportions' (2007) 29 *Human Rights Quarterly* 251

Campbell T, Ewing K and Tomkins A (eds.), *Sceptical Essays on Human Rights* (Oxford University Press, 2001)

Carozza P G, 'Subsidiarity as a Structural Principle of International Human Rights Law' (2003) 97 *American Journal of International Law* 38

Chan C, 'Deference, Expertise and Information-Gathering Powers' (2013) 33 *Legal Studies* 598

Chen T, 'The Standard of Review and the Roles of ICSID Arbitral Tribunals in Investor-State Dispute Settlement' (2012) 5 *Contemporary Asia Arbitration Journal* 23

Cheng T, 'Precedent and Control in Investment Treaty Arbitration' (2006) 30 *Fordham International Law Journal* 1014

Cheyne I, 'Deference and the Use of the Public Policy Exception in International Courts and Tribunals' in L Gruszczynski and W Werner (eds.), *Deference in International Courts and Tribunals: Standard of Review and Margin of Appreciation* (Oxford University Press, 2014) 38

Christie G C, 'What Constitutes a Taking of Property Under International Law?' (1962) 38 *British Yearbook of International Law* 307

Christoffersen J, *Fair Balance: Proportionality, Subsidiarity and Primarity in the European Convention on Human Rights* (Leiden: Martinus Nijhoff, 2009)

Çoban A R, *Protection of Property Rights within the European Convention on Human Rights* (London: Ashgate, 2004)

Cohen-Eliya M and Porat I, 'American Balancing and German Proportionality: The Historical Origins' (2010) 8 *International Journal of Constitutional Law* 263

Proportionality and Constitutional Culture (Cambridge University Press, 2013)

Corten O, *L'utilisation du "raisonnable" par le juge international: discours juridique, raison et contradictions* (Brussels: Emile Bruylant, 1997)

'The Notion of "Reasonableness" in International Law: Legal Discourse, Reason and Contradictions' (1999) 48 *International and Comparative Law Quarterly* 613

Craig P, 'Unreasonableness and Proportionality in UK Law' in E Ellis (ed.), *The Principle of Proportionality in the Laws of Europe* (Oxford: Hart, 1999) 85
  EU Administrative Law (Oxford University Press, 2nd ed., 2012)
  Administrative Law (London: Thomson, 7th ed., 2012)
Crawford J, *The International Law Commission's Articles on State Responsibility: Introduction, Text and Commentaries* (Cambridge University Press, 2002)
  Brownlie's Principles of Public International Law (Oxford University Press, 8th ed., 2012)
Croley S P and Jackson J H, 'WTO Dispute Procedures, Standard of Review, and Deference to National Governments' (1996) 90 *American Journal of International Law* 193
Dalhuisen J H and Guzman A T, 'Expropriatory and Non-Expropriatory Takings under International Investment Law' (2013) *Transnational Dispute Management*
Daly P, *A Theory of Deference in Administrative Law* (Cambridge University Press, 2012)
de Búrca G, 'The Principle of Proportionality and its Application in EC Law' (1993) 13 *Yearbook of European Law* 105
del Moral I D, 'The Increasingly Marginal Appreciation of the Margin-of-Appreciation Doctrine' (2006) 7 *German Law Journal* 611
della Cananea G, 'Reasonableness in Administrative Law' in G Bongiovanni, G Sartor and C Valentini (eds.), *Reasonableness and Law* (Dordrecht: Springer, 2009) 295
de Nanteuil A, *L'expropriation indirecte en droit international de l'investissement* (Paris: Pedone, 2014)
De Sena P, 'Economic and Non-Economic Values in the Case Law of the European Court of Human Rights' in P Dupuy, E Petersmann and F Francioni (eds.), *Human Rights in International Investment Law and Arbitration* (Oxford University Press, 2009) 208
Desierto D A, 'Necessity and "Supplementary Means of Interpretation" for Non-Precluded Measures in Bilateral Investment Treaties' (2010) 31 *University of Pennsylvania Journal of International Law* 827
  Necessity and National Emergency Clauses: Sovereignty in Modern Treaty Interpretation (Leiden: Martinus Nijhoff, 2012)
Desmedt A, 'Proportionality in WTO Law' (2001) *Journal of International Economic Law* 441
Diebold N F, *Non-Discrimination in International Trade in Services* (Cambridge University Press, 2010)
  'Standards of Non-Discrimination in International Economic Law' (2011) 60 *International and Comparative Law Quarterly* 831
Diehl A, *The Core Standard in International Investment Protection: Fair and Equitable Treatment* (Alphen aan den Rijn: Kluwer, 2012)

DiMascio N and Pauwelyn J, 'Nondiscrimination in Trade and Investment Treaties: Worlds Apart or Different Sides of the Same Coin?' (2008) 102 *American Journal of International Law* 48

Dolzer R, 'Indirect Expropriations: New Developments?' (2002) 11 *New York University Environmental Law Journal* 64

Dolzer R and Schreuer C, *Principles of International Investment Law* (Oxford University Press, 2nd ed., 2012)

Du M M, 'Autonomy in Setting Appropriate Level of Protection under the WTO Law: Rhetoric or Reality?' (2010) 13 *Journal of International Economic Law* 1077

Duhaime B, 'Subsidiarity in the Americas: What Room Is There for Deference in the Inter-American System?' in L Gruszczynski and W Werner (eds.), *Deference in International Courts and Tribunals: Standard of Review and Margin of Appreciation* (Oxford University Press, 2014) 289

Dworkin R, *Taking Rights Seriously* (London: Duckworth, 1977)
  'Rights as Trumps' in J Waldron (ed.), *Theories of Rights* (Oxford University Press, 1984)

Ehlermann C and Lockhart N, 'Standard of Review in WTO Law' (2004) 7 *Journal of International Economic Law* 491

Eissen M, 'The Principle of Proportionality in the Case-Law of the European Court of Human Rights' in R S Macdonald, F Matscher and H Petzold (eds.), *The European System for the Protection of Human Rights* (Leiden: Martinus Nijhoff, 1993) 125

Elliott M, 'The HRA 1998 and the Standard of Substantive Review' (2002) 7 *Judicial Review* 97
  'Proportionality and Deference: The Importance of a Structured Approach' in C Forsyth, M Elliott, S Jhaveri, M Ramsden and A Scully Hill (eds.), *Effective Judicial Review: A Cornerstone of Good Governance* (Oxford University Press, 2010) 264

Emberland M, *The Human Rights of Companies: Exploring the Structure of ECHR Protection* (Oxford University Press, 2006)

Emiliou N, *The Principle of Proportionality in European Law: A Comparative Study* (London: Kluwer, 1996)

Engle E, 'History of the General Principle of Proportionality: An Overview' (2012) 10 *Dartmouth Law Journal* 1

Fallon R H Jr., 'Strict Judicial Scrutiny' (2006) 54 *UCLA Law Review* 1267

Fauchald O K, 'The Legal Reasoning of ICSID Tribunals – An Empirical Analysis' (2008) 19 *European Journal of International Law* 301

Feldman D, 'Proportionality and the Human Rights Act 1998' in E Ellis (ed.), *The Principle of Proportionality in the Laws of Europe* (Oxford: Hart, 1999) 117
  'The Impact of Human Rights on the UK Legislative Process' (2004) 25 *Statute Law Review* 91

Finnis J, 'Natural Law and Legal Reasoning' (1990) 38 *Cleveland State Law Review* 1

Fitzmaurice G, 'The Law and Procedure of the International Court of Justice: Treaty Interpretation and Certain Other Treaty Points' (1951) 28 *British Yearbook of International Law* 1

Flett J, 'WTO Space for National Regulation: Requiem for a Diagonal Vector Test' (2013) 16 *Journal of International Economic Law* 37

Fortier Y and Drymer S L, 'Indirect Expropriation in the Law of International Investment: I Know It When I See It, or *Caveat Investor*' (2004) 19 *ICSID Review* 293

Foster C E, 'Burden of Proof in International Courts and Tribunals' (2010) 29 *Australian Yearbook of International Law* 27

　　'Adjudication, Arbitration and the Turn to Public Law "Standards of Review": Putting the Precautionary Principle in the Crucible' (2012) 3 *Journal of International Dispute Settlement* 525

　　'Diminished Ambitions? Public International Legal Authority in the Transnational Economic Era' (2014) 17 *Journal of International Economic Law* 355

　　'A New Stratosphere? Investment Treaty Arbitration as "Internationalized Public Law"' (2015) 64 *International and Comparative Law Quarterly* 461

Franck, S D, 'The Legitimacy Crisis in Investment Treaty Arbitration: Privatizing Public International Law Through Inconsistent Decisions' (2005) 73 *Fordham Law Review* 1521

Franck T M, 'Legitimacy in the International System' (1988) 82 *American Journal of International Law* 705

　　The Power of Legitimacy Among Nations (Oxford University Press, 1990)

　　Fairness in International Law and Institutions (Oxford University Press, 1998)

　　'On Proportionality of Countermeasures in International Law' (2008) 102 *American Journal of International Law* 715

　　'Rights, Balancing and Proportionality' (2010) 4 *Law and Ethics of Human Rights* 230

Frankenburg G, 'Critical Comparisons: Re-thinking Comparative Law' (1985) 26 *Harvard International Law Journal* 411

Freeman E M, 'Regulatory Expropriation Under NAFTA Chapter 11: Some Lessons from the European Court of Human Rights' (2003) 42 *Columbia Journal of Transnational Law* 177

Fuentes X, 'Proportionality Analysis and Disproportionate Damages: *Occidental Petroleum Corporation and Occidental Exploration and Production Company v. The Republic of Ecuador*' (2015) *Journal of World Investment and Trade* 315

Fukunaga Y, 'Standard of Review and "Scientific Truths" in the WTO Dispute Settlement System and Investment Arbitration' (2012) 3 *Journal of International Dispute Settlement* 559

Fuller L L, 'The Forms and Limits of Adjudication' (1978) 92 *Harvard Law Review* 353

Gantz D A, 'An Appellate Mechanism for Review of Arbitral Decisions in Investor-State Disputes: Prospects and Challenges' (2006) 39 *Vanderbilt Journal of Transnational Law* 39

Gardiner R, *Treaty Interpretation* (Oxford University Press, 2010)

Gazzini T, 'General Principles of Law in the Field of Foreign Investment' (2007) 10 *Journal of World Investment and Trade* 103

Gerards J, 'Pluralism, Deference and the Margin of Appreciation Doctrine' (2011) 17 *European Law Journal* 80

'How to Improve the Necessity Test of the European Court of Human Rights' (2013) 11 *International Journal of Constitutional Law* 466

Grando M, *Evidence, Proof and Fact-finding in WTO Dispute Settlement* (Oxford University Press, 2010)

Greer S, *The Margin of Appreciation: Interpretation and Discretion under the European Convention on Human Rights* (Strasbourg: Council of Europe, 2000)

The European Convention on Human Rights: Achievements, Problems and Prospects (Cambridge University Press, 2006)

Gruszczynski L, *Regulating Health and Environmental Risks under WTO Law: A Critical Analysis of the SPS Agreement* (Oxford University Press, 2010)

Gruszczynski L and Vadi V, 'Standard of Review and Scientific Evidence in WTO Law and International Investment Arbitration: Converging Parallels?' in L Gruszczynski and W Werner (eds.), *Deference in International Courts and Tribunals: Standard of Review and Margin of Appreciation* (Oxford University Press, 2014) 152

Gunn T J, 'Deconstructing Proportionality in Limitations Analysis' (2005) 19 *Emory International Law Review* 465

Guzman A T, 'International Tribunals: A Rational Choice Analysis' (2008) 157 *University of Pennsylvania Law Review* 171

'Determining the Appropriate Standard of Review in WTO Disputes' (2009) 42 *Cornell International Law Journal* 45

Habermas J, *Between Facts and Norms: Contributions to a Discourse Theory of Law and Democracy* (Cambridge, MA: MIT Press, W Rehg trans., 1996)

Hamrock K J, 'The *ELSI* Case: Toward an International Definition of "Arbitrary" Conduct' (1992) 27 *Texas International Law Journal* 837

Han X, 'The Application of the Principle of Proportionality in *Tecmed* v. *Mexico*' (2007) 6 *Chinese Journal of International Law* 635

Harbo T, 'The Function of the Proportionality Principle in EU Law' (2010) 16 *European Law Journal* 158

Harris D J, O'Boyle M, Bates E P and Buckley C M, *Law of the European Convention on Human Rights* (Oxford University Press, 3rd ed., 2014)

Harvard Law School, *Draft Convention on the International Responsibility of States for Injuries to Aliens* (Cambridge, MA: Harvard University Press, 1961)

Heiskanen V, 'Arbitrary and Unreasonable Measures' in A Reinisch (ed.), *Standards of Investment Protection* (Oxford University Press, 2008) 87

Henckels C, 'Indirect Expropriation and the Right to Regulate: Revisiting Proportionality Analysis and the Standard of Review in Investor-State Arbitration' (2012) 15 *Journal of International Economic Law* 223

Hertogh M and Halliday S (eds.), *Judicial Review and Bureaucratic Impact: International and Interdisciplinary Perspectives* (Cambridge University Press, 2004)

Hickman T, 'The Reasonableness Principle: Reassessing Its Place in the Public Sphere' (2004) 63 *Cambridge Law Journal* 166

'The Substance and Structure of Proportionality' (2008) *Public Law* 694

Public Law after the Human Rights Act (Oxford: Hart, 2010)

Higgins R, 'The Taking of Property by the State: Recent Developments in International Law' (1982) 176 *Recueil des Cours* 267

Problems and Process: International Law and How We Use It (Oxford University Press, 1994)

Howse R, 'Adjudicative Legitimacy and Treaty Interpretation in International Trade Law: The Early Years of WTO Jurisprudence' in J H H Weiler (ed.), *The EU, the WTO and the NAFTA: Towards a Common Law of International Trade* (Oxford University Press, 2000) 35

Hudec R E, 'GATT/WTO Constraints on National Regulation: Requiem for an "Aim and Effects" Test' (1998) 31 *International Lawyer* 619

Hunt M, 'Sovereignty's Blight: Why Contemporary Public Law Needs the Concept of "Due Deference"' in N Bamworth and P Leyland (eds.), *Public Law in a Multi-Layered Constitution* (Oxford: Hart, 2003) 341

International Centre for Settlement of Investment Disputes Secretariat, *Possible Improvements of the Framework for ICSID Arbitration* (Washington, DC: World Bank Group, 2004)

International Law Commission, *Yearbook of the International Law Commission 1980* (Geneva: International Law Commission, 1981)

Yearbook of the International Law Commission 2001, Volume II, Part Two (Geneva: International Law Commission, 2007)

Jackson V C, 'Being Proportional about Proportionality: Review of Beatty, *The Ultimate Rule of Law*' (2004) 21 *Constitutional Commentary* 803

Jans J J, 'Proportionality Revisited' (2000) 27 *Legal Issues of Economic Integration* 239

Jones D and de Villars A, *Principles of Administrative Law* (Toronto: Carswell, 5th ed., 2009)

Jones T, 'The Devaluation of Human Rights Under the European Convention' (1995) *Public Law* 430

Kapterian G, 'A Critique of the WTO Jurisprudence on "Necessity"' (2010) 59 *International and Comparative Law Quarterly* 89

Katselas A T, 'Do Investment Treaties Prescribe a Deferential Standard of Review?' (2012) 34 *Michigan Journal of International Law* 87

Kaufmann-Kohler G, 'Arbitral Precedent: Dream, Necessity or Excuse?' (2007) 23 *Arbitration International* 357

Kavanagh A, 'Deference or Defiance? The Limits of the Judicial Role in Constitutional Adjudication' in G Huscroft (ed.), *Expounding the Constitution: Essays in Constitutional Theory* (Cambridge University Press, 2008) 184

    Constitutional Review under the UK Human Rights Act (Cambridge University Press, 2009)

    'Defending Deference in Public Law and Constitutional Theory' (2010) 126 *Law Quarterly Review* 222

    'Judicial Restraint in the Pursuit of Justice' (2010) 60 *University of Toronto Law Journal* 23

    'Reasoning about Proportionality under the Human Rights Act 1998: Outcomes, Substance and Process' (2014) 130 *Law Quarterly Review* 235

    'Proportionality and Parliamentary Debates: Exploring Some Forbidden Territory' (2014) 34 *Oxford Journal of Legal Studies* 443

King J, 'The Pervasiveness of Polycentricity' (2008) *Public Law* 101

    'Institutional Approaches to Judicial Restraint' (2008) 28 *Oxford Journal of Legal Studies* 409

    'Proportionality – A Halfway House' (2010) *New Zealand Law Review* 332

    Judging Social Rights (Cambridge University Press, 2012)

Kingsbury B and Schill S W, 'Investor-State Arbitration as Governance: Fair and Equitable Treatment, Proportionality, and the Emerging Global Administrative Law' in A J Van Den Berg (ed.), *50 Years of the New York Convention* (Alphen aan den Rijn: Kluwer, 2009) 5

    'Public Law Concepts to Balance Investors' Rights with State Regulatory Actions in the Public Interest – The Concept of Proportionality' in S W Schill (ed.), *International Investment Law and Comparative Public Law* (Oxford University Press, 2010) 75

Kinnear M, Bjorklund A and Hannaford J, *Investment Disputes Under NAFTA: An Annotated Guide to NAFTA Chapter 11* (Alphen aan den Rijn: Kluwer, 2006)

Kläger R, *'Fair and Equitable Treatment' in International Investment Law* (Cambridge University Press, 2011)

Klatt M and Meister M, *The Constitutional Structure of Proportionality* (Oxford University Press, 2012)

Kleinlein T, 'Judicial Lawmaking by Judicial Restraint? The Potential of Balancing in International Economic Law' (2011) 12 *German Law Journal* 1141

Kretzmer D, 'The Inherent Right to Self Defence and Proportionality in *Jus Ad Bellum*' (2013) 24 *European Journal of International Law* 235

Kriebaum U, 'Regulatory Takings: Balancing the Interests of the Investor and the State' (2007) 8 *Journal of World Investment and Trade* 717

'Is the European Court of Human Rights an Alternative to Investor-State Arbitration?' in P Dupuy, E Petersmann and F Francioni (eds.), *Human Rights in International Investment Law and Arbitration* (Oxford University Press, 2009) 219

Krommendijk J and Morijn J, '"Proportional" by What Measure(s)? Balancing Investor Interests and Human Rights by Way of Applying the Proportionality Principle in Investor-State Arbitration' in P Dupuy, E Petersmann and F Francioni (eds.), *Human Rights in International Investment Law and Arbitration* (Oxford University Press, 2009) 422

Kulick A, 'Review: Stephan W. Schill (ed.). *International Investment Law and Comparative Public Law*' (2011) 22 *European Journal of International Law* 917

Global Public Interest in International Investment Law (Cambridge University Press, 2012)

Kumm M, 'Political Liberalism and the Structure of Rights: On the Place and Limits of the Proportionality Requirement' in G Pavlakos (ed.), *Law, Rights and Discourse: The Legal Philosophy of Robert Alexy* (Oxford: Hart, 2007) 131

Kurtz J, 'The Use and Abuse of WTO Law in Investor-State Arbitration: Competition and Its Discontents' (2009) 20 *European Journal of International Law* 749

'Access to Justice, Denial and Justice and International Investment Law: A Reply to Francesco Francioni' (2009) 20 *European Journal of International Law* 1077

'Adjudging the Exceptional at International Investment Law: Security, Public Order and Financial Crisis' (2010) 59 *International and Comparative Law Quarterly* 325

'The Merits and Limits of Comparativism: National Treatment in International Investment Law and the WTO' in S W Schill (ed.), *International Investment Law and Comparative Public Law* (Oxford University Press, 2010) 243

'The Shifting Landscape of International Investment Law and Its Commentary' (2012) 106 *American Journal of International Law* 686

'On the Evolution and Slow Convergence of International Trade and Investment Law' in G Sacerdoti (ed.), *General Interests of Host States in International Investment Law* (Cambridge University Press, 2014) 104

Lang A, *World Trade Law after Neoliberalism: Reimagining the Global Economic Order* (Oxford University Press, 2011)

Legg A, *The Margin of Appreciation in International Human Rights Law: Deference and Proportionality* (Oxford University Press, 2012)

Leonhardsen E M, 'Looking for Legitimacy: Exploring Proportionality Analysis in Investment Treaty Arbitration' (2011) *Journal of International Dispute Settlement* 1

'Treaty Change, Arbitral Practice and the Search for a Balance: Standards of Review and the Margin of Appreciation in International Investment Law' in L Gruszczynski and W Werner (eds.), *Deference in International Courts and Tribunals: Standard of Review and Margin of Appreciation* (Oxford University Press, 2014) 135

Letsas G, *A Theory of Interpretation of the European Convention on Human Rights* (Oxford University Press, 2007)

Lewans M, 'Deference and Reasonableness Since *Dunsmuir*' (2012) 38 *Queen's Law Journal* 59

Lovric D, *Deference to the Legislature in WTO Challenges to Legislation* (Alphen aan den Rijn: Kluwer, 2010)

Lowenfeld A F, 'The ICSID Convention: Origins and Transformation' (2010) 38 *Georgia Journal of International and Comparative Law* 47

Luban D, 'Incommensurable Values, Rational Choice, and Moral Absolutes' (1990) 38 *Cleveland State Law Review* 65

Macdonald R S, 'The Margin of Appreciation' in R S Macdonald, F Matscher and H Petzold (eds.), *The European System for the Protection of Human Rights* (Dordrecht: Martinus Nijhoff, 1993) 83

Maduro M P, *We the Court: The European Court of Justice and the European Economic Constitution* (Oxford: Hart, 1998)

Mamolea A, 'Good Faith Review' in L Gruszczynski and W Werner (eds.), *Deference in International Courts and Tribunals: Standard of Review and Margin of Appreciation* (Oxford University Press, 2014) 74

Marboe I, *Calculation of Compensation and Damages in International Investment Law* (Oxford University Press, 2009)

Marceau G and Trachtman J P, 'A Map of the World Trade Organization Law of Domestic Regulation of Goods' in G Bermann and P Mavroidis (eds.), *Trade and Human Health and Safety* (Cambridge University Press, 2006) 9

Marks S, 'Civil Liberties at the Margin: the UK Derogation and the European Court of Human Rights' (1995) 15 *Oxford Journal of Legal Systems* 69

Mathis J H, 'Balancing and Proportionality in US Commerce Clause Cases' (2009) 35 *Legal Issues of Economic Integration* 273

Matthews J and Stone Sweet A, 'All Things in Proportion? American Rights Review and the Problem of Balancing' (2011) 60 *Emory Law Journal* 101

Maupin J, 'Differentiating Among International Investment Disputes' in Z Douglas, J Pauwelyn, and J E Viñuales (eds.), *The Foundations of International Investment Law: Bringing Theory into Practice* (Oxford University Press, 2014) 468

Mbengue M M, 'Scientific Fact-finding by International Courts and Tribunals' (2012) 3 *Journal of International Dispute Settlement* 509

McGrady B, 'Necessity Exceptions in WTO Law: Retreaded Tyres, Regulatory Purpose and Cumulative Regulatory Measures' (2009) 12 *Journal of International Economic Law* 153

    Trade and Public Health: The WTO, Tobacco, Alcohol and Diet (Cambridge University Press, 2010)

McHarg A, 'Reconciling Human Rights and the Public Interest: Conceptual Problems and Doctrinal Uncertainty in the Jurisprudence of the European Court of Human Rights' (1999) 62 *Modern Law Review* 671

McKean W A, 'The Meaning of Discrimination in International and Municipal Law' (1970) 44 *British Yearbook of International Law* 177

McLachlan C, Shore L and Weiniger M, *International Investment Arbitration: Substantive Principles* (Oxford University Press, 2007)

McNair A, *International Law Opinions*, Volume 2 (Cambridge University Press, 1956)

McRae D, 'The WTO Appellate Body: A Model for an ICSID Appeals Facility?' (2010) 1 *Journal of International Dispute Settlement* 371

Mead D, 'Outcomes Aren't All: Defending Process-Based Review of Public Authority Decisions under the Human Rights Act' (2012) *Public Law* 61

Meron T, *Human Rights and Humanitarian Norms as Customary Law* (Oxford University Press, 1989)

Michaels R, 'The Functionalist Method of Comparative Law' in M Reimann and R Zimmermann (eds.), *The Oxford Handbook of Comparative Law* (Oxford University Press, 2006) 339

Miles K, *The Origins of International Investment Law: Empire, Environment and the Safeguarding of Capital* (Cambridge University Press, 2013)

Miles T J and Sunstein C R, 'The Real World of Arbitrariness Review' (2008) 75 *University of Chicago Law Review* 761

Mitchell A D, 'Proportionality and Remedies in WTO Disputes' (2007) 17 *European Journal of International Law* 985

Mitchell A D and Henckels C, 'Variations on a Theme: Comparing the Concept of "Necessity" in International Investment Law and WTO Law' (2013) 14 *Chicago Journal of International Law* 93

Moloo R and Jacinto J, 'Environmental and Health Regulation: Assessing Liability Under Investment Treaties' (2011) 29 *Berkeley Journal of International Law* 101

    'Standards of Review and Reviewing Standards: Public Interest Regulation in International Investment Law' in K P Sauvant (ed.), *Yearbook of International Investment Law and Policy 2011–2012* (Oxford University Press, 2013) 539

Montt S, *State Liability in Investment Treaty Arbitration: Global Constitutional and Administrative Law and the BIT Generation* (Oxford: Hart, 2009)

Mostafa B, 'The Sole Effects Doctrine, Police Powers and Indirect Expropriation under International Law' (2008) 15 *Australian International Law Journal* 267

Mountfield H, 'Regulatory Expropriations in Europe: The Approach of the European Court of Human Rights' (2002) 11 *New York University Environmental Law Journal* 136

Muchlinski P, *Multinational Enterprises and the Law* (Oxford University Press, 2nd ed., 2007)

NAFTA Free Trade Commission, *Note of Interpretation of Certain Chapter 11 Provisions* (2001)

Neumann J and Türk E, 'Necessity Revisited: Proportionality in World Trade Organization Law After *Korea-Beef, EC-Asbestos* and *EC-Sardines*' (2003) 37 *Journal of World Trade* 199

Newcombe A and Paradell L, *Law and Practice of Investment Treaties: Standards of Treatment* (Alphen aan den Rijn: Kluwer, 2009)

Newton M and May L, *Proportionality in International Law* (Oxford University Press, 2013)

New Zealand Government, 'Government Moves Forward with Plain Packaging of Tobacco Products', media release, 19 February 2013, www.beehive.govt.nz/release/government-moves-forward-plain-packaging-tobacco-products

Oesch M, *Standards of Review in WTO Dispute Resolution* (Oxford University Press, 2003)

Organisation for Economic Cooperation and Development, *Draft Convention on the Protection of Foreign Property and Resolution of the Council of the OECD on the Draft Convention* (Paris: OECD, 1967)

National Treatment for Foreign-Controlled Enterprises (Paris: OECD, 1992)

'*Indirect Expropriation' and the 'Right to Regulate'* in International Investment Law (Paris: OECD, 2004)

Ortino F, *Basic Legal Instruments for the Liberalisation of Trade: A Comparative Analysis of EC and WTO Law* (Oxford: Hart, 2004)

'The Social Dimension of International Investment Agreements: Drafting a New BIT/MIT Model?' (2005) 7 *International Law FORUM du Droit International* 243

'From "Non-Discrimination" to "Reasonableness:" A Paradigm Shift in International Economic Law?' (2005) 1 *New York University School of Law Jean Monnet Working Papers*

'Legal Reasoning of International Investment Tribunals: A Typology of Egregious Failures' (2012) 3 *Journal of International Dispute Settlement* 31

'The Investment Treaty System as Judicial Review' (2013) 24 *American Review of International Arbitration* 437

Paine J 'The Project of System-Internal Reform in International Investment Law: An Appraisal' (2015) 6 *Journal of International Dispute Settlement* 332

Panaccio C, 'In Defence of Two-Step Balancing and Proportionality in Rights Adjudication' (2011) 24 *Canadian Journal of Law and Jurisprudence* 109

Paparinskis M, 'Inherent Powers of ICSID Tribunals: Broad and Rightly So' in I Laird and T Weiler (eds.), *Investment Treaty Arbitration and International Law* (New York: JurisNet, 2012) 11

    The International Minimum Standard and Fair and Equitable Treatment (Oxford University Press, 2013)

Pauwelyn J, 'Comment: The Unbearable Lightness of Likeness' in M Panizzon, N Pohl and P Sauvé (eds.), *GATS and the Regulation of International Trade in Services* (Cambridge University Press, 2008) 358

    'At the Edge of Chaos? Foreign Investment Law as a Complex Adaptive System, How It Emerged and How It Can Be Reformed' (2014) 29 *ICSID Review* 372

Peel J, 'Of Apples and Oranges (and Hormones in Beef): Science and the Standard of Review in WTO Disputes under the SPS Agreement' (2012) 61 *International and Comparative Law Quarterly* 427

Perkams M, 'The Concept of Indirect Expropriation in Comparative Public Law – Searching for Light in the Dark' in S W Schill (ed.), *International Investment Law and Comparative Public Law* (Oxford University Press, 2010) 107

Peterson L E, 'Liability Ruling in *Oxy* v *Ecuador* Arbitration Puts Spotlight on Need for States to Mete Out Treatment that is Proportionate' (2012) *Investment Arbitration Reporter*

    'After Settling Some Awards, Argentina Takes More Fractious Path in Bond-Holders Case, with New Bid to Disqualify Arbitrators' (2013) *Investment Arbitration Reporter*

Pirker B, *Proportionality Analysis and Judicial Review: A Comparative Study in Domestic Constitutional, European and International Economic Law* (Groningen: Europa, 2013)

Pita C, 'Right to Property, Investments and Environmental Protection: The Perspectives of the European and Inter-American Courts of Human Rights' in T Treves, F Seatzu and S Trevisanut (eds.), *International Investment Law and Common Concern* (New York: Taylor and Francis, 2013) 553

Poole T, 'Of Headscarves and Heresies: The *Denbigh High School* Case and Public Authority Decision Making under the Human Rights Act' (2005) *Public Law* 685

Popelier P and Van De Heyning C, 'Procedural Rationality: Giving Teeth to the Proportionality Analysis' (2013) 9 *European Constitutional Law Review* 230

Porges A and Trachtman J P, 'Robert Hudec and Domestic Regulation: The Resurrection of Aim and Effects' (2003) 37 *Journal of World Trade* 783

Potestà M, 'Legitimate Expectations in Investment Treaty Law: Understanding the Roots and the Limits of a Controversial Concept' (2013) 28 *ICSID Review* 88

Qin, J Y, 'Defining Non-Discrimination Under the Law of the World Trade Organization' (2005) 23 *Boston University International Law Journal* 215

Radi Y, 'Realizing Human Rights in Investment Treaty Arbitration: A Perspective from within the International Investment Law Toolbox' (2012) 37 *North Carolina Journal of International Law and Commercial Regulation* 1107

Ranieri N W, 'Investors' Rights, Legal Concepts and Public Policy in the NAFTA Context' in L E Trakman and N W Ranieri (eds.), *Regionalism in International Investment Law* (Oxford University Press, 2013) 400

Ranjan P, 'Using the Public Law Concept of Proportionality to Balance Investment Protection with Regulation in International Investment Law: A Critical Reappraisal' (2014) 3 *Cambridge Journal of International and Comparative Law* 853

Ratner S R, 'Regulatory Takings in Institutional Context: Beyond the Fear of Fragmented International Law' (2008) 102 *American Journal of International Law* 475

Raz J, *The Morality of Freedom* (Oxford: Clarendon Press, 1986)

Engaging Reason (Oxford University Press, 2001)

Regan D H, 'Further Thoughts on the Role of Regulatory Purpose Under Article III of the General Agreement on Tariffs and Trade: A Tribute to Bob Hudec' (2003) 37 *Journal of World Trade* 737

'The Meaning of "Necessary" in GATT Article XX and GATS Article XIV: The Myth of Cost–Benefit Balancing' (2007) 6 *World Trade Review* 347

Reinisch A, 'Expropriation' in P Muchlinski, F Ortino and C Schreuer (eds.), *The Oxford Handbook on International Investment Law* (Oxford University Press, 2008) 407

'Necessity in Investment Arbitration' (2010) 41 *Netherlands Yearbook of International Law* 137

Rivers J, 'A Theory of Constitutional Rights and the British Constitution' in R Alexy, *A Theory of Constitutional Rights* (Oxford University Press, J Rivers trans., 2002) xvii

'Proportionality and Variable Intensity of Review' (2006) 65 *Cambridge Law Journal* 174

'Proportionality, Discretion and the Second Law of Balancing' in G Pavlakos (ed.), *Law, Rights and Discourse: The Legal Philosophy of Robert Alexy* (Oxford: Hart, 2007) 167

'Proportionality and Discretion in International and European Law' in N Tsagourias (ed.), *Transnational Constitutionalism: European and International Models* (Cambridge University Press, 2007) 107

'The Presumption of Proportionality' (2014) 77 *Modern Law Review* 409

Roberts A, 'Power and Persuasion in Investment Treaty Arbitration: The Dual Role of States' (2010) 104 *American Journal of International Law* 179

'The Next Battleground: Standards of Review in Investment Treaty Arbitration' in A J Van Den Berg (ed.), *Arbitration – The Next Fifty Years*, ICCA Congress Series No. 16 (Alphen aan den Rijn: Kluwer, 2012) 170

'Clash of Paradigms: Actors and Analogies Shaping the Investment Treaty System' (2013) 107 *American Journal of International Law* 45

Roessler F, 'Beyond the Ostensible – A Tribute to Professor Robert Hudec's Insights Under the National Treatment Provisions of the General Agreement on Tariffs and Trade' (2003) 37 *Journal of World Trade* 771

Sabahi B and Duggal K, '*Occidental Petroleum v Ecuador* (2012): Observations on Proportionality, Assessment of Damages and Contributory Fault' (2013) 28 *ICSID Review* 279

Sacerdoti G, 'BIT Protections and Economic Crises: Limits to Their Coverage, the Impact of Multilateral Financial Regulation and the Defence of Necessity' (2013) 28 *ICSID Review* 351

'The Application of BITs in Time of Economic Crisis: Limits to their Coverage, Necessity and the Relevance of WTO Law' in G Sacerdoti (ed.), *General Interests of Host States in International Investment Law* (Cambridge University Press, 2014) 3

'Trade and Investment Law: Institutional Differences and Substantive Similarities' (2014) 9 *Jerusalem Review of Legal Studies* 1

Salacuse J W, *The Law of Investment Treaties* (Oxford University Press, 2010)

Sauter W, 'Proportionality in EU Law: A Balancing Act?' (2013) 15 *Cambridge Yearbook of European Legal Studies* 439

Schill S W, 'Revisiting a Landmark: Indirect Expropriation and Fair and Equitable Treatment in the ICSID Case *Tecmed*' (2006) 3 *Transnational Dispute Management*

'International Investment Law and the Host State's Power to Handle Economic Crises – Comment on the ICSID Decision in *LG&E* v. *Argentina*' (2007) 24 *Journal of International Arbitration* 265

The Multilateralization of International Investment Law (Cambridge University Press, 2009)

'International Investment Law and Comparative Public Law – An Introduction' in S W Schill (ed.), *International Investment Law and Comparative Public Law* (Oxford University Press, 2010) 3

'Fair and Equitable Treatment, the Rule of Law, and Comparative Public Law' in S W Schill (ed.), *International Investment Law and Comparative Public Law* (Oxford University Press, 2010) 151

'Enhancing International Investment Law's Legitimacy: Conceptual and Methodological Foundations of a New Public Law Approach' (2011) 52 *Virginia Journal of International Law* 57

'Deference in Investment Treaty Arbitration: Re-Conceptualizing the Standard of Review' (2012) 3 *Journal of International Dispute Settlement* 577

'General Principles of Law and International Investment Law' in T Gazzini and E De Brabandere (eds.), *International Investment Law – The Sources of Rights and Obligations* (Leiden: Martinus Nijhoff, 2012) 133

'Cross-Regime Harmonization through Proportionality Analysis: The Case of International Investment Law, the Law of State Immunity and Human Rights' (2014) 27 *ICSID Review* 87

'The Sixth Path: Reforming Investment Law from Within' in J E Kalicki and A Joubin-Bret (eds), *Reshaping the Investor-State Dispute Settlement System: Journeys for the 21st Century* (Leiden: Brill Nijhoff, 2015) 621

Schill S and Briese R, '"If the State Considers": Self-Judging Clauses in International Dispute Settlement' (2009) 13 *Max Planck United Nations Yearbook* 61

Schneiderman D, *Constitutionalizing Economic Globalization* (Cambridge University Press, 2008)

'The Global Regime of Investor Rights: Return to the Standards of Civilised Justice?' (2014) 5 *Transnational Legal Theory* 60

Schønberg S J, *Legitimate Expectations in Administrative Law* (Oxford University Press, 2000)

Schreuer C, *The ICSID Convention: A Commentary* (Cambridge University Press, 2nd ed., 2009)

Schueler B, 'Methods of Application of the Proportionality Principle in Environmental Law' (2008) 35 *Legal Issues of Economic Integration* 231

Schwarze J, *European Administrative Law* (London: Sweet and Maxwell, revised 1st ed., 2006)

Shaffer G and Trachtman J, 'Interpretation and Institutional Choice at the WTO' (2011) 52 *Virginia Journal of International Law* 103

Shany Y, 'Toward a General Margin of Appreciation Doctrine in International Law?' (2006) 16 *European Journal of International Law* 907

Shaw M, *International Law* (Cambridge University Press, 6th ed., 2008)

Shirlow E, 'Deference and Indirect Expropriation Analysis in International Investment Law: Observations on Current Approaches and Frameworks for Future Analysis' (2014) 29 *ICSID Review* 595

Sinclair I, *The Vienna Convention on the Law of Treaties* (Manchester University Press, 2nd ed., 1984)

Sloane R D, 'On the Use and Abuse of Necessity in the Law of State Responsibility' (2012) 106 *American Journal of International Law* 447

Sornarajah M, *The International Law on Foreign Investment* (Cambridge University Press, 3rd ed., 2010)

'Evolution or Revolution in International Investment Arbitration? The Descent into Normlessness' in C Brown and K Miles (eds.), *Evolution in Investment Treaty Law and Arbitration* (Cambridge University Press, 2011) 631

Spears S, 'The Quest for Policy Space in a New Generation of International Investment Agreements' (2010) 13 *Journal of International Economic Law* 1037

Stone J, 'Arbitrariness, the Fair and Equitable Treatment Standard, and the International Law of Investment' (2012) 25 *Leiden Journal of International Law* 77

Stone Sweet A, *The Judicial Construction of Europe* (Oxford University Press, 2004)

'Investor-State Arbitration: Proportionality's New Frontier' (2010) 4 *Law and Ethics of Human Rights* 47

'Arbitration and Judicialization' (2011) 1 *Oñati Socio-Legal Series* 16

Stone Sweet A and della Cananea G, 'Proportionality, General Principles of Law, and Investor-State Arbitration: A Response to José Alvarez' (2014) 46 *New York University Journal of International Law and Politics* 911

Stone Sweet A and Grisel F, 'Transnational Investment Arbitration: From Delegation to Constitutionalization?' in P Dupuy, E Petersmann and F Francioni (eds.), *Human Rights in International Investment Law and Arbitration* (Oxford University Press, 2009) 118

Stone Sweet A and Matthews J, 'Proportionality Balancing and Global Constitutionalism' (2008) 47 *Columbia Journal of Transnational Law* 72

Sullivan E T and Frase R S, *Proportionality Principles in American Law: Controlling Excessive Government Actions* (Oxford University Press, 2009)

Sunstein C, *After the Rights Revolution: Reconceiving the Regulatory State* (Cambridge, MA: Harvard University Press, 1990)

Sykes A O, *Product Standards for Internationally Integrated Goods Markets* (Washington, DC: Brookings, 1995)

'The Least Restrictive Means' (2003) 70 *University of Chicago Law Review* 403

Taggart M, 'Proportionality, Deference, *Wednesbury*' (2008) 1 *New Zealand Law Review* 423

Tams C J, 'An Appealing Option? The Debate about an ICSID Appellate Mechanism' (2006) 57 *Martin-Luther-Universität Halle-Wittenburg Beiträge zum Transnationalen Wirtschaftsrecht*

Thomas R, *Legitimate Expectations and Proportionality in Administrative Law* (Hart: Oxford, 2000)

Tienhaara K, 'Regulatory Chill and the Threat of Arbitration: A View from Political Science' in C Brown and K Miles (eds.), *Evolution in Investment Treaty Law and Arbitration* (Cambridge University Press, 2011) 607

Tomuschat C, 'The European Court of Human Rights and Investment Protection' in C Binder, U Kriebaum, A Reinisch and S Wittich (eds.), *International Investment Law for the 21st Century: Essays in Honour of Christoph Schreuer* (Oxford University Press, 2009) 636

Trachtman J P, 'Trade and . . . Problems, Cost-Benefit Analysis and Subsidiarity' (1998) 9 *European Journal of International Law* 32

'Regulatory Jurisdiction and the WTO' (2007) 10 *Journal of International Economic Law* 631

Tridimas T, 'Proportionality in Community Law: Searching for the Appropriate Standard of Scrutiny' in E Ellis (ed.), *The Principle of Proportionality in the Laws of Europe* (Oxford: Hart, 1999) 65

The General Principles of EU Law (Oxford University Press, 2nd ed., 2006)

Tsakyrakis S, 'Proportionality: An Assault on Human Rights?' (2009) 7 *International Journal of Constitutional Law* 468

United Nations Conference on Trade and Development, *National Treatment* (Geneva: UNCTAD, 1999)

The Protection of National Security in IIAs (Geneva: UNCTAD, 2009)

Fair and Equitable Treatment: A Sequel (Geneva: UNCTAD, 2012)

Investment Policy Framework for Sustainable Development (Geneva: UNCTAD, 2012)

World Investment Report 2012: Towards a New Generation of Investment Policies (Geneva: UNCTAD, 2012)

Expropriation: A Sequel (Geneva: UNCTAD, 2012)

Recent Developments in Investor-State Dispute Settlement (ISDS) (Geneva: UNCTAD, 2014)

World Investment Report 2014: Investing in the SDGs: An Action Plan (Geneva: UNCTAD, 2014)

Recent Trends in IIAs and ISDS (Geneva: UNCTAD, 2015)

Vadi V, 'Critical Comparisons: The Role of Comparative Law in Investment Treaty Arbitration' (2010) 39 *Denver Journal of International Law and Policy* 67

Vadi V and Gruszczynski L, 'Standards of Review in International Investment Law and Arbitration: Multilevel Governance and the Commonweal' (2013) 16 *Journal of International Economic Law* 613

Van Aaken A, 'International Investment Law Between Commitment and Flexibility: A Contract Theory Analysis' (2009) 12 *Journal of International Economic Law* 507

'Defragmentation of Public International Law Through Interpretation: A Methodological Proposal' (2009) 16 *Indiana Journal of Global Legal Studies* 483

'Primary and Secondary Remedies in International Investment Law and National State Liability: A Functional and Comparative View' in S W Schill (ed.), *International Investment Law and Comparative Public Law* (Oxford University Press, 2010) 721

'Control Mechanisms in International Investment Law' in Z Douglas, J Pauwelyn and J E Viñuales (eds.), *The Foundations of International Investment Law: Bringing Theory into Practice* (Oxford University Press, 2014) 409

Van Aaken A and Kurtz J, 'Prudence or Discrimination? Emergency Measures, the Global Financial Crisis and International Economic Law' (2009) 12 *Journal of International Economic Law* 859

Van Damme I, *Treaty Interpretation by the WTO Appellate Body* (Oxford University Press, 2009)

Van den Bossche P, 'Looking for Proportionality in WTO Law' (2008) 35 *Legal Issues of Economic Integration* 283

Van Dijk P, van Hoof G, Van Rijn A and Zwaak L, *Theory and Practice of the European Convention on Human Rights* (Oxford: Intersentia, 4th ed., 2006)

Van Gerven W, 'The Effect of Proportionality on the Actions of Member States of the European Community: National Viewpoints from Continental Europe' in E Ellis (ed.), *The Principle of Proportionality in the Laws of Europe* (Oxford: Hart, 1999) 37

Van Harten G, *Investment Treaty Arbitration and Public Law* (Oxford University Press, 2007)

    'Investment Treaty Arbitration, Procedural Fairness and the Rule of Law' in S W Schill (ed.), *International Investment Law and Comparative Public Law* (Oxford University Press, 2010) 627

    Sovereign Choices and Sovereign Constraints: Judicial Restraint in Investment Treaty Arbitration (Oxford University Press, 2013)

    'Investment Arbitrators' Evident Lack of Restraint' (2014) 5 *Journal of International Dispute Settlement* 1

Van Harten G and Loughlin M, 'Investment Treaty Arbitration as a Species of Global Administrative Law' (2006) 17 *European Journal of International Law* 121

Verhoosel G, *National Treatment and WTO Dispute Settlement: Adjudicating the Boundaries of Regulatory Autonomy* (Oxford: Hart 2002)

Vierdag E W, *The Concept of Discrimination in International Law: With Special Reference to Human Rights* (Dordrecht: Springer Netherlands, 1973)

Viñuales J E, 'Foreign Investment and the Environment in International Law: An Ambiguous Relationship' (2010) 80 *British Yearbook of International Law* 244

von Staden A, 'Deference or No Deference, That is the Question: Legitimacy and Standards of Review in Investor-State Arbitration' (2012) 2 *Investment Treaty News* 3

    'The Democratic Legitimacy of Judicial Review Beyond the State: Normative Subsidiarity and Judicial Standards of Review' (2012) 10 *International Journal of Constitutional Law* 1023

Vranes E, *Trade and the Environment: Fundamental Issues in International Law, WTO Law, and Legal Theory* (Oxford University Press, 2009)

Wagner M, 'Law Talk v. Science Talk: The Languages of Law and Science in WTO Proceedings' (2012) 35 *Fordham International Law Journal* 151

'Regulatory Space in International Investment Law and International Trade Law' (2015) 36 *University of Pennsylvania Journal of International Law* 1

Waibel M, 'Two Worlds of Necessity in ICSID Arbitration: *CMS* and *LG&E*' (2007) 20 *Leiden Journal of International Law* 637

'Opening Pandora's Box: Sovereign Bonds in International Arbitration' (2007) 101 *American Journal of International Law* 711

Wälde T W, 'Investment Arbitration under the Energy Charter Treaty: An Overview of Selected Key Issues Based on Recent Litigation Experience' in N Horn and S Kröll (eds.), *Arbitrating Foreign Investment Disputes* (The Hague: Kluwer, 2004) 193

Webber G C N, *The Negotiable Constitution: On the Limitation of Rights* (Cambridge University Press, 2009)

'Proportionality, Balancing and the Cult of Constitutional Rights Scholarship' (2010) 23 *Canadian Journal of Law and Jurisprudence* 179

Weeramantry J R, *Treaty Interpretation in Investment Arbitration* (Oxford University Press, 2012)

Weiler J H H, 'The Rule of Lawyers and the Ethos of Diplomats: Reflections on the Internal and External Legitimacy of WTO Dispute Settlement' (2002) 13 *American Review of International Arbitration* 177

'Comment: *Brazil – Measures Affecting Imports of Retreaded Tyres*' (2009) 8 *World Trade Review* 137

Weiner A S, 'Indirect Expropriation: The Need for a Taxonomy of "Legitimate" Regulatory Purposes' (2003) 5 *International Law FORUM du droit international* 166

White R C A and Ovey C, *The European Convention on Human Rights* (Oxford University Press, 5th ed., 2010)

Whytock C A, 'Legal Origins, Functionalism, and the Future of Comparative Law' (2009) 34 *Brigham Young University Law Review* 1879

Wildhaber L, 'The Protection of Legitimate Expectations in European Human Rights Law' in M Monti, Prinz N von und zu Liechtenstein, B Versterdorf, J Westbrook and L Wildhaber (eds.), *Economic Law and Justice in Times of Globalisation: Festschrift for Carl Baudenbacher* (Sinzheim: Nomos Verlagsgesellschaft, 2007) 253

Wildhaber L, Hjartarson A and Donnelly S, 'No Consensus on Consensus? The Practice of the European Court of Human Rights' (2011) 33 *Human Rights Law Journal* 248

Yannaca-Small K, 'Indirect Expropriation and the Right to Regulate: How to Draw the Line?' in K Yannaca-Small (ed.), *Arbitration Under International Investment Agreements: A Guide to the Key Issues* (Oxford University Press, 2010) 445

Young A L, 'Will You, Won't You, Will You Join the Deference Dance?' (2014) 34 *Oxford Journal of Legal Studies* 375

Yourow H C, 'The Margin of Appreciation Doctrine in the Dynamics of the European Human Rights Jurisprudence' (1988) 3 *Connecticut Journal of International Law* 111

Zhou W, '*US–Clove Cigarettes* and *US–Tuna II (Mexico)*: Implications for the Role of Regulatory Purpose Under Article III:4 of the GATT' (2012) 15 *Journal of International Economic Law* 1075

Zleptnig S, 'The Standard of Review in WTO Law: An Analysis of Law, Legitimacy and the Distribution of Legal and Political Authority' (2002) 6 *European Integration Online Papers*

Zweigert K, 'Des solutions identiques par des voies différentes (Quelques observations en matière de droit comparé)' (1966) 18 *Revue internationale de droit comparé* 5

Zweigert K and Kötz H, *Introduction to Comparative Law* (Oxford University Press, 3rd ed., T Weir trans., 1998)

INDEX

arbitrariness
  arbitrary measures clauses in
    investment treaties, 71
  as breach of fair and equitable
    treatment, 70–1, 120–2
  ELSI case, 121–2
  as method of review, 73, 120–3
Argentine economic crisis, 3–4, 87–97,
  105–6, 110–2, 139–40, 147–8,
  175

balancing
  as concept between state and
    investor interests, 6–7, 74,
    113–15, 117, 124, 174
  fair balance concept in ECtHR case
    law, 64–5
  proportionality *stricto sensu* and, 24,
    27–8, 62, 160, 168
  in US constitutional law, 17

comparative law
  domestic legal systems and, 16–18
  general principles of law and,
    19–20
  role of, 10–20
  selection of comparators, 12–16
Court of Justice of the European Union
  (CJEU)
  derogation clauses, 15, 49–50, 81,
    96–7, 129, 132, 152
  mandatory requirements, 15, 49, 58,
    132, 152
  proportionality analysis and
    legitimacy of regulatory objective,
      49–50
  necessity test, 58–9

proportionality *stricto sensu,*
  62–4, 164–5, 184–5
suitability test, 54
standard of review, factors
  influencing
  activist approach, 14
  European consensus, 14, 50, 58,
    62–3, 133
  strategic considerations, 184–5
customary international law
  customary plea of necessity, 87–92,
    95, 111, 153
  expropriation, 75–6, 173–4
  minimum standard of treatment of
    aliens, 102, 144, 181–2

deference
  Alexy, theory of, 35–6
  definition of, 34–5
  democratic legitimacy as basis for,
    41–2
  developing countries, impact of
    deferential approach, 41–3
  institutional competence and
    expertise as basis for, 38–43
  proportionality analysis, relationship
    to, 6, 31, 45–6, 193–4
  regulatory autonomy and proximity
    as basis for, 37–8, 42
  standard of review, relationship to,
    34
  uncertainty and, 22, 29, 34–46, 43,
    49–50, 54–7, 59, 62, 68, 91, 109,
    123, 128, 135, 138–40, 143,
    145–8, 156, 158, 168, 171,
    186–7, 189–90, 192, 194
  v. non-justiciability, 187–8

CAMBRIDGE STUDIES IN INTERNATIONAL AND COMPARATIVE LAW

Books in the series

Proportionality and Deference in Investor-State Arbitration: Balancing Investment Protection and Regulatory Autonomy
Caroline Henckels

International Law and Governance of Natural Resources in Conflict and Post-Conflict Situations
Daniëlla Dam-de Jong

Proof of Causation in Tort Law
Sandy Steel

Taking Economic, Social and Cultural Rights Seriously in International Criminal Law
Evelyne Schmid

Climate Change Litigation: Regulatory Pathways to Cleaner Energy?
Jacqueline Peel and Hari Osofsky

Mestizo International Law: A Global Intellectual History 1842–1933
Arnulf Becker Lorca

Sugar and the Making of International Trade Law
Michael Fakhri

Strategically-created Treaty Conflicts and the Politics of International Law
Surabhi Ranganathan

Investment Treaty Arbitration as Public International Law: Procedural Aspects and Implications
Eric De Brabandere

The New Entrants Problem in International Fisheries Law
Andrew Serdy

Substantive Protection under Investment Treaties: A Legal and Economic Analysis
Jonathan Bonnitcha

Popular Governance of Post-Conflict Reconstruction: The Role of International Law
Matthew Saul

Evolution of International Environmental Regimes: The Case of Climate Change
Simone Schiele

Judges, Law and War: The Judicial Development of International Humanitarian Law
Shane Darcy

Religious Offence and Human Rights: The Implications of Defamation of Religions
Lorenz Langer

Forum Shopping in International Adjudication: The Role of Preliminary Objections
Luiz Eduardo Ribeiro Salles

CPSIA information can be obtained
at www.ICGtesting.com
Printed in the USA
LVHW052310030119
602644LV00017B/415/P

9 781107 458178